Lacy wire jewelry

Melody MacDuffee

Kalmbach Books
21027 Crossroads Circle
Waukesha, Wisconsin 53186
www.Kalmbach.com/Books

Published in 2010
14 13 12 11 10   1 2 3 4 5

Manufactured in the United States of America

ISBN: 978-0-87116-293-9

Publisher's Cataloging-in-Publication Data

MacDuffee, Melody.
Lacy wire jewelry / Melody MacDuffee
p. : ill. ; cm.
ISBN: 978-0-87116-293-9
1. Jewelry making–Handbooks, manuals, etc. 2. Wire jewelry–Handbooks, manuals, etc. 3. Wire jewelry–Patterns.
I. Title.

TT212 .M33 2010
739.27

Contents

Introduction

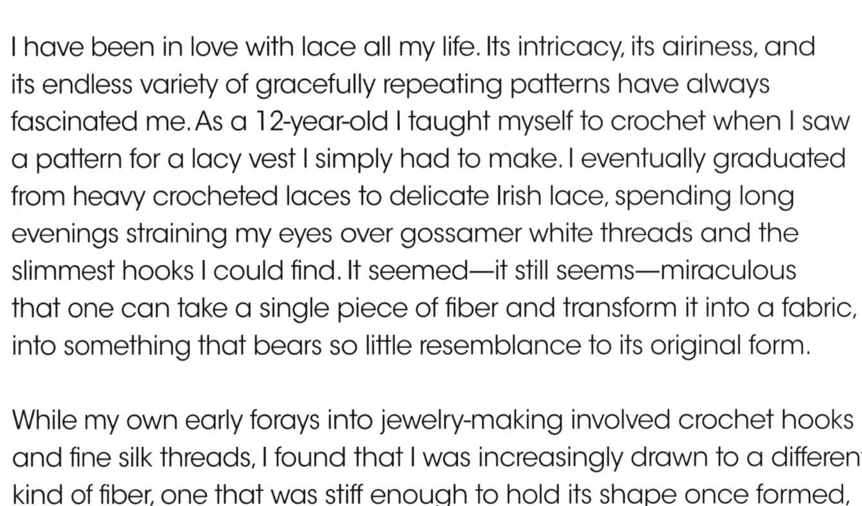

I have been in love with lace all my life. Its intricacy, its airiness, and its endless variety of gracefully repeating patterns have always fascinated me. As a 12-year-old I taught myself to crochet when I saw a pattern for a lacy vest I simply had to make. I eventually graduated from heavy crocheted laces to delicate Irish lace, spending long evenings straining my eyes over gossamer white threads and the slimmest hooks I could find. It seemed—it still seems—miraculous that one can take a single piece of fiber and transform it into a fabric, into something that bears so little resemblance to its original form.

While my own early forays into jewelry-making involved crochet hooks and fine silk threads, I found that I was increasingly drawn to a different kind of fiber, one that was stiff enough to hold its shape once formed, to bear the weight of beads without sagging, and to lend itself to three-dimensional constructions.

I began crocheting with wire, but I couldn't get the effect or precision I was looking for. My favorite pieces of jewelry have always been the metal equivalent of lace—filigrees—and I wanted to make jewelry that looked more like that. I considered learning smithing, casting, and soldering. But fiber is my natural medium, and processes involving heat simply didn't beckon to me. I longed to create lacy jewelry using a process I have always enjoyed: the simple transformation of one long piece of fiber into something complex, structured and completely new.

This book is the result of that ongoing desire. It is filled with lacy wire jewelry projects that require no heat, no expensive equipment, and no hard-to-acquire skills. Instead, these pieces are made using, almost exclusively, the three inexpensive tools most jewelry makers already own: wire cutters, roundnose pliers, and chainnose pliers. As for the skills involved, if you can wrap a piece of wire around a pen or a nail or a knitting needle, you can learn to make lacy wire jewelry. While some of the moves may feel a bit awkward at first, a little practice is all you need.

To make it easy for you to learn, I've created a series of ***Technical Basics*** *(p. 86) that are the building blocks for every project in the book as well as an excellent way to practice your techniques. Take note of the* ***Technical Basics Reference*** *list at the beginning of each project, and refresh your skills before you begin.*

So relax, play, and have fun. I hope you enjoy creating lacy wire jewelry as much as I do!

Melody MacDuffee

ch.1 Filigree

Pearl & Gold Earrings

Nothing is classier—or more classic—than pearls and gold. These dainty, feather-light earrings will quickly become your new favorites.

Materials

- approx. 10 ft. (3.05 m) 28-gauge craft wire or dead-soft wire, gold
- 9 in. (22.9 cm) 20-gauge half-hard wire, gold
- **38** 3 mm freshwater pearls, white
- **2** 4 mm jump rings, gold
- pair of earring wires, gold

Tools

- roundnose pliers
- chainnose pliers
- wire cutters

Dimensions

dangle is approx. 1½ in. x 2 in. (38 x 51 mm)

Technical Basics Reference

- Making Frames: Basic Frame, p. 86
- Anchoring Wires, p. 87
- Making Base Rows: Unbeaded Outer Base Rows and Unbeaded Inner Base Rows p. 87
- Finishing Off, p. 87
- Building onto Base Rows: Unbeaded Arches and Beaded Arches, p. 88

Preparation

1 Cut 20-gauge wire in half. Cut 28-gauge wire into 2 ft. (61 cm) lengths.

Frames

2 Using 20-gauge wire, make two round frames (*Basic Frame*). Using chainnose pliers, make a 45° bend ½ in. (13 mm) from each end. Using roundnose pliers, curl ends into loops toward back **(a)**.

Base Outer Row

3 Anchor one piece of 28-gauge wire near top of frame *(Anchoring Wires)*. Make base outer row of 37 unbeaded arches *(Unbeaded Outer Base Rows)*. Do not clip tails **(b)**.

Base Inner Row

4 Turn frame over and work back in the other direction, making an inner base row of 37 arches *(Unbeaded Inner Base Rows)*. Finish off *(Finishing Off)* **(c)**.

Second Outer Row

5 Anchor new wire to base outer row at the ninth arch from top. Make the first unbeaded arch into the next base row arch *(Unbeaded Arches and Beaded Arches)*. Make an unbeaded arch into the next arch. Using a pearl, make a one-bead arch into the next arch.

6 Make an unbeaded arch into next arch followed by a one-bead arch into next arch.

7 Repeat Step 6 six times.

8 Make an unbeaded arch into each of next two arches. Finish off **(d)**.

Third Outer Row

9 Anchor wire to second arch of second outer row.

10 Make an unbeaded arch into each of next eight unbeaded arches. Finish off **(e)**.

Fourth Outer Row

11 Anchor wire to second arch of third outer row. Make an unbeaded arch into each of next five unbeaded arches. Do not clip tails **(f)**.

Fifth Outer Row

12 Turn frame over and work back in the other direction, beginning by anchoring wire in first unbeaded arch. Make a one-bead arch into next unbeaded arch.

13 Make a 3-bead arch into each of next two unbeaded arches. Make a 1-bead arch into next unbeaded arch. Finish off **(g)**.

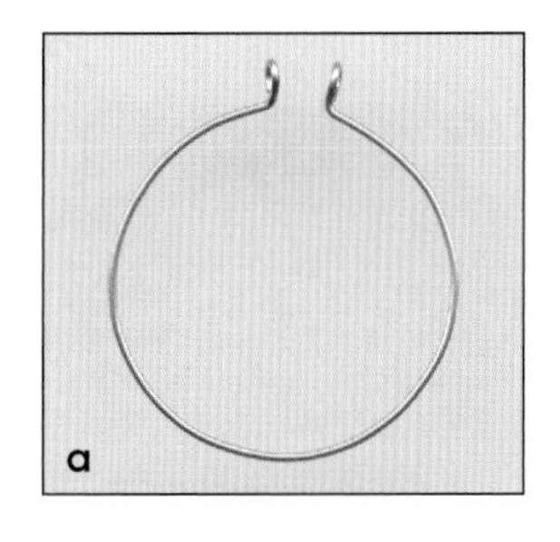

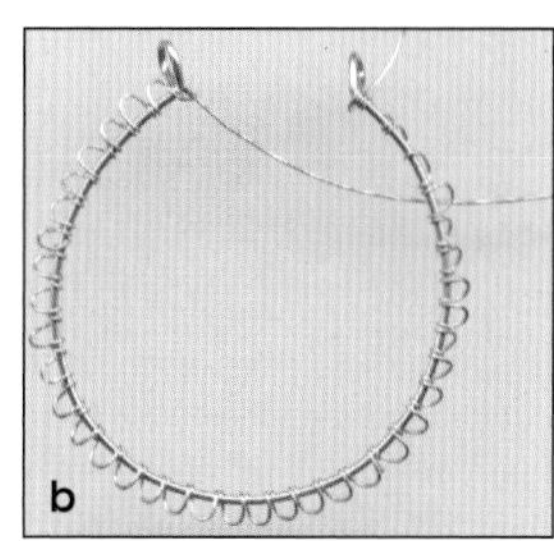

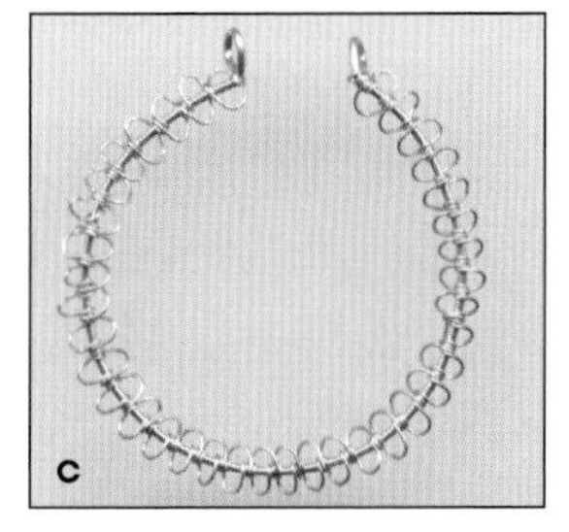

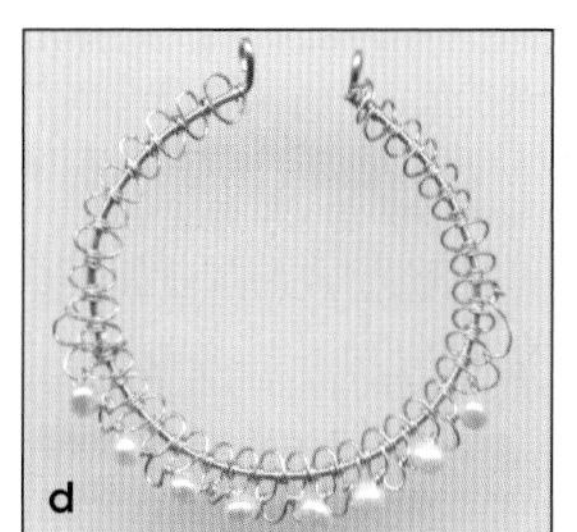

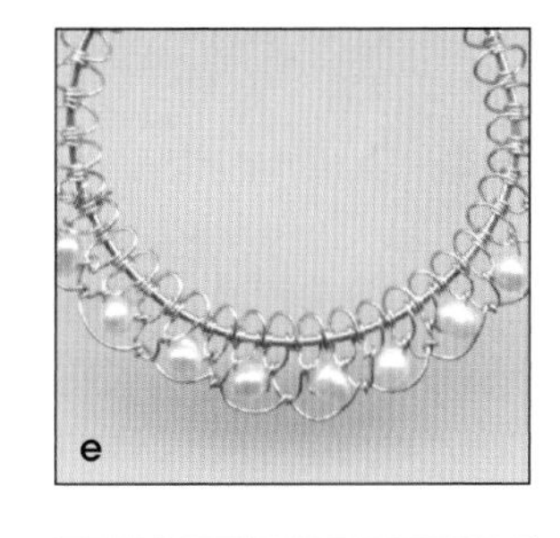

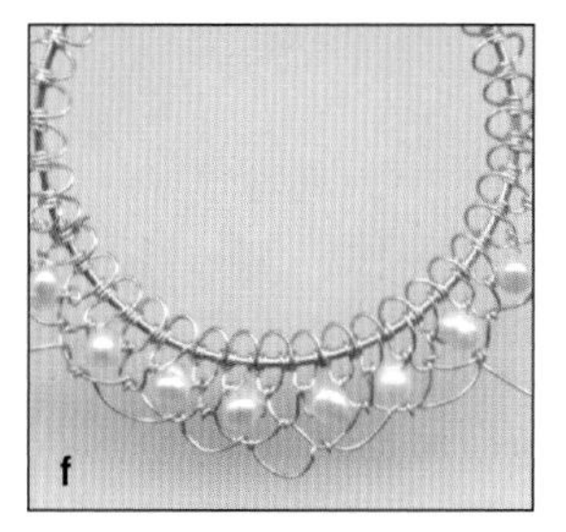

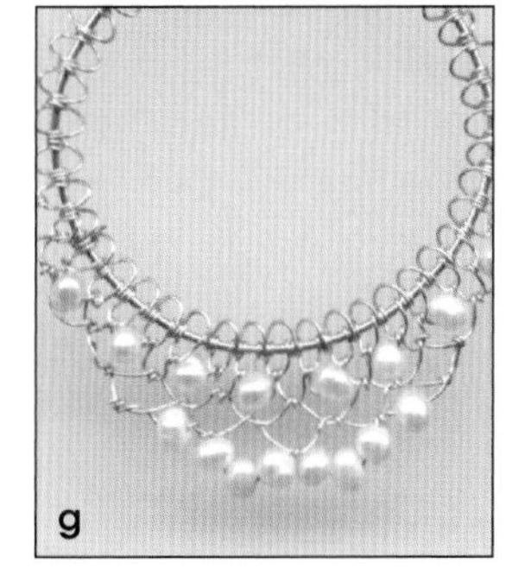

Sixth Outer Row

14 Anchor wire between second and third beads of the first 3-bead arch. Make a 3-bead arch between first and second beads of next 3-bead arch. Finish off **(h)**.

Finishing

15 Gently reshape hoop if needed so that the two loops at top lie close together.

16 Insert a jump ring through both loops. Attach an earring wire. Make a second earring to match the first.

Krobo Barrette

This colorful barrette will be the delight of any young girl ... and many not so young! Made of copper wire and hand-painted recycled-glass beads created by the Krobo people of Ghana, it's a bright, cheerful, and completely unique addition to a collection of hair ornaments.

Materials
- 2½ ft. (76.2 cm) 20-gauge dead-soft wire, copper
- approx. 9 ft. (27.4 m) 24-gauge dead-soft wire, copper
- **8** 10 x 18 mm painted Krobo recycled glass tube-shaped beads
- **45–50** Krobo recycled glass E beads, **9–10** each of **5** colors
- 3 in. (76 mm) metal barrette

Tools
- roundnose pliers
- chainnose pliers
- wire cutters

Dimensions
approx. 1½ x 4¼ in. (38 x 108 mm)

Technical Basics Reference
- Anchoring Wires, p. 87
- Finishing Off, p. 87
- Making Base Rows: Beaded Outer Base Rows, p. 87

Preparation

1 Cut 24-gauge wire into 3-ft. (91.4 cm) lengths. Remove the spring from the back of the barrette.

2 Anchor a piece of 24-gauge wire to end hole of barrette *(Anchoring Wires)* **(a)**. Wrap wire once around end portion of barrette and then diagonally across to other side of latch **(b)**. Wrap once straight around barrette again, and then diagonally back to end section. Wrap once more around end section **(c)**.

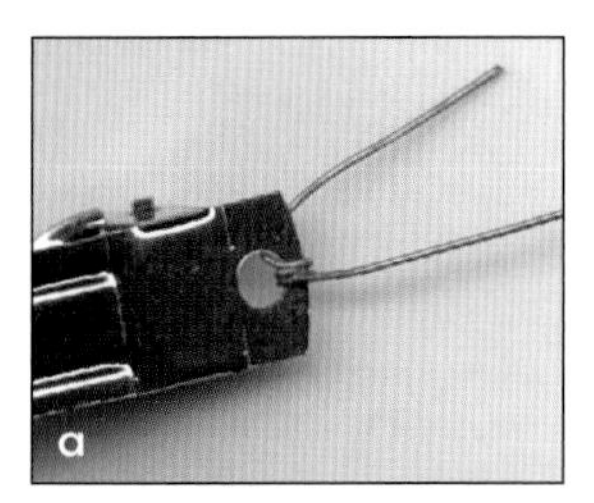
a

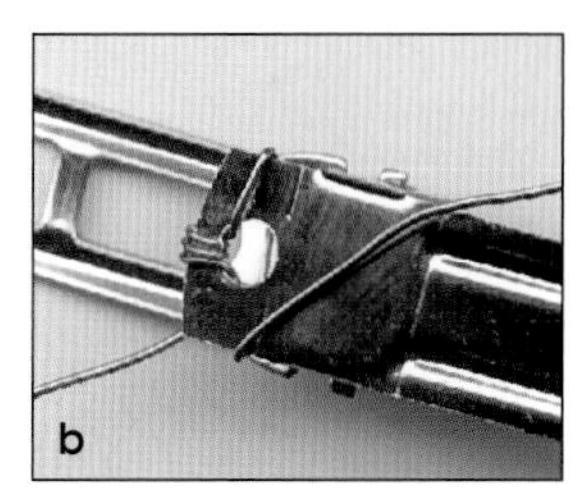
b

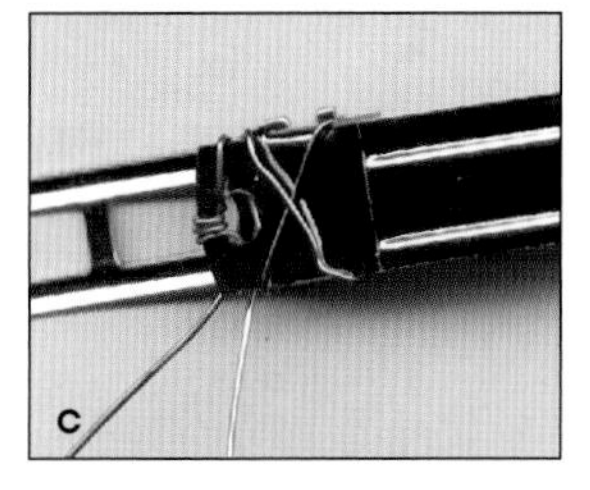
c

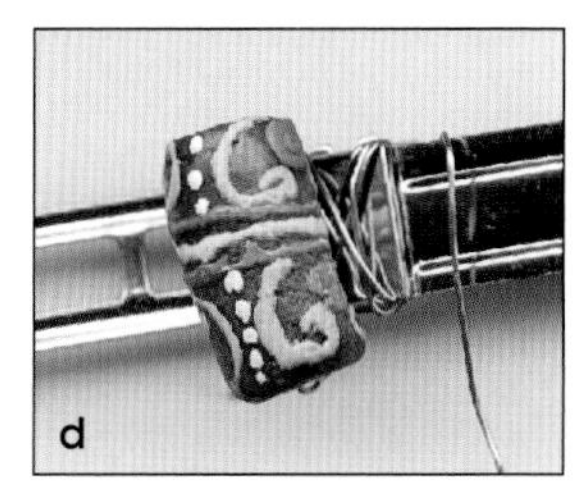
d

Base

3 String a tube bead on the wire. Set bead evenly across end of barrette and pull wire tightly around and under barrette. String wire through bead again and wrap twice around barrette only.

4 Bring wire diagonally across to other side of latch. Wrap wire around barrette twice **(d)**.

5 Repeat Steps 3 and 4 six times.

6 Bring wire across latch and wrap twice around end of barrette. String a tube bead. Set the bead evenly across end of barrette and pull wire tightly around under the barrette. String wire through bead again and wrap twice around barrette only.

7 Bring wire diagonally back to main section and wrap around twice between last two beads. Finish off *(Finishing Off)* **(e,f)**.

e

f

Frame

8 String 20-gauge wire through the end bead, centering the wire through the bead. Using chainnose pliers, bend wires 45° on each side so they are parallel to short side of bead. Bend wires again so they are parallel to long side of bead **(g)**.

9 Bend wires again parallel with short side of bead, and again at a point even with the hole. Gently pull wires through hole one at a time up to last bends. Bend wires again at point where they exit the bead, and again even with the hole of the third bead. Gently pull the wires one at a time through hole in the third bead until even with last bends **(h)**.

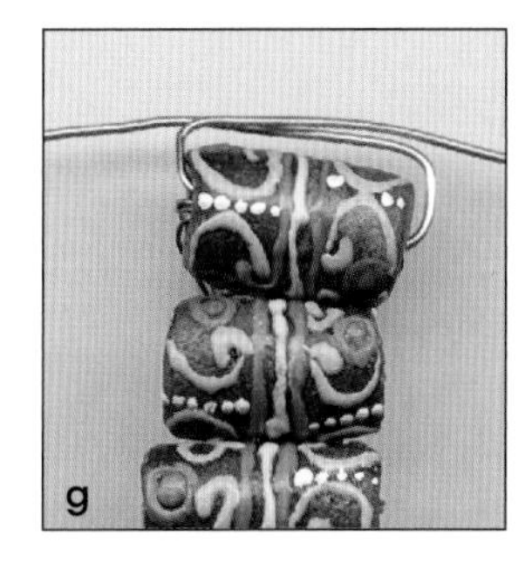
g

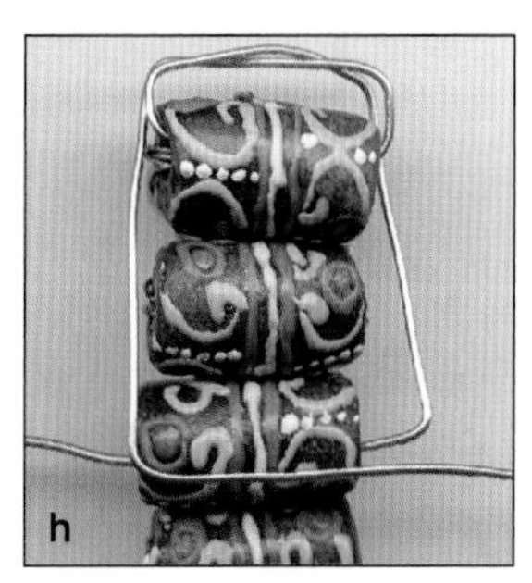
h

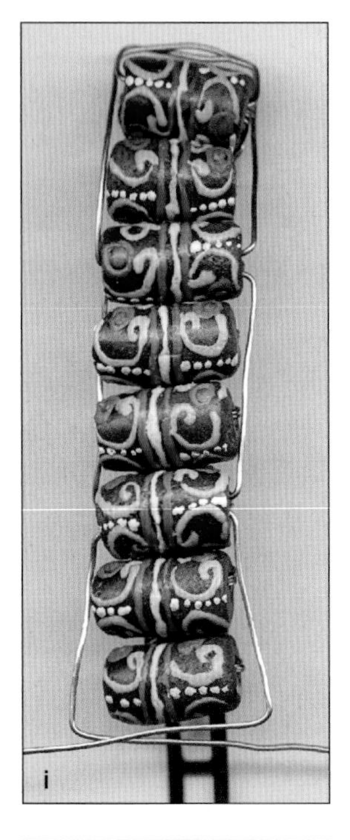

i

j

k

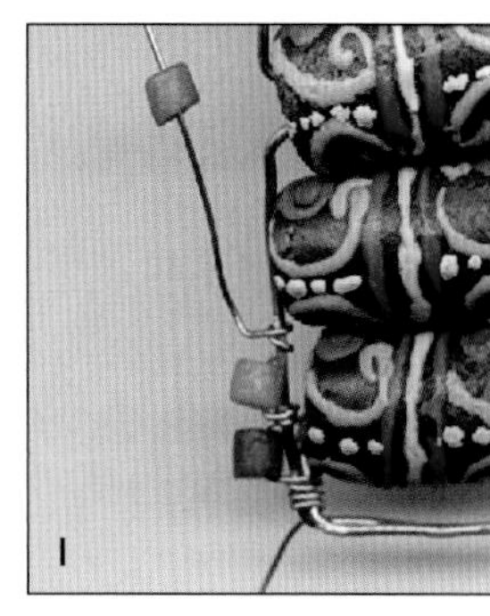

l

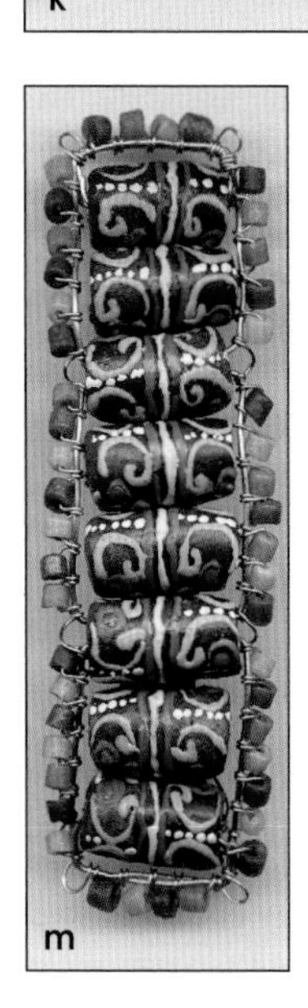

m

n

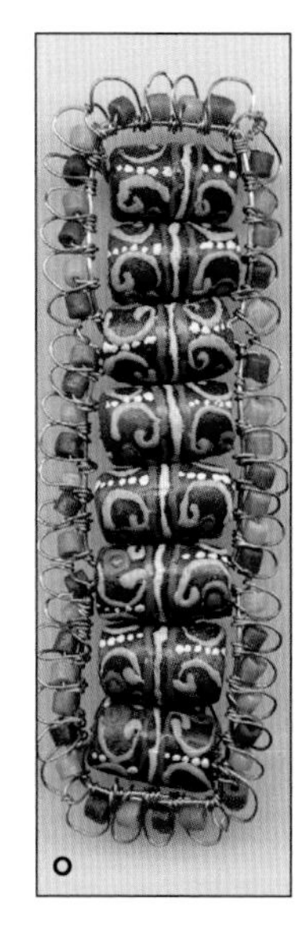

o

10 Bend wires again at point where they exit the bead, and again even with hole of sixth bead. Gently pull wires one at a time through the hole in the sixth bead until even with the bends.

11 Bend wires again at point where they exit the bead, and again even with end of last bead so that they lie across its long side **(i)**. Bend wires again to lie across ends of bead, and again even with hole of last bead. Gently pull wires one at a time through hole up to last bends. Bend them again toward end of barrette and clip tails about ¼ in. (6.5 mm) from hole **(j)**.

Base Outer Row

12 Anchor a piece of 24-gauge wire around both wires of frame at corner as shown **(k)**.

13 Using E beads, make 5–7 one-bead arches in first frame section (*Beaded Outer Base Rows*).

Note: To get these cylindrical beads to sit more or less straight, bend the wire at a 45° angle ¼ in. from base prior to stringing each bead **(l)**.

14 Make an unbeaded arch into next frame section by using roundnose pliers to curve wire slightly close to anchor point and then drawing wire through under frame just after corner of new section. Coil around frame twice. Make 5–7 one-bead arches into same frame section. Make an unbeaded arch into next frame section. Make 5–7 one-bead arches into same frame section. Make an unbeaded arch at corner. Make four one-bead arches across end of barrette. Make an unbeaded arch at corner.

15 Repeat Steps 13 and 14. Do not clip tails **(m)**.

Second Outer Row

16 Make an unbeaded arch into place just after next beaded arch of base row, placing coils on top of previous coils on frame **(n)**. Repeat until you reach the unbeaded base-row arch. Make an unbeaded arch into unbeaded base-row arch.

17 Repeat Step 16 around the entire frame. Finish off **(o)**. Reattach the spring.

Turquoise & Tigereye Earrings

The warmth of turquoise and the mellow tones of tigereye work well together with the rich brilliance of golden wires. A matte finish on the stones keeps these earrings casual.

Materials

- approx. 8 ft. (24.4 m) 28-gauge craft wire or dead-soft wire, gold
- 6 in. (15.2 cm) 20-gauge half-hard wire, gold
- **12** 2 x 4 mm rondelles, hessonite garnet
- **12** 2 x 4 mm rondelles, turquoise
- **60** 2 mm round beads, tigereye
- pair of earring wires, gold

Tools

- roundnose pliers
- chainnose pliers
- wire cutters

Dimensions

dangle is approx. 2 x 1¼ in. (51 x 32 mm)

Technical Basics Reference

- Making Frames: Basic Frame, p. 86
- Anchoring Wires, p. 87
- Making Base Rows: Unbeaded Outer Base Rows, p. 87
- Finishing Off, p. 87
- Building onto Base Rows: Anchoring, Unbeaded Arches, and Beaded Arches, p. 88

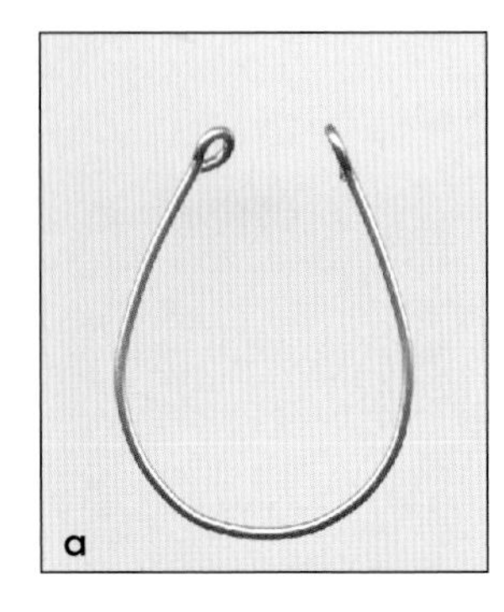

Preparation
1 Cut 20-gauge wire in half. Cut 28-gauge wire into 2-ft. (61 cm) lengths.

Frames
2 Using a piece of 20-gauge wire, make a basic frame in a teardrop shape *(Basic Frame)*. Using roundnose pliers, make loops at top of frame toward back side. Tip loops forward to center them on wire **(a)**.

Base Outer Row
3 Anchor a piece of 28-gauge wire near top of frame *(Anchoring Wires)*.

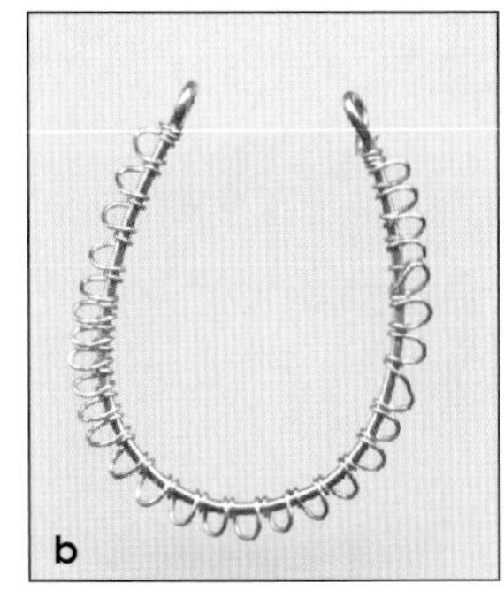

4 Make an outer base filigree row of 29 unbeaded arches *(Unbeaded Outer Base Rows)*. Finish off *(Finishing Off)* **(b)**.

Second Outer Row
Note: Use tigereye beads throughout.

5 Anchor a piece of 28-gauge wire in first unbeaded arch of base outer row.

6 Make an unbeaded arch into each of next two unbeaded arches of base outer row (*Anchoring, Unbeaded Arches,* and *Beaded Arches*). Make a one-bead arch into each of next two unbeaded arches of base outer row.

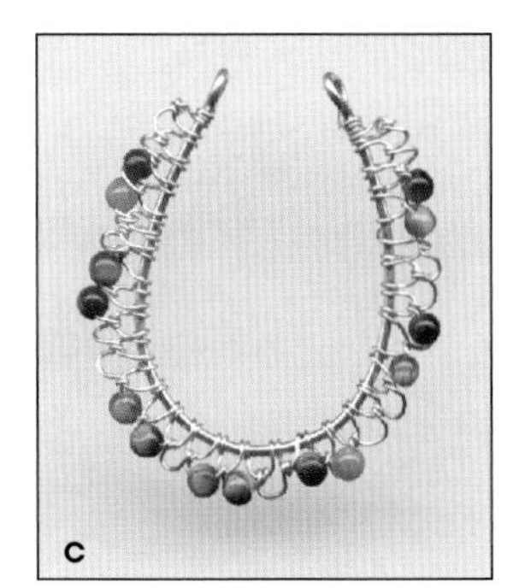

7 Repeat Step 6 twice.

8 Make an unbeaded arch into next arch. Make a one-bead arch into each of next two arches. Make an unbeaded arch into next arch.

9 Make a one-bead arch into each of next two unbeaded arches. Make an unbeaded arch into each of next two unbeaded arches.

10 Repeat Step 9 twice. Finish off **(c)**.

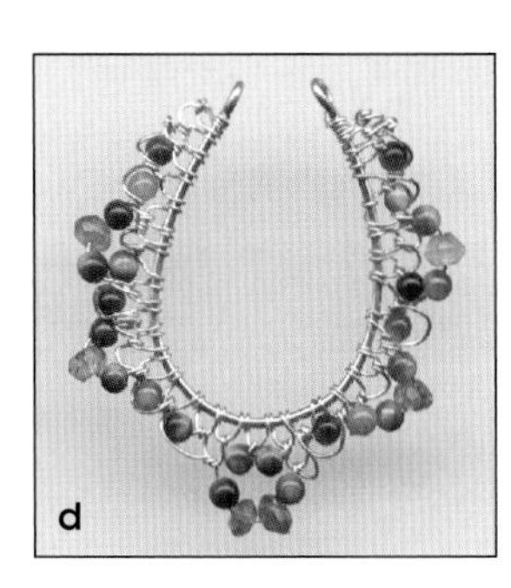

Third Outer Row
11 Anchor a piece of 28-gauge wire in second unbeaded arch of second outer row. Make unbeaded arches into places after each of next two beaded arches, coiling over previous coils.

12 Using a tigereye, a hessonite, and a tigereye, make a 3-bead arch into the place between next pair of beaded arches. Make an unbeaded arch into the place after bead on next beaded arch. Repeat one time.

13 Make an unbeaded arch into next unbeaded arch. Using a tigereye, two hessonites, and a tigereye, make a 4-bead arch into next unbeaded arch. Make an unbeaded arch into the places just prior to the beads on each of next two beaded arches.

14 Using a tigereye, a hessonite, and a tigereye, make a 3-bead arch into place just prior to bead on next beaded arch. Make an unbeaded arch into the place just prior to bead on next beaded arch. Using a tigereye, a hessonite, and a tigereye, make a triple-beaded arch into the place just prior to the bead on the next beaded arch. Make an unbeaded arch into the place just prior to the bead on the next beaded arch. Make an unbeaded arch into next unbeaded arch. Finish off **(d)**.

Fourth Outer Row

15 Anchor a piece of 28-gauge wire in first arch of third outer row. Make an unbeaded arch into next unbeaded arch.

16 Make an unbeaded arch into place between first tigereye and rondelle; another in between rondelle and next tigereye; and another just after next tigereye. Make an unbeaded arch into next unbeaded arch.

17 Repeat Step 16.

18 Make an unbeaded arch into next unbeaded arch. Make an unbeaded arch into place just after each of next three beads. Make an unbeaded arch into each of next two unbeaded arches. Make an unbeaded arch into place just prior to each of next three beads. Make an unbeaded arch into next unbeaded arch. Make an unbeaded arch into place just prior to each of next three beads. Make an unbeaded arch into each of next two unbeaded arches. Finish off **(e)**.

e

Fifth Outer Row

19 Anchor a piece of 28-gauge wire in second arch of fourth outer row. Make an unbeaded arch into each of next two unbeaded arches. Using a turquoise rondelle, make a one-bead arch into next unbeaded arch. Make an unbeaded arch into each of next four unbeaded arches. Using a turquoise rondelle, make a one-bead arch into next unbeaded arch. Make an unbeaded arch in place just after next tigereye. Using a tigereye, a turquoise rondelle, and a tigereye, make a 3-bead arch into place just prior to next tigereye. Make an unbeaded arch into next unbeaded arch. Using a turquoise rondelle, make a one-bead arch into next unbeaded arch. Make an unbeaded arch into each of next four unbeaded arches. Using a turquoise rondelle, make a beaded arch into next unbeaded arch. Make an unbeaded arch into each of next two unbeaded arches. Finish off **(f)**.

f

Top

20 Using a 2-in. (51 mm) piece of 28-gauge wire, string two round tigereyes, one top frame loop, a turquoise rondelle, the next loop, and two more tigereyes. Bring the tails of wire together and, using them as one wire, wire wrap a loop at the top of the earring **(g)**.

g

21 Attach an earring wire. Make a second earring to match the first.

Krobo Painted Bead Cuff Bracelet

This cuff bracelet, both lacy and substantial, is a harmonious blend of traditional African beads and oxidized copper. The wire lace has slight variations in the sizes and shapes of its loops and is the perfect counterpart for these slightly irregular, wonderfully colorful beads.

Materials
- approx. 18 ft. (5.5 m) 24-gauge dead-soft wire, copper
- 4 ft. (1.2 m) 20-gauge half-hard wire, copper
- **3** overlapping circlets of memory wire
- **10** 9 x 18 mm painted Krobo recycled glass tube-shaped beads
- **50** Krobo recycled glass E beads, black
- **66** Krobo recycled glass E beads, green
- **48** 2 mm round copper beads or 11º seed beads

Tools
- roundnose pliers
- chainnose pliers
- wire cutters

Dimensions
approx. 1⅛ x 8 in. (2.9 x 20.3 cm)

Technical Basics Reference
- Anchoring Wires, p. 87
- Finishing Off, p. 87
- Making Base Rows: Beaded Outer Base Rows, p. 87
- Building onto Base Rows: Unbeaded Arches, p. 88

Frame

1 Curl a small loop at one end of each piece of memory wire. Cut 24-gauge wire into 3-ft. (91.4 cm) lengths. Cut 20-gauge wire into 2-ft. (61 cm) lengths.

2 Anchor a piece of 20-gauge wire to a piece of memory wire next to the loop (*Anchoring Wires*). String a tube bead onto the memory wire.

3 Using chainnose pliers, bend 20-gauge wire 45° so it lies parallel to long side of bead. Bend it again at other end of bead and coil twice around memory wire **(a, b)**. Repeat to attach nine more beads.

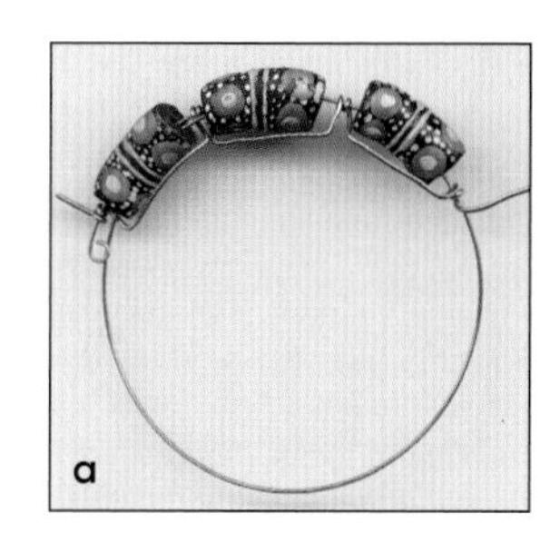

a

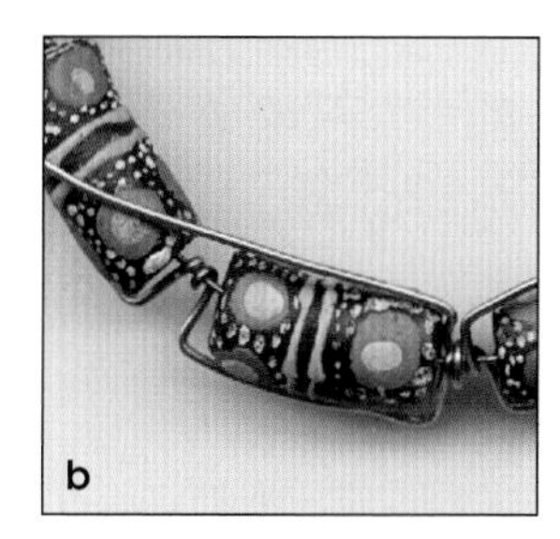

b

4 Make a half-turn in the wire and repeat the wiring in Step 3 on other side of beads. Finish off *(Finishing Off)* **(c)**.

Base Outer Row

5 Anchor a piece of 24-gauge wire on frame at first corner made. Using black E beads, make five one-bead arches in first frame section *(Beaded Outer Base Rows)*. Using a green E bead, make a one-bead arch into next frame section.

Note: To get these cylindrical beads to sit more or less straight, bend the wire at a 45° angle ¼ in. (6.5 mm) from base prior to stringing each bead **(d)**.

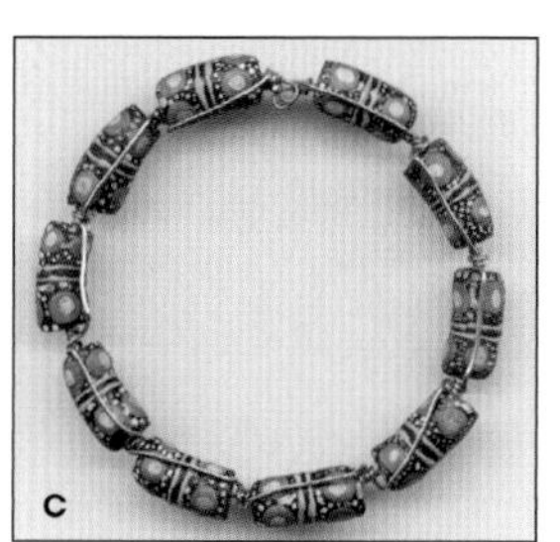

c

6 Repeat Step 5 eight times. Use black E beads to make five one-bead arches in last frame section. Finish off.

Second Outer Row

7 Anchor a piece of 24-gauge wire to frame at first corner made, coiling it on top of previous coil. Make an unbeaded arch into place just prior to bead in each of next four beaded arches (*Unbeaded Arches*). Make an unbeaded arch into place just after green E bead.

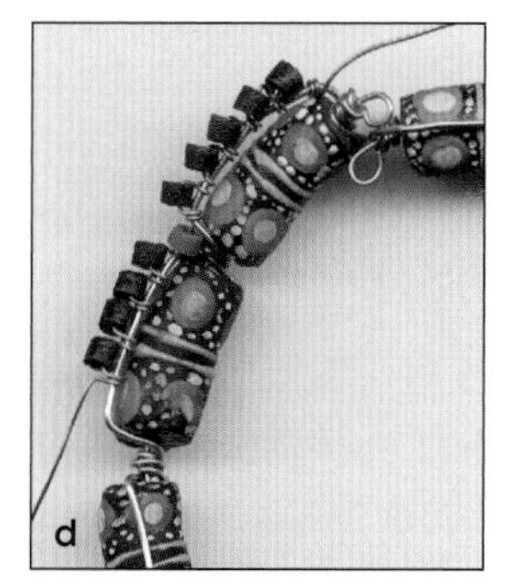

d

8 Repeat Step 7 nine times, working final arch over previous coil on frame. Finish off.

Third Outer Row

9 Line a piece of memory wire up along outer edge of bracelet. Anchor a piece of 24-gauge wire to first unbeaded arch on second outer row, coiling around memory wire next to its loop at the same time.

10 Using a green E bead, make a one-bead arch on the memory wire only. Coil twice more around both the memory wire and the next unbeaded arch.

11 Using a round copper bead, repeat Step 10.

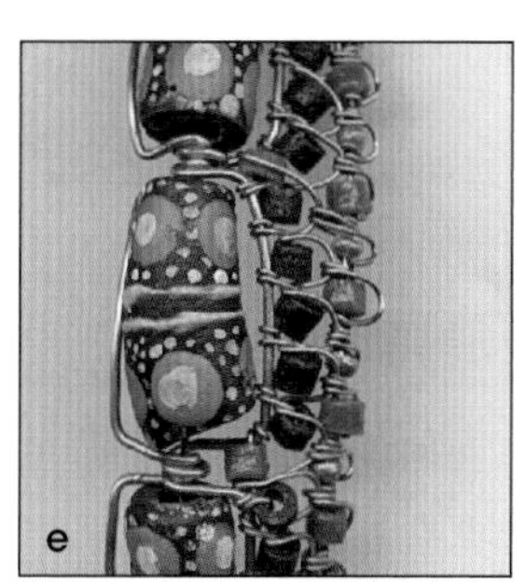

e

12 Repeat Steps 10–11 to end **(e)**, using chainnose pliers as needed to pull memory wire through as tightly as possible. Finish off.

13 Repeat Steps 5–12 on other side of bracelet.

14 Anchor a piece of 24-gauge wire to frame at first corner made, coiling it on top of previous coils. Make an unbeaded arch into each arch to end. Repeat on other side of bracelet. Finish off.

Multigemstone Earrings

Tiny gemstone beads of tourmaline, amethyst, iolite, and garnet come together in a dainty web of silver wires. This lightweight earring pair nevertheless packs a heavy punch.

Materials
- approx. 8 ft. (2.4 m) 28-gauge craft or dead-soft wire, silver
- 6 in. (15.2 cm) 20-gauge half-hard wire, silver
- Gemstones:
  44 A: 1.5 x 2 mm faceted rondelles, pink tourmaline
  32 B: 2 mm rounds, garnet
  28 C: 2 mm rounds, iolite
  18 D: 2 x 4 mm faceted rondelles, amethyst
- pair of earring wires, silver

Tools
- roundnose pliers
- chainnose pliers
- wire cutters

Dimensions
dangle is approx. 1¾ x 1 in. (44 x 25.5 mm)

Technical Basics Reference

- Making Frames: Basic Frame, p. 86
- Anchoring Wires, p. 87
- Making Base Rows: Unbeaded Outer Base Rows, p. 87
- Finishing Off, p. 87
- Building onto Base Rows: Beaded Arches and Unbeaded Arches, p. 88

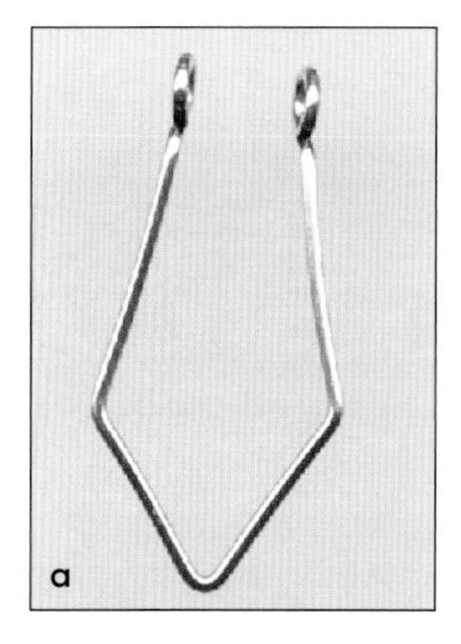

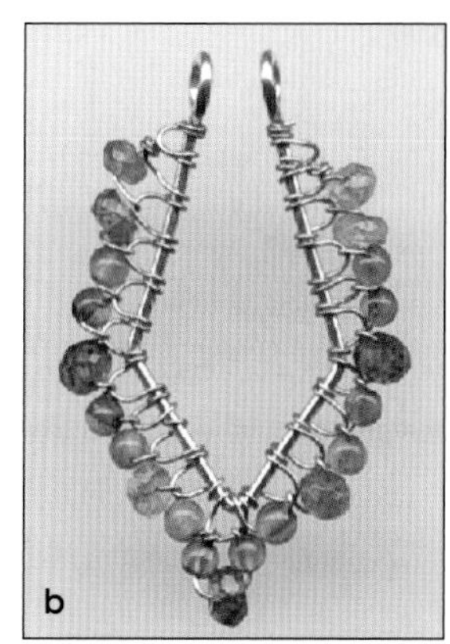

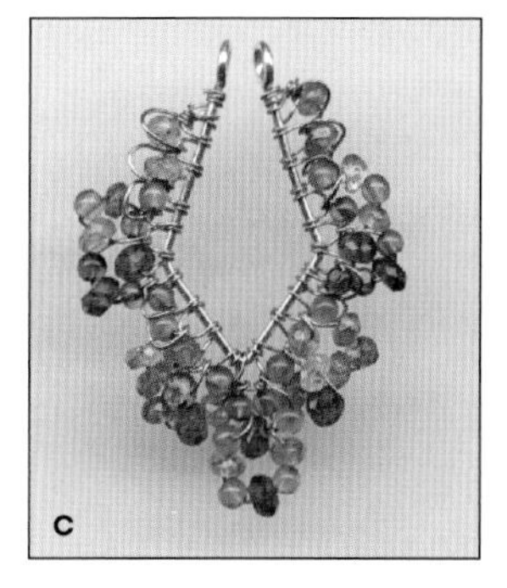

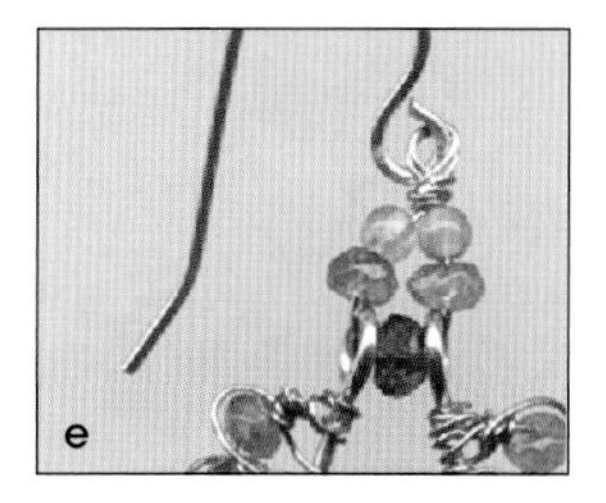

Preparation

1 Cut 28-gauge wire into 2-ft. (61 cm) pieces.

2 Cut 20-gauge wire in half. Make frames (*Basic Frame*). Bend wires at center and then ⅜ in. (9.5 mm) from center on each side. Make loops on each end toward back. Tip loops forward to center on wire **(a)**.

Base Outer Row

3 Anchor a piece of 28-gauge wire near top of frame *(Anchoring Wires)*. Make a base outer row of 21 unbeaded arches *(Unbeaded Outer Base Rows)*, placing 6 arches above outer bends, 4 on short sides, and 1 at bottom center. Finish off *(Finishing Off)*.

Second Outer Row

4 Anchor a piece of 28-gauge wire in second unbeaded arch of base outer row. Make a one-bead arch into each of next nine unbeaded arches of base outer row *(Beaded Arches)* with gemstones: A, A, B, C, D, C, B, A, B. Make a 3-bead arch into bottom center arch with: C, D, and C. Make a one-bead arch into each of next 9 unbeaded arches of base outer row with: B, A, B, C, D, C, B, A, A. Finish off **(b)**.

Third Outer Row

5 Anchor a piece of 28-gauge wire over the anchor for the second outer row.

Make unbeaded arches into spaces between each of next 3 pairs of beaded arches, coiling over previous coils (*Building onto Base Rows: Unbeaded Arches*).

With A, B, and A, make a 3-bead arch into space between next pair of beaded arches.

With C, D, and C, make a 3-bead arch into space between next pair of beaded arches.

Make unbeaded arches into spaces between each of next 2 pairs of beaded arches.

With 3 As, make a 3-bead arch into space between next pair of beaded arches.

With A, D, and A, make a 3-bead arch into space between next pair of beaded arches.

With a B, make a one-bead arch into space between next pair of beaded arches.

With A, B, D, B, and A, make a 5-bead arch into space between next pair of beaded arches (after bottom center D).

With a B, make a one-bead arch into space between next pair of beaded arches.

With A, D, and A, make a 3-bead arch into space between next pair of beaded arches.

With 3 As, make a 3-bead arch into space between next pair of beaded arches.

Make unbeaded arches into spaces between each of next two pairs of beaded arches.

With C, D, and C, make a 3-bead arch into space between next pair of beaded arches.

With A, B, and A, make a 3-bead arch into space between next pair of beaded arches.

Make unbeaded arches into spaces between each of next 3 pairs of beaded arches. Finish off **(c)**.

Fourth Outer Row

6 Anchor a piece of 28-gauge wire between the top A and D beads in the fourth 3-bead arch from the top. Make an unbeaded arch into the space after the D. Skip the space after the B. Make unbeaded arches into the spaces after each of the next 5 beads. Skip the space after the A (prior to the next D). Make another unbeaded arch into the space after the D. Finish off **(d)**. Nudge arches around frame for an even look.

7 Using a scrap of 28-gauge wire, string a B, C, a top frame loop, D, and a loop. String a C and a B. Bring the tails together and, using them as one wire, wire wrap a loop at the top of the earring.

8 Attach an earring wire to the dangle **(e)**. Make a second earring to match the first.

Multicolored Chandelier Earrings

Festive and glamorous, these chandelier earrings have it all—movement, color, and lots of shimmer.

Materials
- 16 in. (40.6 cm) 20-gauge half-hard wire, gold
- approx. 10 ft. (3.0 m) 28-gauge craft wire or dead-soft wire, gold
- **42** 26-gauge headpins, gold
- 4 mm fire-polished crystal beads:
  - **10** olive green
  - **12** coral
  - **8** purple
  - **8** gold
  - **10** taupe/beige
- **16** 3 mm fire-polished beads, coral
- 4 grams 15º metallic gold charlottes or seed beads
- pair of earring wires, gold

Tools
- roundnose pliers
- chainnose pliers
- wire cutters

Dimensions
dangle is approx.
2 x 1⅜ in. (51 x 35 mm)

Technical Basics Reference

- Making Frames: Basic Frame, p. 86
- Anchoring Wires, p. 87
- Finishing Off, p. 87
- Building onto Base Rows: Anchoring and Unbeaded Arches, p. 88
- Attaching Laces to Frames, p. 91

Preparation

1 Cut two 3-in. (76 mm) and two 5-in. (12.7 cm) pieces of 20-gauge wire. Cut 28-gauge wire into 2-ft. (61 cm) lengths.

Frames

2 Using 20-gauge wire pieces, make two 5-in. and two 3-in. round frames *(Basic Frame)*. Using chainnose pliers, bend last ½ in. (13 mm) at top on either side of frames 45° upwards. Using roundnose pliers, curl vertical ends into loops toward back side **(a)**.

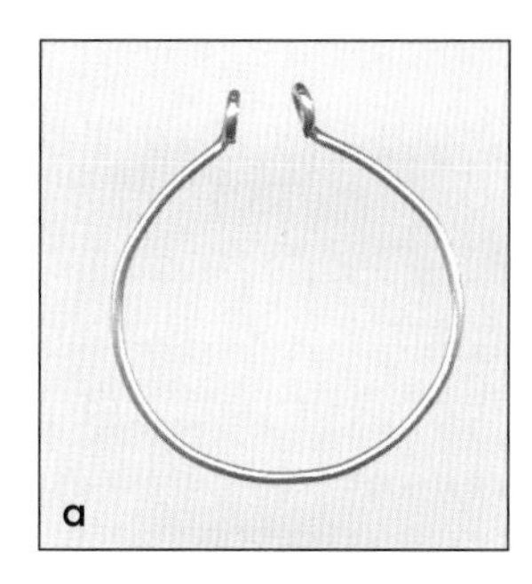
a

Base Outer Row

3 Anchor a piece of 28-gauge wire to a small frame just below its loop *(Anchoring Wires)*. Coil tightly around frame seven more times.

4 Using gold charlottes, make two one-bead arches, eleven 3-bead arches and two one-bead arches *(Beaded Outer Base Row)*. Coil wire tightly eleven times around frame. Finish off *(Finishing Off)* **(b)**.

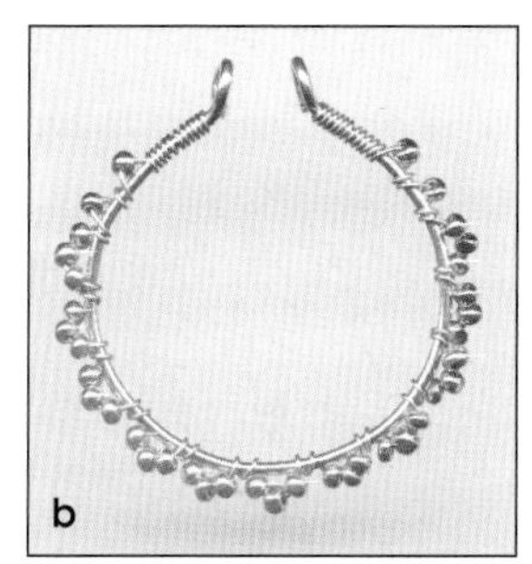
b

5 Nudge arches around frame so that they are evenly spaced, with an equal number on each side of frame and one at bottom center point.

Second Outer Row

6 Anchor a piece of 28-gauge wire to fourth arch at top right (i.e. the second triple bead arch).

7 Make an unbeaded arch into each of next eight arches of base outer row *(Anchoring* and *Unbeaded Arches)*. Do not clip tails **(c)**.

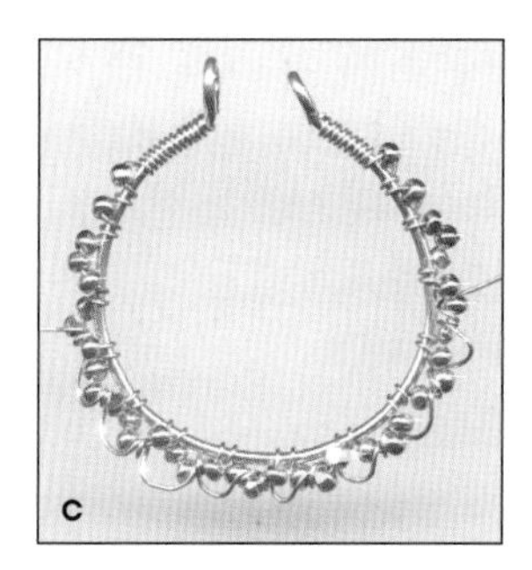
c

Third Outer Row

8 Turn frame over. Anchor wire in unbeaded arch just made. Using 3 mm fire-polished beads, and working back in opposite direction, make a one-bead arch into each of next three unbeaded arches. Make a 2-bead arch into next unbeaded arch. Make a one-bead arch into each of next three unbeaded arches. Finish off **(d)**.

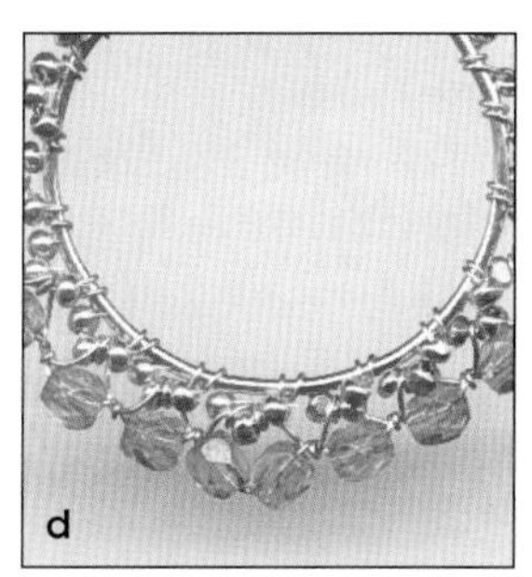
d

Fourth Outer Row

9 Anchor a piece of 28-gauge wire in same arch where you anchored the third outer row.

10 Using charlottes, make a 5-bead arch over each of next three beaded arches, coiling over the coils made previously for third row. Make another 5-bead arch into the spot between the two 3 mm beads on the 2-bead arch. Make a 5-bead arch over each of next four beaded arches **(e)**. Finish off.

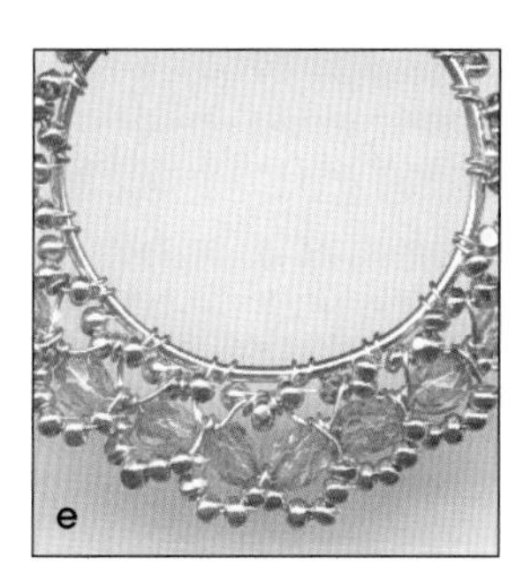
e

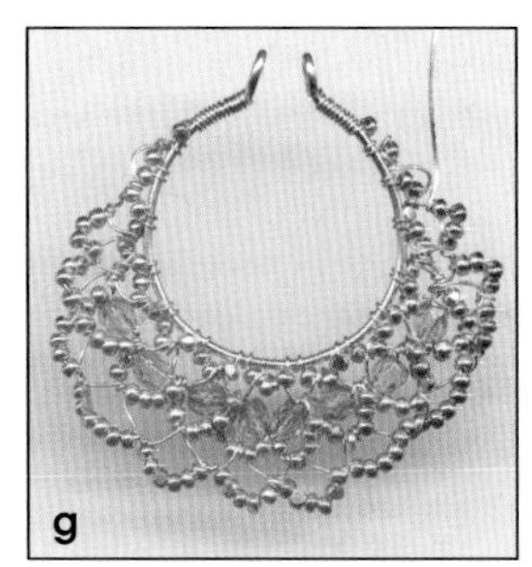

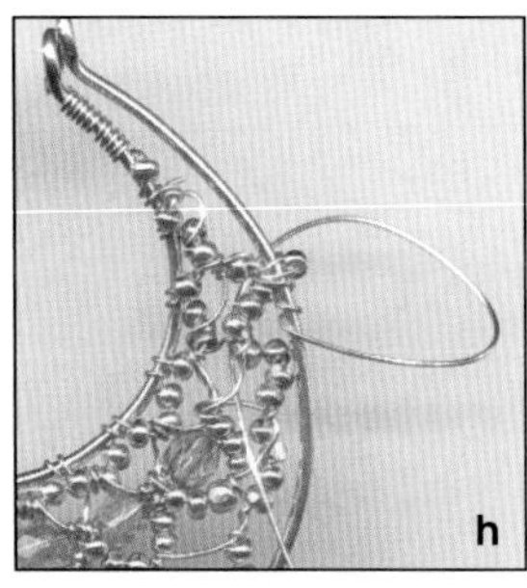

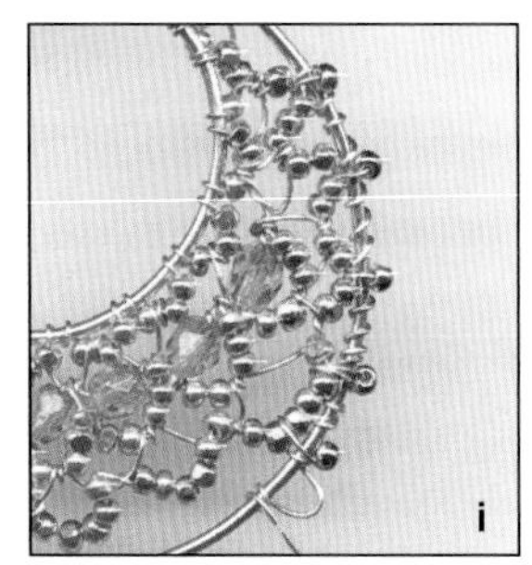

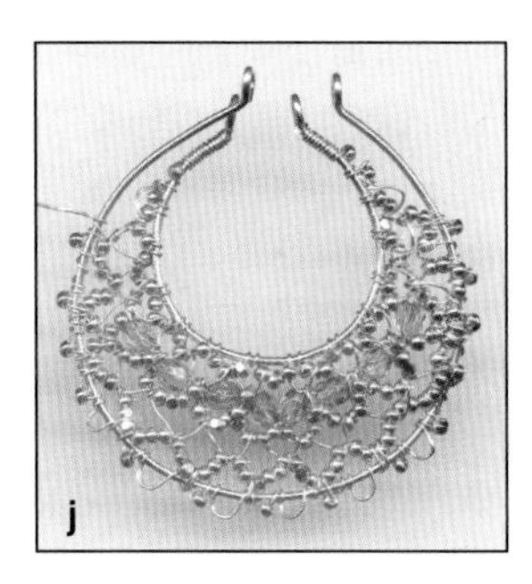

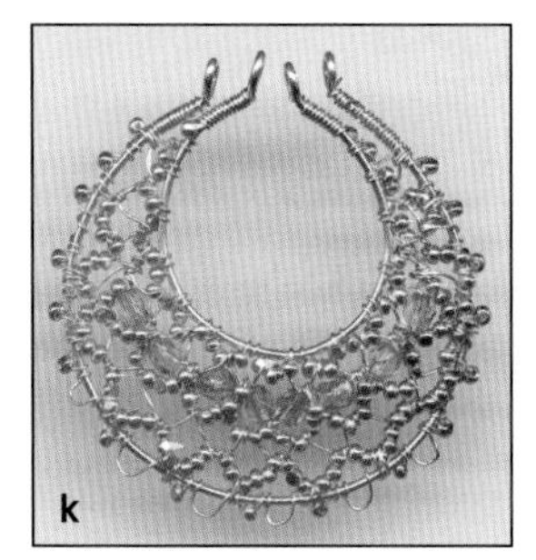

Fifth Outer Row

11 Anchor a piece of 28-gauge wire in second beaded arch on base outer row.

12 Make an unbeaded arch into each of next two beaded arches on base outer row. Make an unbeaded arch into first unbeaded arch on second row. Make an unbeaded arch into each beaded arch on fourth row. Make an unbeaded arch into last unbeaded arch on second row. Make an unbeaded arch into each of next two beaded arches on base outer row **(f)**. Finish off.

Sixth Outer Row

13 Anchor a piece of 28-gauge wire to second unbeaded arch on fifth row. Using charlottes, make a 4-bead arch into each of next three unbeaded arches. Make a 6-bead arch into each of next six unbeaded arches. Make a 4-bead arch into each of next three unbeaded arches **(g)**. Finish off.

Outer Frame and Seventh Outer Row

14 Attach a large frame to outer edge of filigree at each arch on the sixth row *(Attaching Laces to Frames)*, adding a 1-charlotte arch or an unbeaded arch where indicated **(h–j)**. Continue coiling and attaching lace to top of outer frame.

15 Anchor a piece of 28-gauge wire just under loop on other side of outer frame and coil down to point where filigree is attached **(k)**. Nudge the two frames as needed to get them (and their top loops) lined up evenly.

16 String a doubled piece of 28-gauge wire through one top loop on the outer frame. String a 4 mm olive bead. String the top loop on the inner frame. String a 4 mm coral bead. String the second loop on the inner frame. String a 4 mm olive bead. String the second loop on the outer frame **(l)**. Even up the tails. Using all four thicknesses of wire as one, wire wrap a loop at the top of the earring.

17 Using headpins and wrapped loops, wire wrap three remaining 4 mm beads to each of the seven unbeaded arches on seventh row as shown in **(m)**.

18 Attach an earring wire. Make a second earring to match the first.

ch.2

Inset Bezel

Gray Crazy Lace Agate Necklace

This crazy lace agate cabochon in subtle pale gray, yellow, and rose hues nestles inside a delicately wrought webbing of fine silver for a lace-within-lace necklace. The sparkle of faceted crystals accents a wonderfully feminine filigree chain.

Materials
- approx. 6 ft. (1.8 m) 28-gauge dead-soft wire, silver
- 6 in. (15.2 cm) 20-gauge half-hard wire, silver
- 20 x 45 mm marquise-shaped crazy lace cabochon
- 2 g 11º seed beads, silver lined
- 4 mm bicone crystal, silver or gray
- **44** 3 mm fire-polished beads, in 3–4 colors from cabochon
- 16 in. (40.6 cm) filigree chain, silver
- lobster claw clasp
- soldered jump ring

Tools
- roundnose pliers
- chainnose pliers
- wire cutters

Pendant Dimensions
approx. 2¼ x ⅞ in. (57 x 22 mm)

Technical Basics Reference
- Making Frames: Inset Bezel Frame, p. 86
- Making Base Rows: Unbeaded Inner Base Rows and Unbeaded Outer Base Rows p. 87
- Anchoring Wires, p. 87
- Finishing Off, p. 87
- Finishing Bezels: Lacing Up Bezels, p. 88
- Inset Bezels: Rearranging Rows Upright, p. 87
- Finishing Bezels: Tightening Bezels around Cabochons, p. 88
- Building onto Base Rows: Anchoring and Unbeaded Arches, p. 88

Preparation

1 Cut 28-gauge wire into 2-ft. (61 cm) pieces.

2 Using 20-gauge wire, make basic frame *(Inset Bezel Frame)* **(a)**.

Note: All arches are unbeaded.

Base Outer Row

3 Anchor 28-gauge wire to frame *(Anchoring Wires)* and make a 34-arch base outer row *(Unbeaded Outer Base Rows)*. Do not clip tails **(b)**.

Base Inner Row

4 Turn frame over and, working in the other direction, make a 34-arch base inner row *(Unbeaded Inner Base Rows)*. Do not clip tails **(c)**.

5 Rearrange rows *(Rearranging Rows Upright)* **(d)**.

6 Bring wire up through first arch of what is now back outer row of arches and anchor. Lace up back side of the bezel *(Lacing Up Bezels)*. Finish off *(Finishing Off)* **(e)**.

Second Outer Row

7 Join a piece of 28-gauge wire in first arch of what is now front row of arches. Make a second row *(Anchoring and Unbeaded Arches)* **(f)**.

8 Insert cabochon. Tighten bezel around cabochon *(Tightening Bezels around Cabochons)*.

Note: If cabochon is not secure in bezel, remove the cabochon, add an unbeaded outer row onto top row of the bezel, reinsert cabochon, and repeat tightening process **(g)**.

Finishing the Necklace

9 Cut chain into four 1-in. (25.5 mm) and two 6-in. (15.2 cm) pieces.

10 Wire wrap a loop to end link of a 1-in. chain piece. String wire end through one top frame loop, a bicone, and the remaining frame loop. Wire wrap to end link of a 1-in. chain piece.

11 Using three 3-in. (76 mm) pieces of 28-gauge wire as one, wire wrap a loop to an end link of 1-in. chain. String two seed beads, three fire-polished beads, and two seed beads on each of the three pieces of wire. Using all three wires as one, wire wrap a loop into a new 1-in. chain piece. Give "beaded bead" a half twist to create spiral effect **(h)**.

12 Repeat Step 11 on other side of necklace.

13 Repeat Steps 11 and 12, but connect to the 1-in. chain piece and a 6-in. chain piece.

14 Attach clasp on one end and soldered ring on other with smaller version of "beaded bead" made of two fire-polished beads on each of two pieces of 28-gauge wire.

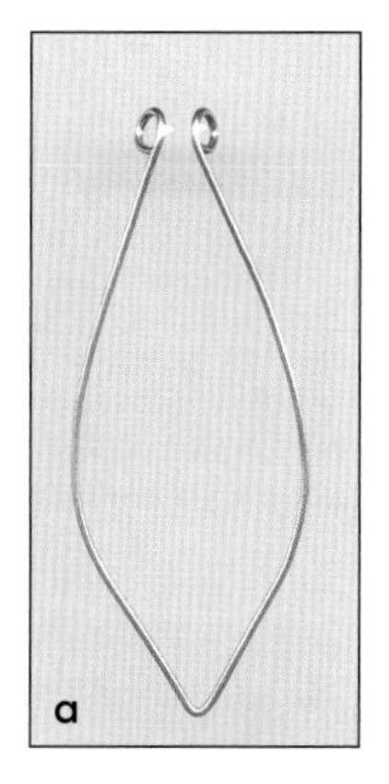
a

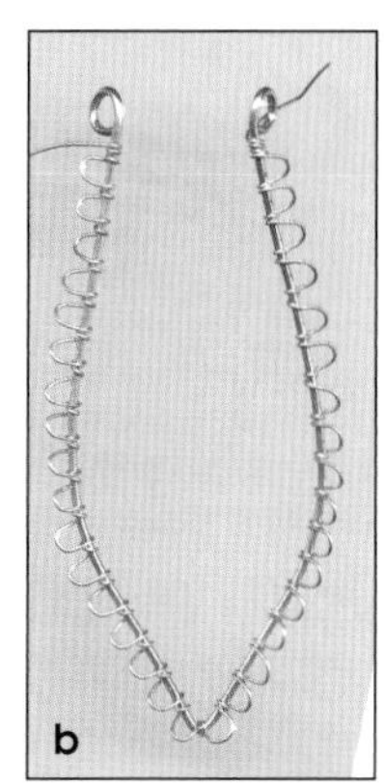
b

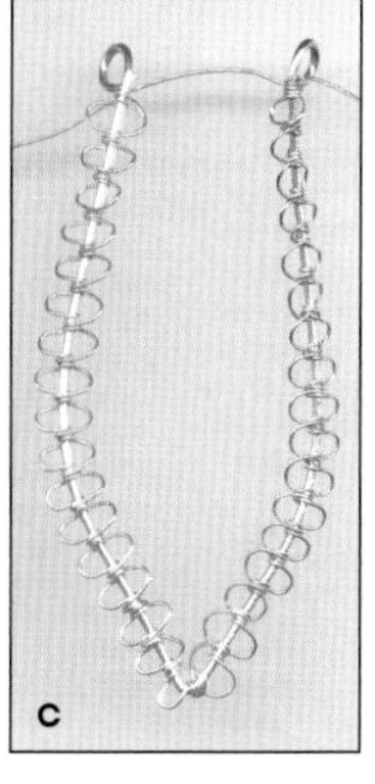
c

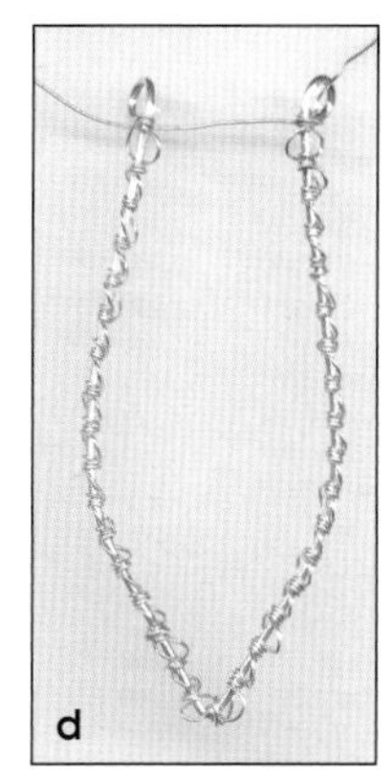
d

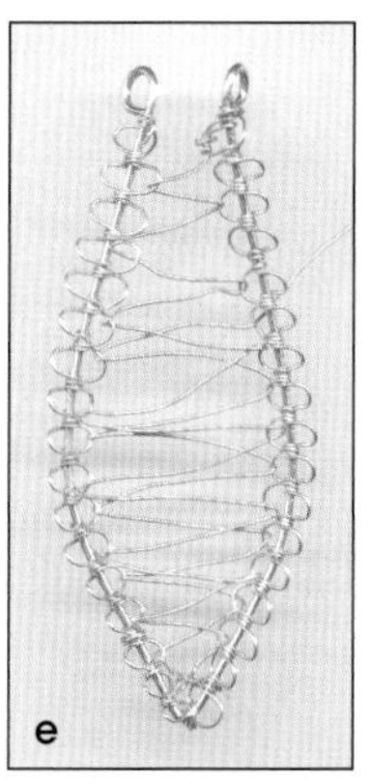
e

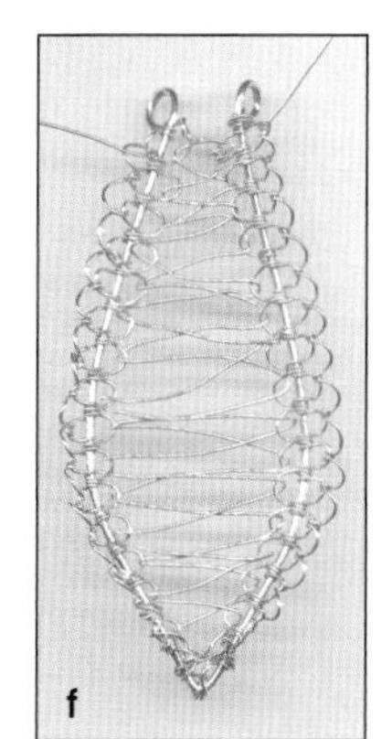
f

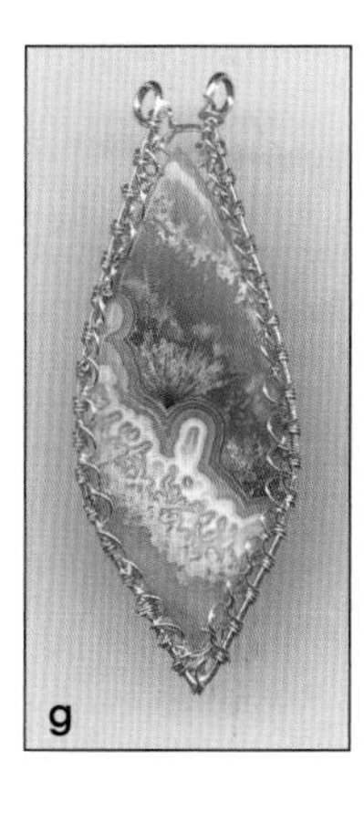
g

h

Green Plume Agate Necklace

This copper wire and West African bead necklace evokes the subtle mysteries of the rain forest. In keeping with the weight and size of the beads, the lacy bezel is made of heavier, 24-gauge wire.

Materials
- 6 in. (15.2 cm) 16-gauge wire, copper
- 1 ft. (30.5 cm) 18-gauge wire, copper
- approx. 5 ft. (1.5 m) 22-gauge wire, copper
- approx. 16 ft. (4.9 m) 24-gauge wire, copper
- 25 x 30 mm triangular plume agate cabochon
- **2** 16 mm Krobo recycled glass round beads, blue-green
- **8** 12 mm Krobo recycled glass round beads, amber
- **2** 8 mm Krobo recycled glass round beads, dark brown
- **12** 3 x 10 mm Krobo recycled glass rondelles, blue-green
- **6** 3 x 10 mm Krobo recycled glass rondelles, amber
- **31** Krobo recycled glass E beads, caramel
- **28** Krobo recycled glass cone beads, caramel
- **22** 2 x 4 mm heishi beads, copper
- **18** 11º seed beads, metallic bronze
- **2** crimp beads, copper
- flexible beading wire, .018 or .019

Tools
- roundnose pliers
- chainnose pliers
- wire cutters
- small hammer
- anvil

Pendant Dimensions
approx. 1½ x 1¼ in. (38 x 32 mm)

Necklace Length
approx. 20 in. (50.8 cm)

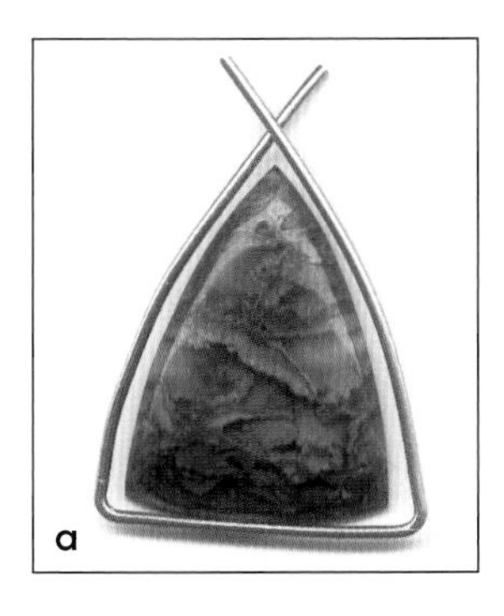
a

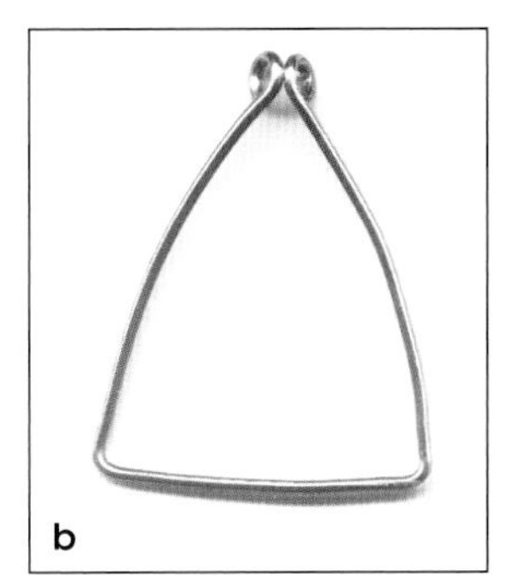
b

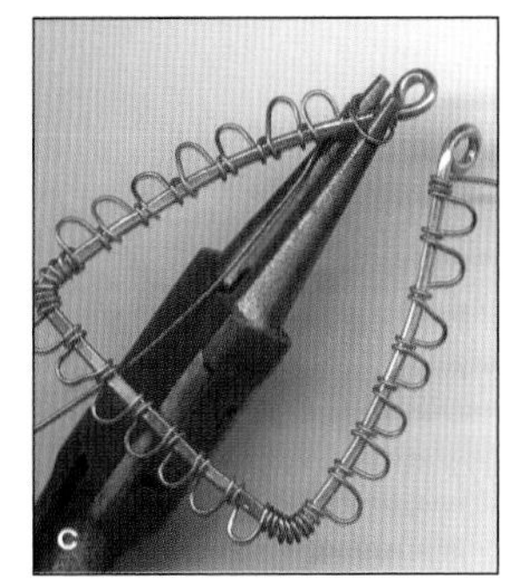
c

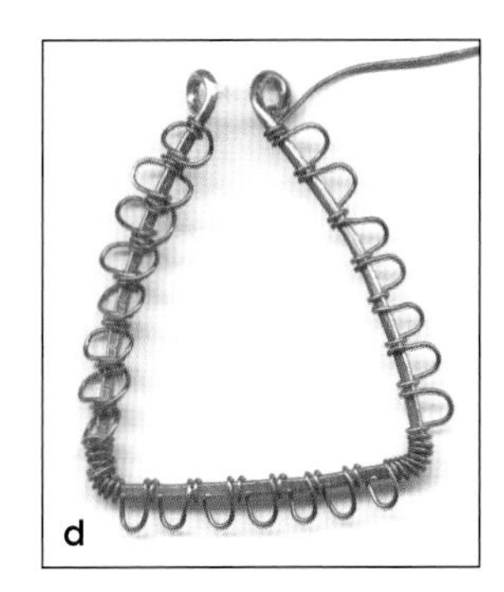
d

Preparation

1 Cut 24-gauge wire into 2-ft. (61 cm) pieces. Cut 22-gauge wire into 15-in. (38.1 cm) pieces.

Bezel

2 Using 16-gauge wire, make basic inset bezel frame *(Inset Bezel Frame)* to fit cabochon. Turn loops at top towards back of frame **(a, b)**.

Note: All arches are unbeaded.

Base Outer Row

3 Anchor a piece of 24-gauge wire to frame *(Anchoring Wires)* and make a 7-arch base outer row *(Unbeaded Outer Base Rows)*. Make five coils at the corner. Make a 7-arch base outer row, five coils at the corner, and a 7-arch base outer row.

Base Inner Row

4 Turn frame over and, working in opposite direction, make 21-arch base inner row *(Unbeaded Inner Base Rows)*. Finish off *(Finishing Off)* **(c, d)**.

Finishing the Bezel

5 Rearrange rows upright *(Rearranging Rows Upright)* **(e)**. Anchor wire in last arch made and lace up back side of bezel *(Lacing Up Bezels)*. Finish off **(f)**.

6 Insert cabochon. Tighten bezel around cabochon *(Tightening Bezels around Cabochons)*.

Note: If cabochon is not secure in bezel, remove cabochon, add a second outer row onto what is now top row of bezel, reinsert cabochon, and tighten again **(g)**.

e

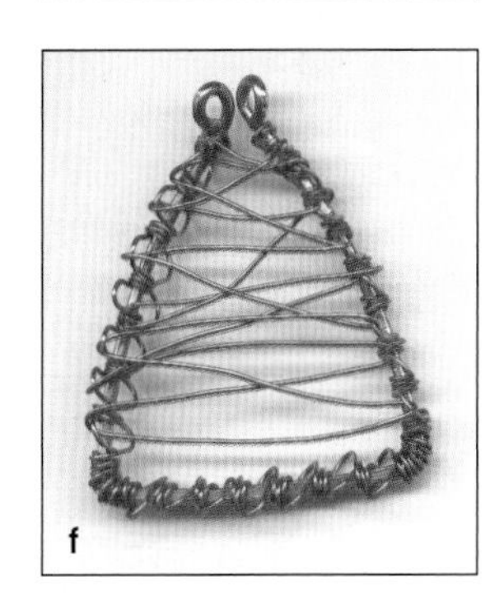
f

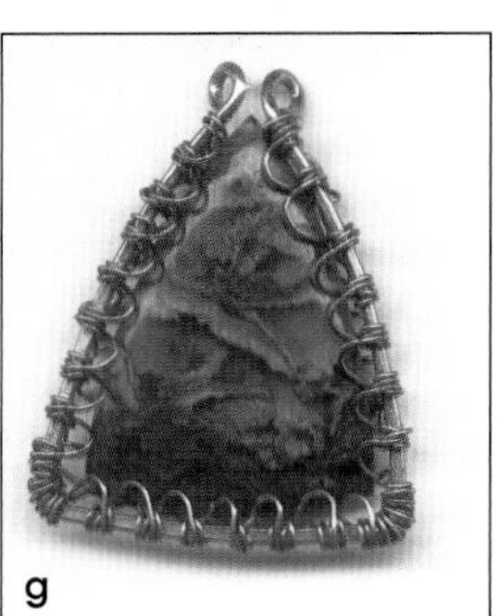
g

Technical Basics Reference

- Making Frames: Inset Bezel Frame, p. 86
- Finishing Off, p. 87
- Finishing Bezels: Tightening Bezels around Cabochons, p. 88
- Making Base Rows: Unbeaded Outer Base Rows and Unbeaded Inner Base Rows, p. 87
- Rearranging Rows Upright, p. 87
- Clasps: Spiral Point Clasp, p. 92

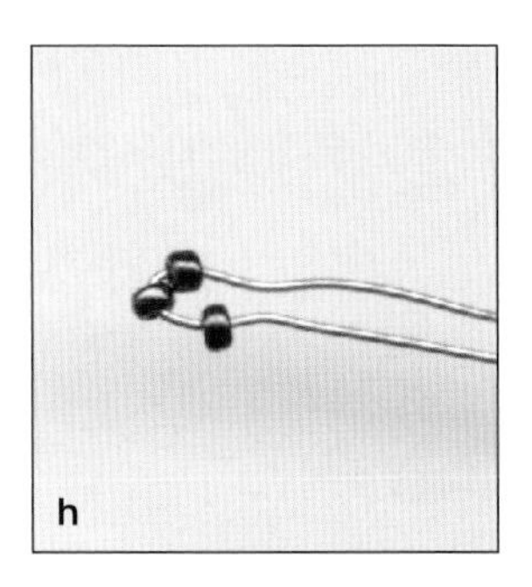
h

i

Drops (make six):

7 Using a piece of 24-gauge wire, string and center three seed beads **(h)**. Bring wire ends together and string a cone bead from the narrow end and a 12 mm amber round bead. Using roundnose pliers, form a loop **(i)**. Coil doubled wire around and around top of bead until almost used up **(j, k)**. Wind remaining wire down diagonally around bead and into space between round bead and cone bead. Clip tails **(l)**.

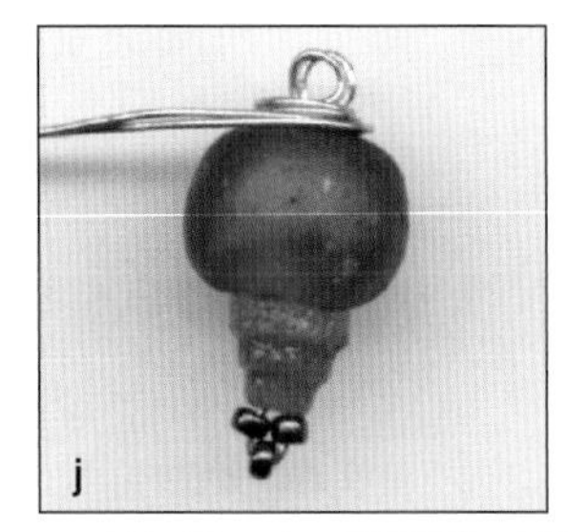
j

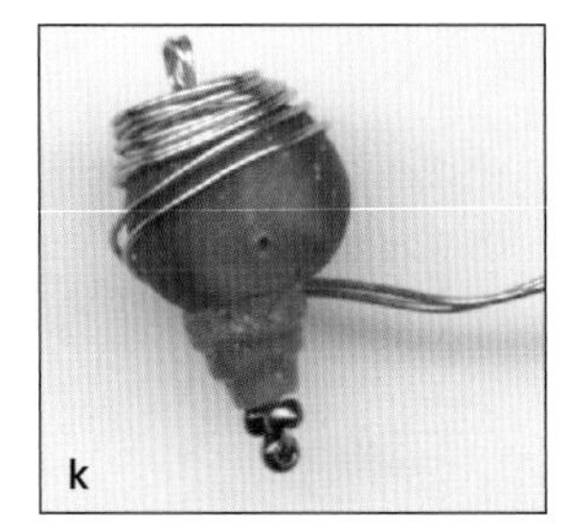
k

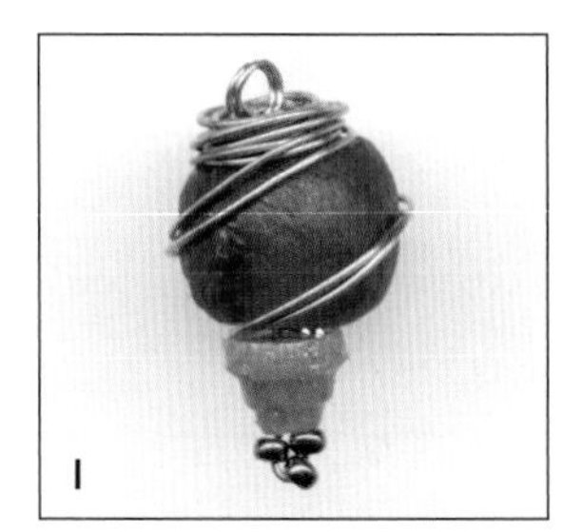
l

m

Capped Beads (make two):

8 Using 22-gauge wire, make a 12 mm spiral at one end, leave a 4-in. (10.2 cm) gap, and make a second 12 mm spiral at the other end **(m)**. Place a spiral over one end of a 12 mm round. Coil straight part of wire down around bead **(n)**. Flip second coil over to cap other end of bead **(o)**.

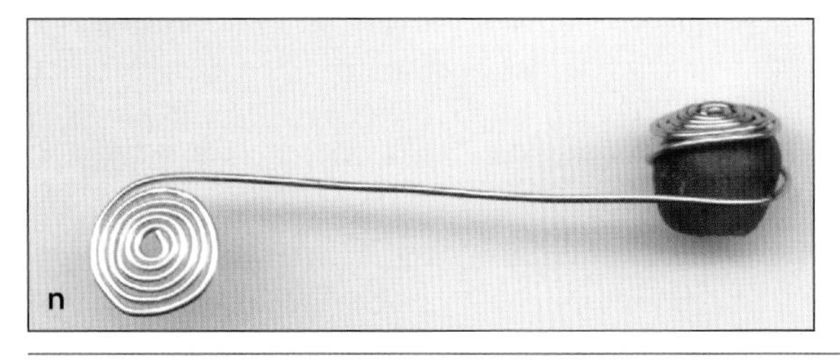
n

o

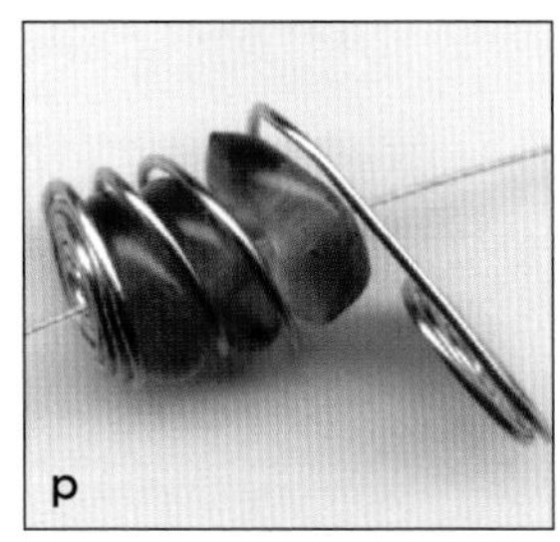
p

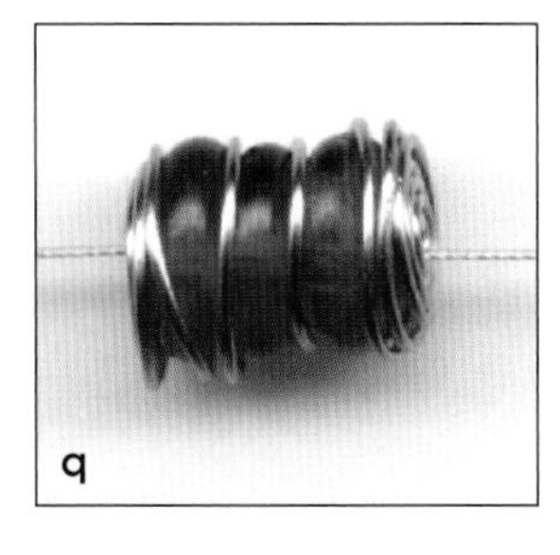
q

Capped Bead Triplet (make two):

9 Using 22-gauge wire, make a 12 mm spiral at one end, leave a 6-in. (15.2 cm) gap, and make a 12 mm spiral at the other end. Place one spiral over one end of a stack of three rondelles. Coil straight part of wire down around beads **(p)**. Flip second coil over to cap other end of beads **(q)**.

Note: String beads after first coil has been made to keep them evenly stacked.

Clasp

10 Using 18-gauge wire, make a spiral point clasp *(Spiral Point Clasp)*.

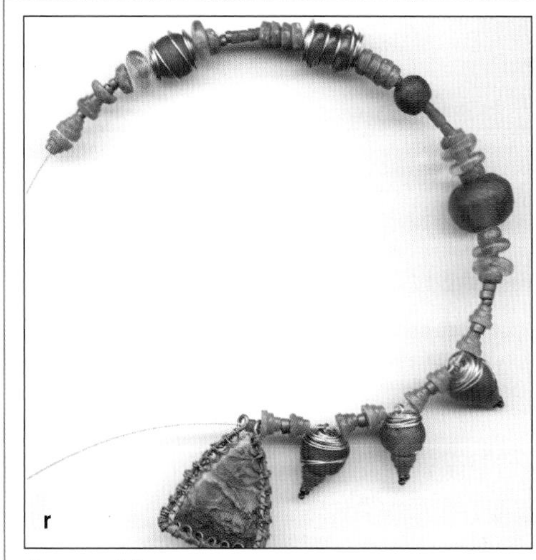
r

Assembly

11 String beads on flexible beading wire as shown **(r)**, repeating on the other side. Attach clasp with crimp beads.

Turquoise Ring & Bracelet

Turquoise, turquoise, and more turquoise: This lacy wire bezel lets the beauty of the stone speak for itself. The ring is easy to size and comfortable to wear, and the bracelet is constructed as a series of linked bezels.

Materials

RING

- approx. 6 ft. (1.8 m) 28-gauge dead-soft wire, gold
- 1 ft. (30.5 cm) 20-gauge half-hard wire, gold
- 13 x 18 mm turquoise cabochon

BRACELET

- 3½ ft. (1 m) 20-gauge half-hard wire, gold
- approx. 15 ft. (4.6 m) 28-gauge dead-soft wire, gold
- 20 x 20 mm square cabochon, turquoise
- **6** 15 x 20 mm oval cabochons, turquoise

Tools (both projects)

- roundnose pliers
- chainnose pliers
- wire cutters

Dimensions

RING: approx. 1 x ⅞ in. (25.5 x 22 mm)

BRACELET: approx. 7¾ in. (19.7 cm)

Technical Basics Reference

- Making Frames: Inset Ring Bezel Frame, p. 86
- Anchoring Wires, p. 87
- Making Base Rows: Unbeaded Outer Base Rows and Unbeaded Inner Base Rows, p. 87
- Finishing Off, p. 87
- Rearranging Rows Upright, p. 87
- Finishing Bezels: Lacing Up Bezels and Tightening Bezels around Cabochons, p. 88
- Building onto Base Rows: Anchoring and Unbeaded Arches, p. 88
- Jump Rings: Single Jump Rings, p. 92
- Clasps: Basic Hook-and-Eye Clasp, p. 92

a

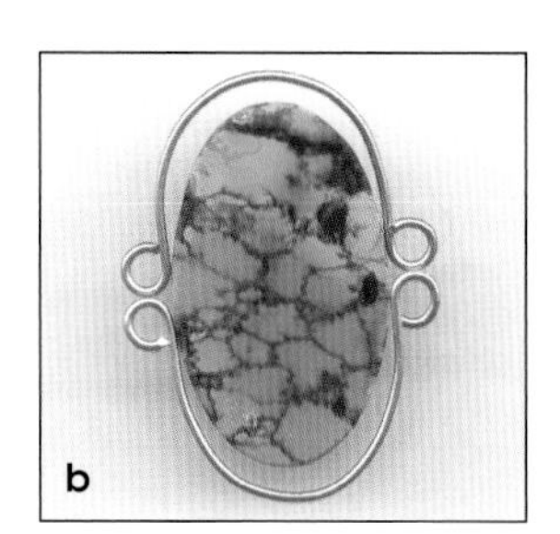
b

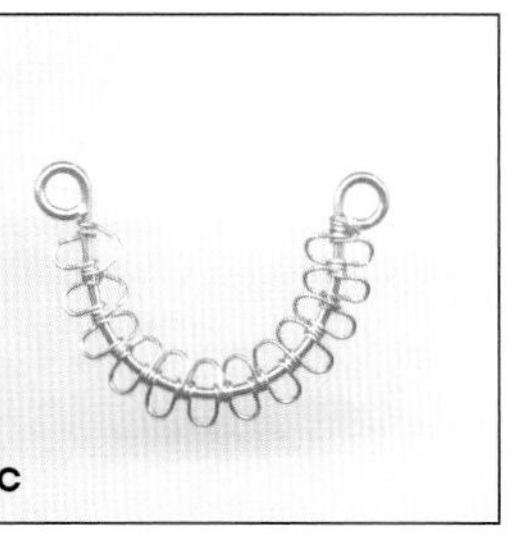
c

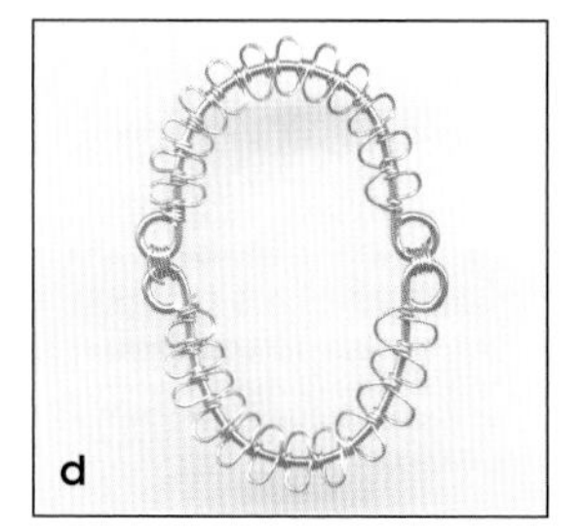
d

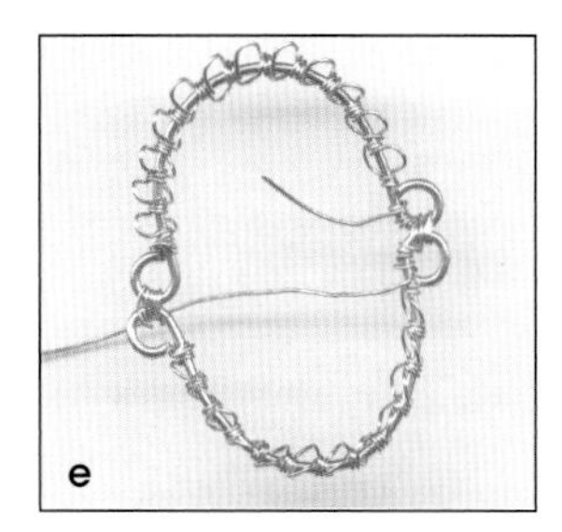
e

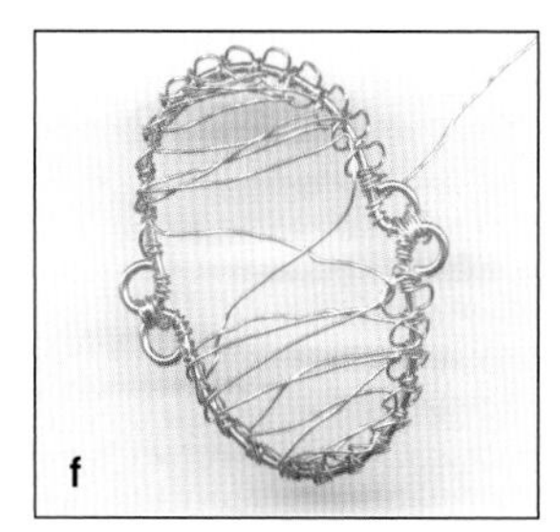
f

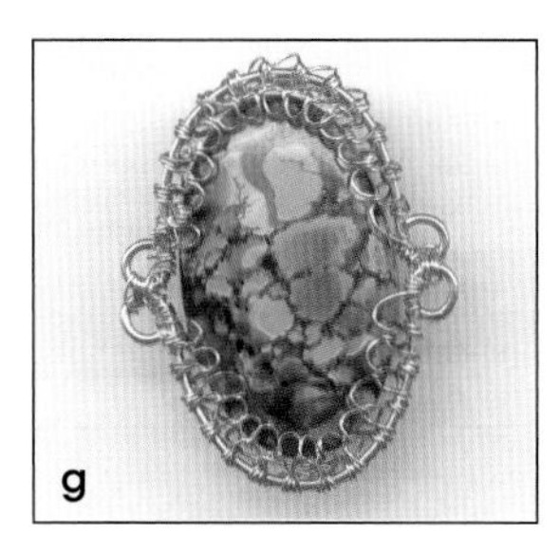
g

h

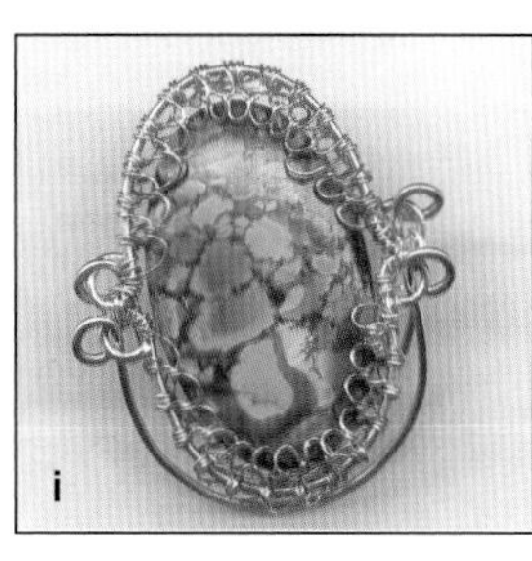
i

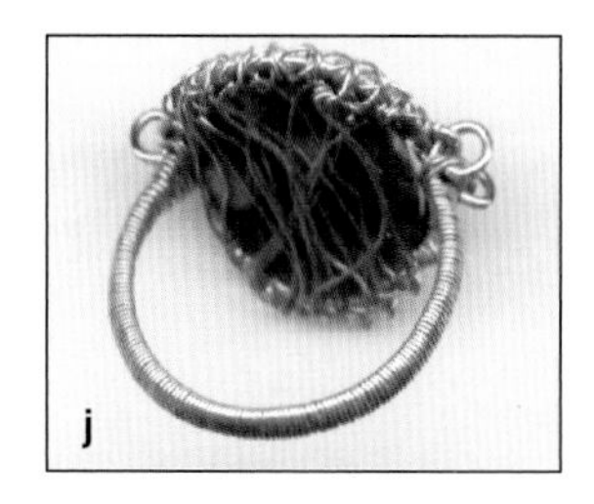
j

Turquoise Ring

Preparation

1 Cut 20-gauge wire into two 2-in. (51 mm) and two 4-in. (10.2 cm) pieces. Cut 28-gauge wire in half.

Bezel

2 Using 2-in. pieces, make basic ring frame (two frame halves) (*Inset Ring Bezel Frame*). Do not join frame halves together **(a, b)**.

Note: All arches are unbeaded.

Base Outer Row

3 Anchor 28-gauge wire to one frame half *(Anchoring Wires)* and make a 12-arch base outer row *(Unbeaded Outer Base Rows)*. Turn frame over and, working back in opposite direction, make a 12-arch base inner row *(Unbeaded Inner Base Rows)*. Finish off *(Finishing Off)* **(c)**. Repeat for other frame half.

4 Join two halves of the frame together *(Inset Ring Beaded Frame)* **(d)**.

5 Rearrange rows *(Rearranging Rows Upright)*. Lace up back side of bezel *(Lacing Up Bezels)*. Finish off **(e, f)**.

Second Outer Row

6 Anchor wire on either side of bezel on first arch of what is now front row of arches. Make an 11-arch second row on one side *(Anchoring* and *Unbeaded Arches)*. Repeat on opposite side.

7 Insert cabochon. Tighten bezel around cabochon *(Tightening Bezels around Cabochons)*.

Note: If cabochon is not secure in bezel, remove cabochon, add another unbeaded outer row onto what is now the top row of the bezel, reinsert cabochon, and repeat tightening process **(g)**.

Ring Band and Assembly

8 Using 4-in. pieces of 20-gauge wire, form two ring band sections. Insert ends of one band section up through frame loops. Curl loops at ends of band section towards outside of "U" shape. Repeat for other ring section **(h)**.

9 Clip short bits from ends of loops as needed for sizing ring band and curl loops down around frame loops **(i)**.

10 Anchor 28-gauge wire to ring band loops on one side of ring bands. Coil tightly and evenly around both ring band wires all the way to opposite set of ring band loops. Finish off in loops **(j)**.

Turquoise Bracelet

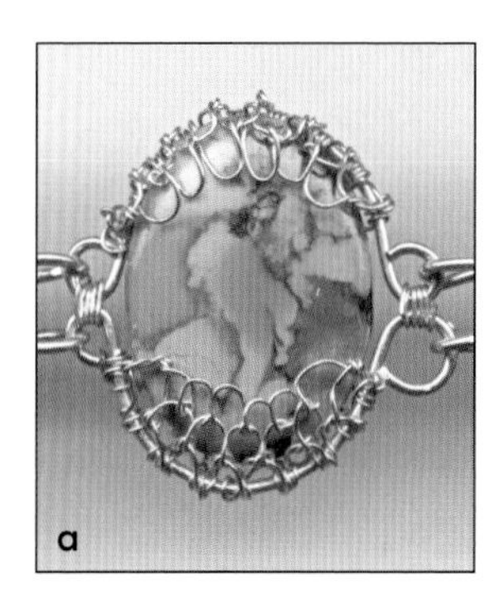
a

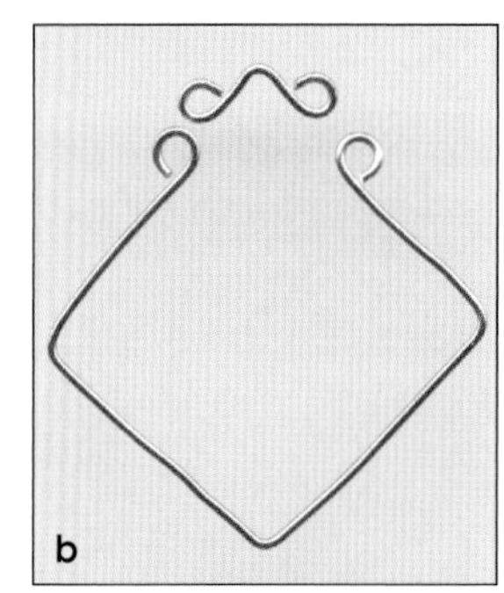
b

c

d

Preparation

1 Cut 20-gauge wire into 12 2-in. (51 cm) pieces, one 4-in. (10.2 cm) piece, one 1-in. (25.5 mm) piece, and one 13-in. (33 cm) piece. Cut 28-gauge wire into 2-ft. (61 cm) lengths.

Note: All arches are unbeaded.

Oval Bezels (make six)

Note: For general help with these oval bezels, see Turquoise Ring, Steps 3–7. Exact instructions for the bezels in this project are as follows:

2 Using 2-in. pieces of 20-gauge wire, make six basic oval ring frames (12 frame halves) *(Inset Ring Bezel Frame)*. Do not join frame halves together.

3 Anchor 28-gauge wire to a frame *(Anchoring Wires)*. Make an 8-arch base outer row *(Unbeaded Outer Base Rows)*. Do not clip tails.

4 Turn frame over and, working back in opposite direction, make an 8-arch base inner row *(Unbeaded Inner Base Rows)*. Do not clip tails.

5 Turn and anchor wire in last arch made. Working back in opposite direction, add a 7-arch second outer row *(Anchoring* and *Unbeaded Arches)*.

6 Turn and anchor wire in last arch made. Working back in opposite direction, add a 6-arch third outer row as above. Finish off *(Finishing Off)*.

7 Repeat Steps 3–6 for other half of frame.

8 Join frame halves together *(Inset Ring Bezel Frame)*. Rearrange rows of arches *(Rearranging Rows Upright)*. Anchor a piece of 28-gauge wire in any arch at back of bezel. Lace up back side *(Lacing Up Bezels)*. Finish off.

9 Insert cabochon. Tighten bezel around cabochon *(Tightening Bezels around Cabochons)* **(a)**.

Diamond-Shaped Bezel

10 Using the 4-in. piece of 20-gauge wire, bend at a 45° angle at halfway point. Bend again on either side about 7/8 in. (22 mm) from first bend. Trim wires so that they just meet at top of frame. Curl loops towards outside of frame. Using 1-in piece of 20-gauge wire, bend at a 45° angle at halfway point. Curl a loop towards outside of "V" shape on each side **(b)**.

11 Anchor a piece of 28-gauge wire to small frame section. Make a 3-arch base outer row. Turn and, working in opposite direction, make a 3-arch base inner row.

12 Turn. Anchor wire in last arch made. Working back in opposite direction, make a 2-arch second outer row. Finish off **(c)**.

13 Anchor a scrap of wire to frame loop on small frame. Make an arch into last arch made. Make an arch into next arch. Make an arch into other frame loop. Finish off **(d)**.

14 Anchor a piece of 28-gauge wire to large frame. Make a 21-arch base outer row (three arches on each short side, six on each long side, and one at each corner) **(e)**.

15 Turn and, working in opposite direction, make a 21-arch base inner row **(f)**.

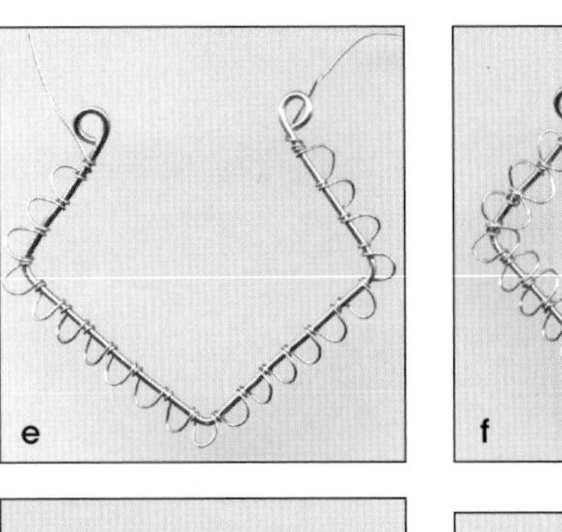
e

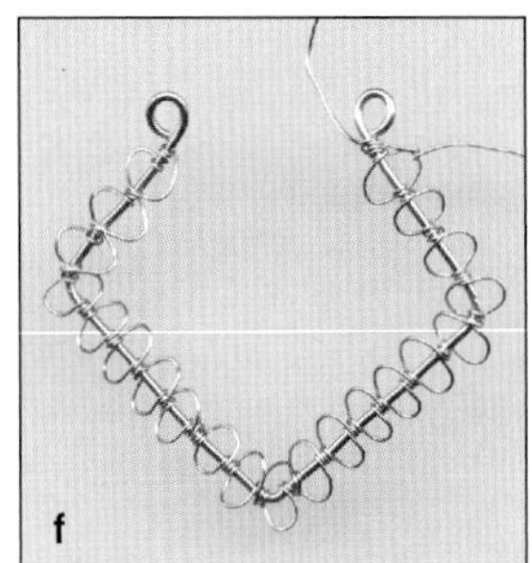
f

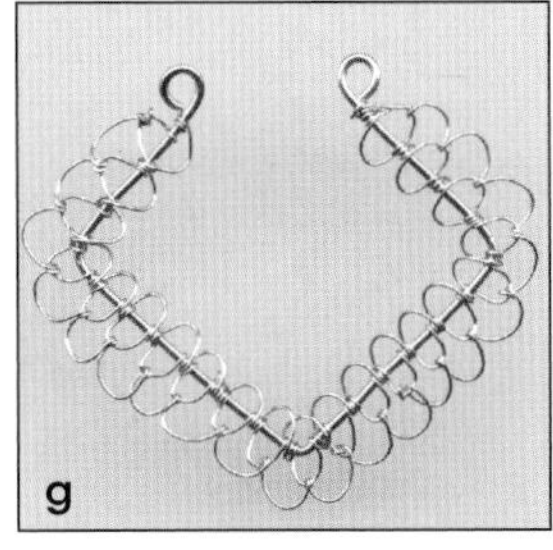
g

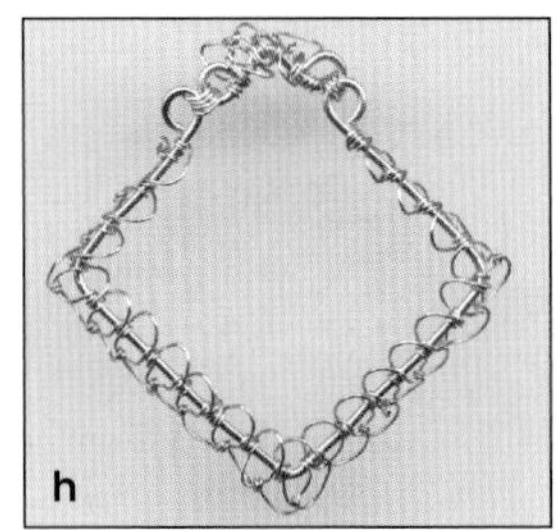
h

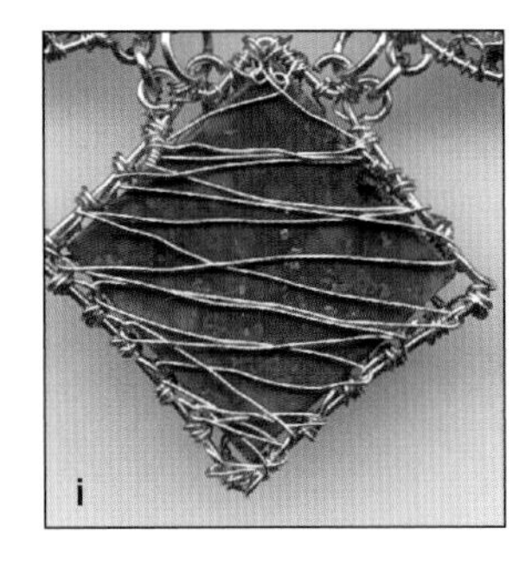
i

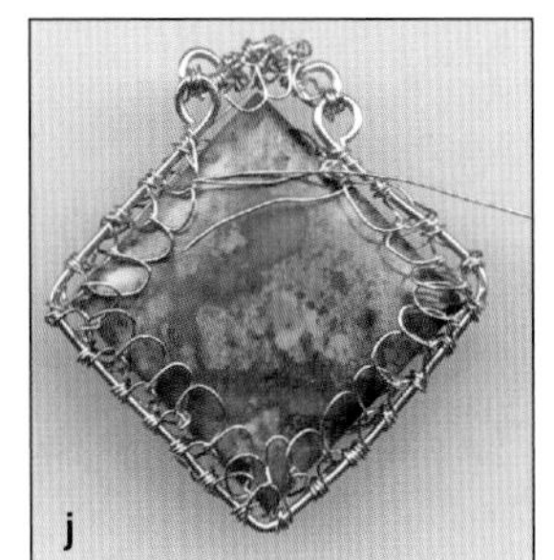
j

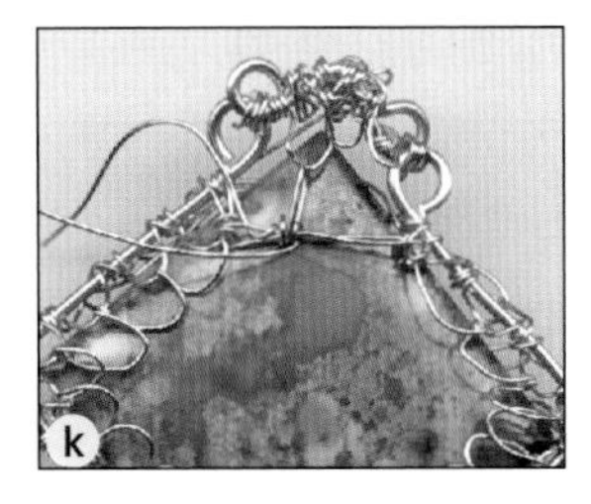
k

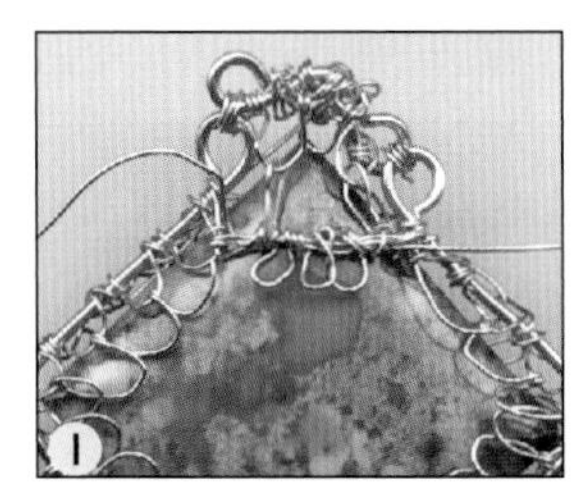
l

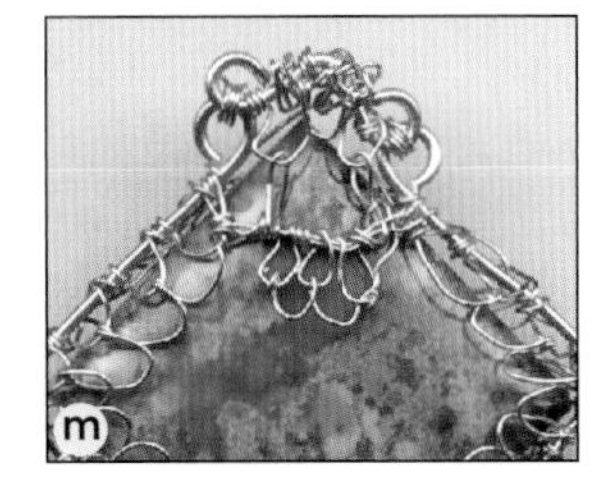
m

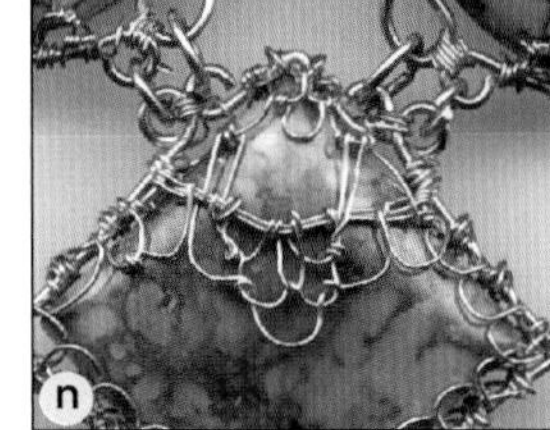
n

16 Turn. Anchor wire in last arch made. Working back in opposite direction, make a 20-arch second outer row. Finish off **(g)**.

17 Join the two frame sections together **(h)**.

18 Anchor a new piece of 28-gauge wire in any arch at back of frame and lace up bezel. Finish off.

19 Insert cabochon. Tighten bezel around cabochon **(i)**.

20 Anchor a piece of 28-gauge wire to first arch on base outer row of large frame. Carry wire straight across to last arch on opposite side. Coil twice tightly around top of arch. Carry wire back to starting point. Coil around at beginning point **(j)**.

21 Carry wire to first outer arch on small frame. Bring it through arch and carry back to doubled straight wire section just made. Coil around straight section twice. Make three arches along doubled straight wire section. Carry wire to third outer arch on small frame. Carry wire back to doubled straight wire section. Coil twice around doubled wire. Do not clip tails **(k, l)**.

22 Bring wire up through last arch made and anchor. Make an arch into each of next two arches. Finish off **(m)**.

23 Anchor a piece of 28-gauge wire to first arch on second outer row of frame. Make an arch onto doubled wire section prior to last wire join. Make an arch into each of next two arches. Make an arch onto doubled wire section. Make an arch into last arch on second outer row of frame. Finish off **(n)**.

Assembly

24 With 20-gauge wire, make 22 jump rings (*Single Jump Rings*) and a curlicue hook (*Basic Hook and Eye Clasp*).

25 Attach bezels with jump rings, using two jump rings between each pair of bezels and at ends **(n)**.

26 Attach a jump ring to both jump rings at each end. Attach two more rings to each end of bracelet, attaching the hook clasp at one end.

ch.3

Wrap around Bezel

Simple & Fancy Ammonite Necklaces

Materials

SIMPLE AMMONITE NECKLACE

- 1⅛ x 1⅜ in. (29 x 35 mm) ammonite slice
- 3–4 ft. (91.4–121.9 cm) 24-gauge wire, copper
- 5–6 in. (12.7–15.2 cm) 18-gauge wire, copper
- 2½ ft. (76.2 cm) 1.5 mm leather cord, brown
- **2–4** beads for leather ends

FANCY AMMONITE NECKLACE

- 1½ x 1¾ in. (38 x 44 mm) ammonite slice
- approx. 4 ft. (121.9 cm) 24-gauge wire, copper
- 4½ ft. (137.2 cm)18-gauge wire, copper
- **4** 11 x 14 mm Tibetan alabaster beads, browns and golds
- **12** 10 x 3 mm shallow-dome Afghani bead caps, copper
- **12** 3 x 10 mm Krobo recycled glass rondelles, amber
- **6** Krobo recycled glass cones, caramel
- **2** 12 x 12 mm Krobo recycled glass rounds, dark amber
- **2** 8 mm Krobo recycled glass rounds, light amber
- **2** 8 mm Krobo recycled glass rounds, dark amber
- **4** 6 mm Krobo recycled glass rounds, burgundy
- **8** 4 mm fire-polished beads (or E beads), gold

Tools
(both projects)

- roundnose pliers
- chainnose pliers
- wire cutters

Pendant Dimensions
(both projects)

approx. 1¼ x 1½ in. (32 x 38 mm) or 1½ in. x 1¾ in. (38 x 44 mm)

Necklace length

FANCY AMMONITE NECKLACE:
19 in. (48.3 cm)

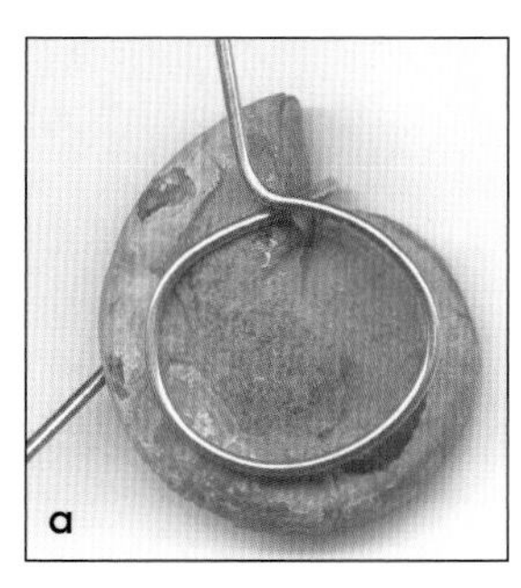

a

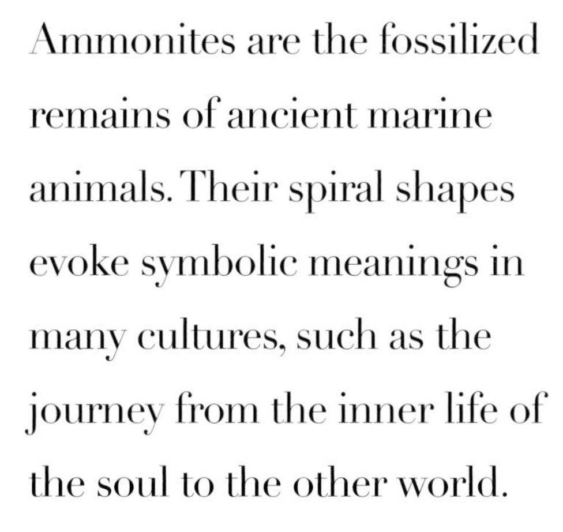

Ammonites are the fossilized remains of ancient marine animals. Their spiral shapes evoke symbolic meanings in many cultures, such as the journey from the inner life of the soul to the other world.

Technical Basics Reference
- Making Frames: Wraparound Bezel Frame, p. 86
- Anchoring Wires, p. 87
- Making Base Rows: Unbeaded Outer Base Rows, p. 87
- Building onto Base Rows, p. 88
- Finishing Off, p. 87
- Finishing Bezels: Tightening Bezels around Cabochons, p. 88
- Jump Rings: Single Jump Rings, p. 92
- Spiral Point Motif, p. 93
- Clasps: Spiral Point Clasp, p. 92

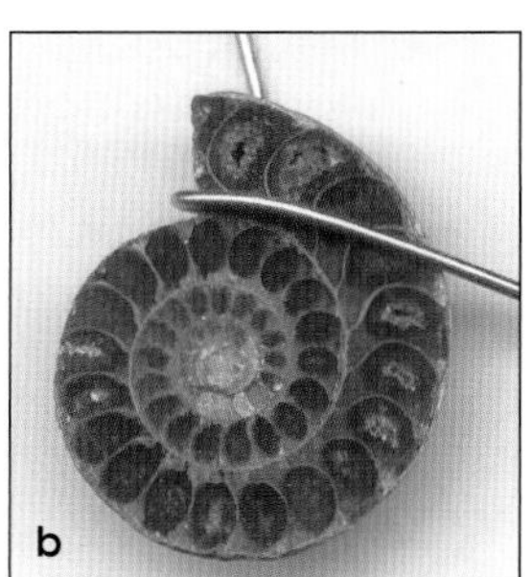

b

Simple Ammonite Necklace

1 Using 18-gauge wire, make a wraparound bezel frame *(Wraparound Bezel Frame)* **(a)**.

2 Bend one end of wire around in front and across top section of ammonite **(b)**. Clip to about 1 in. (25.5 mm) and, using roundnose pliers, curl a spiral from tail end inward **(c)**. Remove the fossil.

c

3 Anchor a 24-gauge wire firmly around both wires at top of frame to close frame *(Anchoring Wires)*. Make a base outer row of arches *(Unbeaded Outer Base Rows)*, forming as many arches as necessary (for a 1-in. ammonite, start with about 18 arches; for a 1½ in./38 mm, about 28). Do not clip tails **(d, e)**.

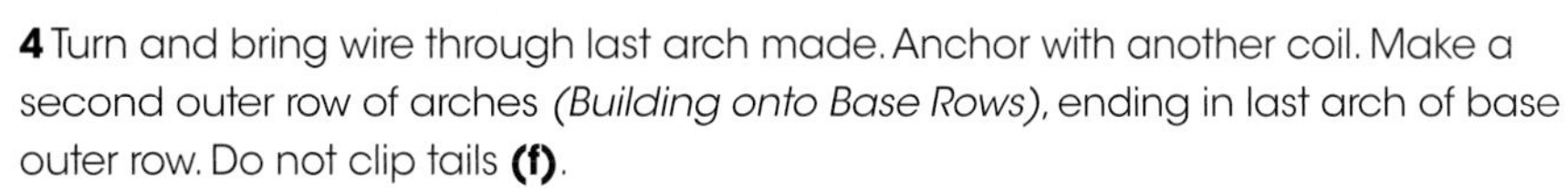

4 Turn and bring wire through last arch made. Anchor with another coil. Make a second outer row of arches *(Building onto Base Rows)*, ending in last arch of base outer row. Do not clip tails **(f)**.

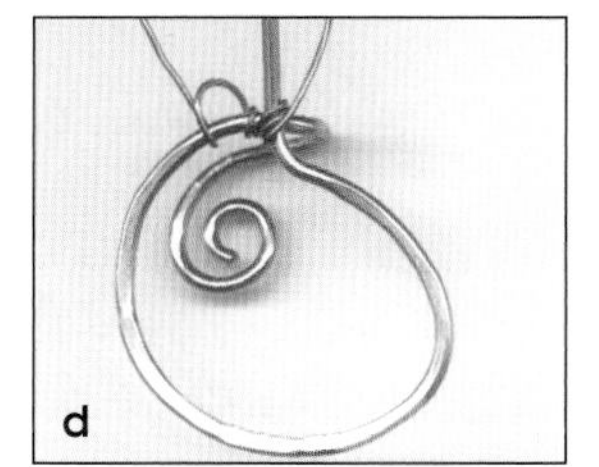

d

5 Repeat Step 4 for third outer row.

6 Continue building outer rows on each other until lace is wide enough to wrap up and over front edges of ammonite **(g)**. Finish off *(Finishing Off)*. Using your fingers, gently press edges of lace around front of ammonite. Tighten lace around ammonite *(Tightening Bezels around Cabochons)* **(h)**.

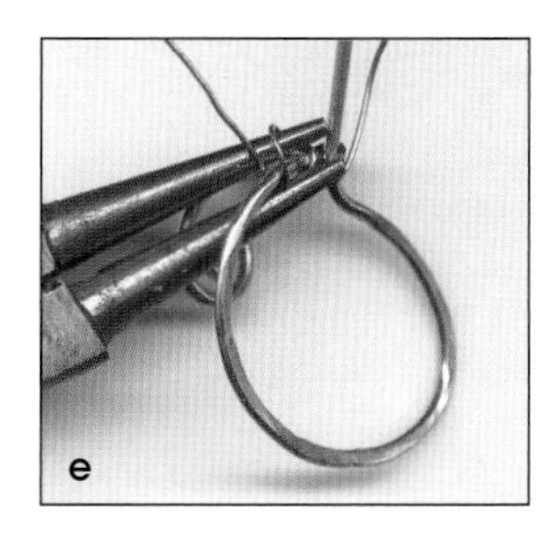

e

7 Clip tail to about 1 in. Using roundnose pliers, curl a spiral from tail end forward, making the inner curl large enough to string leather through **(i)**.

8 String spiral on leather. Tie overhand knot 1½ in. from each end. String one or two beads on each end and tie overhand knot to secure in place. With a 3-in. (76 mm) piece of cord, tie a square knot around both pieces of leather just loosely enough that the leather pieces can slide when pulled. Knot and trim the ends.

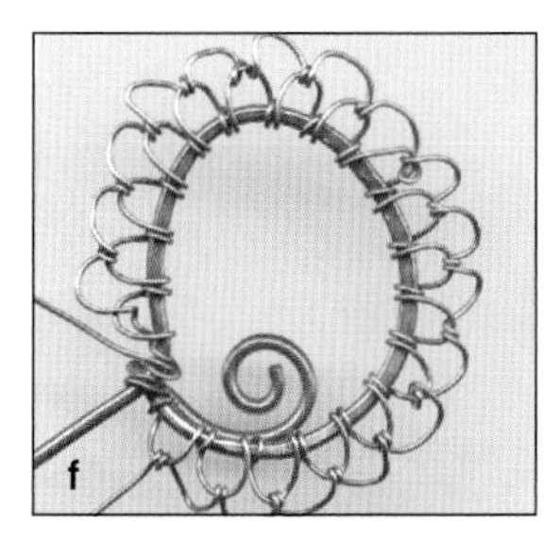

f

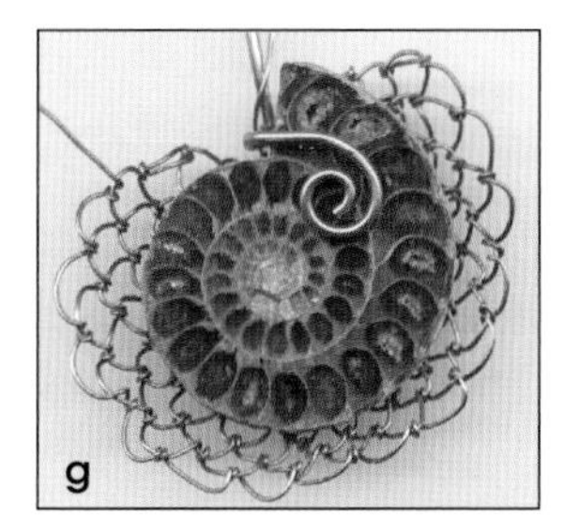

g

h

i

a

b

c

d

e

f

Fancy Ammonite Necklace

1 Cut 18-gauge wire into four equal pieces. Using one piece and the 24-gauge wire, follow steps 1–7 of the Simple Ammonite Necklace instructions.

2 With a piece of 18-gauge wire, make 20 jump rings *(Single Jump Rings)*.

3 Curl a loop on one end of a piece of 18-gauge wire. String a 4 mm burgundy Krobo round bead. Bend the wire slightly and string the top coil of bezel. String a 4 mm burgundy round. Clip excess wire and curl a loop **(a)**.

Spiral Rondelle Unit (make two)

4 With a scrap piece of 18-gauge wire, make a spiral point motif *(Spiral Point Motif)*. Add three Krobo rondelles. Clip excess wire to ⅜ in. (9.5 mm) and curl a loop **(b)**.

Tibetan Alabaster Unit (make four):

5 Curl a loop at one end of a scrap piece of 18-gauge wire. String a 4 mm gold fire-polished bead, a bead cap upside down, a Tibetan alabaster bead, another bead cap, and another gold fire-polished bead. Clip excess wire to ⅜ in. and curl a loop **(c)**.

Burgundy Connector (make two)

6 Curl a loop at one end of a scrap piece of 18-gauge wire. String a 4 mm burgundy Krobo round bead. Clip excess wire to ⅜ in. and curl a loop **(d)**.

Krobo Bead Unit (make two)

7 Make a spiral point motif at one end of a scrap piece of 18-gauge wire. String a bead cap, a 12 mm Krobo round dark amber bead, and another bead cap. Clip excess wire to ⅜ in. and curl a loop **(e)**.

Rondelle Connector (make two)

8 Curl a loop at one end of a scrap piece of 18-gauge wire. String three Krobo rondelles. Clip excess wire to ⅜ in. and curl a loop.

Dark Amber Connector (make two)

9 Curl a loop at one end of a scrap piece of 18-gauge wire. String an 8 mm Krobo dark amber bead. Clip excess wire to ⅜ in. and curl a loop.

Cone Bead Connector (make two)

10 Curl a loop at one end of a scrap piece of 18-gauge wire. String three Krobo cone beads. Clip excess wire to ⅜ in. and curl a loop **(f)**.

Light Amber Connector (make two)

11 Curl a loop at one end of a scrap piece of 18-gauge wire. String an 8 mm Krobo light amber bead. Clip excess wire to ⅜ in. and curl a loop.

Clasp

12 Make a spiral point clasp *(Spiral Point Clasp)* with 18-gauge wire.

Assembly

13 Use jump rings to connect components on each side of the pendant as follows: spiral rondelle unit, Tibetan alabaster unit, burgundy connector, Krobo bead unit, Tibetan alabaster unit, rondelle connector, dark amber connector, cone bead connector, light amber connector, clasp half.

Shell Pendant

A lacy wire bezel can turn the simplest object into an unusual and lovely piece of jewelry. This shell, caught in a golden net, becomes a necklace fit for a mermaid ... or a princess.

Materials
- 1⅛ x 2 in. (29 x 51 mm) shell
- approx. 4 ft. (122.5 cm) 28-gauge wire, gold
- 8 in. (20.3 cm) 20-gauge wire, gold
- 20 in. (50.8 cm) chain, gold
- lobster claw clasp, gold
- 6 mm split ring or jump ring, gold

Tools
- roundnose pliers
- chainnose pliers
- wire cutters

Pendant Dimensions
approx. 1⅛ in. x 2 in. (29 x 51 mm)

Technical Basics Reference
- Making Frames: Wraparound Bezel Frame, p. 86
- Anchoring Wires, p. 87
- Making Base Rows: Unbeaded Outer Base Rows, p. 87
- Building onto Base Rows: Anchoring and Unbeaded Arches, p. 88
- Finishing Bezels: Tightening Bezels around Cabochons, p. 88

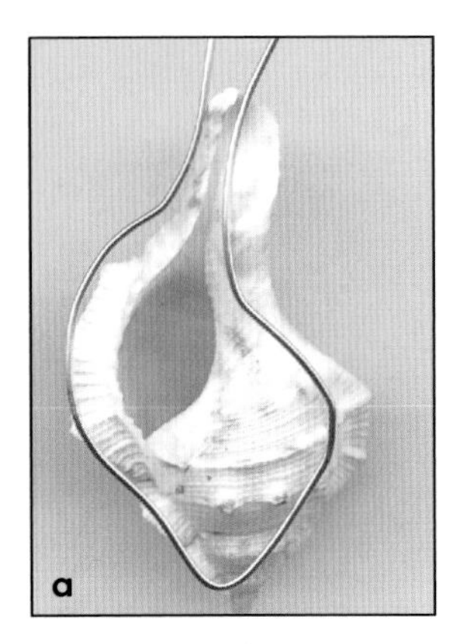

a

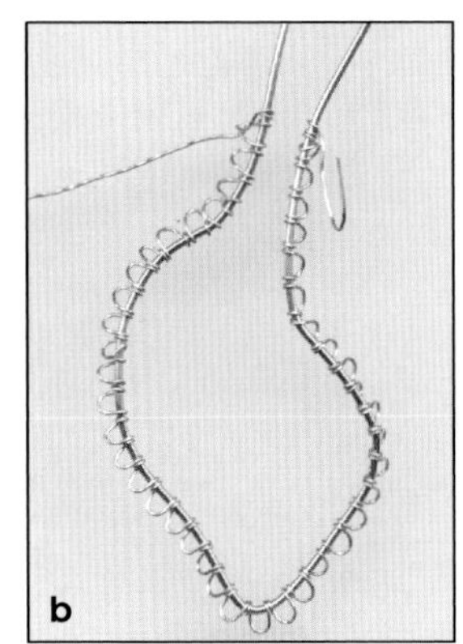

b

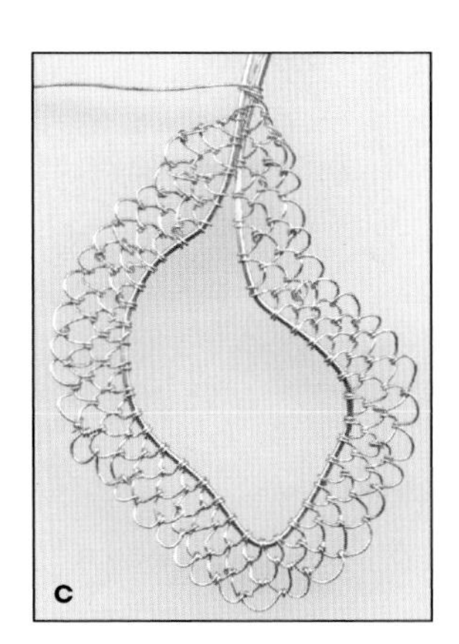

c

d

e

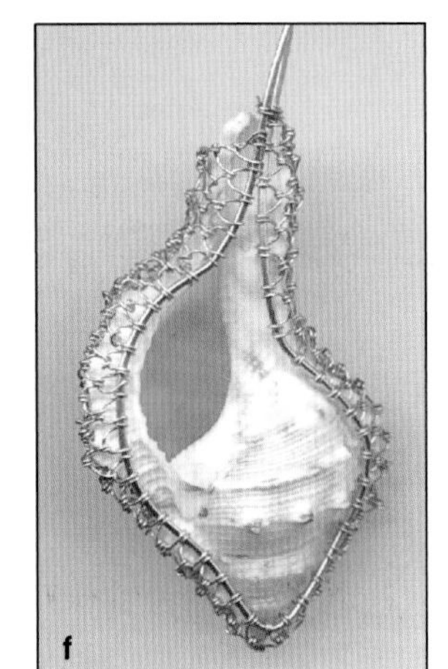

f

g

Bezel Frame

1 Using 20-gauge wire, make a wraparound bezel frame *(Wraparound Bezel Frame)* in shape of open side of shell **(a)**.

2 Cut 28-gauge wire into 2-ft. (61 cm) lengths. Anchor a 28-gauge wire firmly around one wire at top of frame *(Anchoring Wires)*. Make a base outer row of unbeaded arches *(Unbeaded Outer Base Rows)*, forming as many arches as necessary for the size of the shell (for a 1⅛ in x 2 in./29 x 51 mm shell, about 42 small arches). Do not clip tails **(b)**.

3 Turn and bring wire through last arch made. Anchor with another coil. Make a second outer row of arches *(Anchoring* and *Unbeaded Arches)*, ending in last arch of base outer row. Do not clip tails.

4 Repeat Step 3 for third outer row.

5 Continue building outer rows on each other until lace is wide enough to wrap up and over front edges of shell. Finish off *(Finishing Off)*.

6 Using a scrap of 28-gauge wire, coil several times around top of frame just above top arches to close frame **(c)**. Finish off.

7 Gently press edges of lace around front of shell **(d)**.

8 Tighten lace around shell *(Tightening Bezels around Cabochons)* **(e, f)**.

9 Clip any excess wire from top of frame and curl loops towards front side of shell **(g)**.

Finishing

10 Thread chain through top frame loops. Attach clasp and ring.

ch. 4 Beaded Bezels

Crazy Lace Agate Necklace

Materials

- 2 ft. (91.4 cm) 20-gauge half-hard wire, gold
- approx. 20 ft. (6 m) 28-gauge dead-soft wire, gold
- 30 mm cabochon, round or marquise-shaped brown and gold crazy lace
- **2** 20 x 27 mm diamond-shaped cabochons, brown and gold crazy lace
- **2** 12 x 18 mm teardrop-shaped cabochons, brown and gold crazy lace
- **4** 4 mm bicone crystals, copper
- **2** 4 mm bicone crystals, dark brown
- **2** 4 mm bicone crystals, smoky quartz
- **2** 6 mm round crystals, light amber
- **4** 2 x 4 mm rondelles, citrine
- **4** 3 mm rounds, smoky quartz
- **3** 2.5 mm rounds, yellow jade
- **130** (approx.) 2–4 mm beads in mixed colors and shapes, including: gemstone, glass, metal, etc.; gold, bronze, dark green, light green, turquoise, amber, brown; round, rondelle, bicone, barrel, seed beads
- 4 g 15º charlottes, gold
- 2 ft. (60.9 cm) 1.5 mm leather cord, metallic gold
- **2** fold-over crimps
- lobster claw clasp and 6 mm soldered jump ring, gold

Tools

- roundnose pliers
- chainnose pliers
- wire cutters

Dimensions of Front Section

approx. 9 x 2 in. (22.9 x 51 cm)

Technical Basics Reference

- Making Frames: Inset Ring Bezel Frame, p. 86 and Unbeaded Inner Base Rows, p. 87
- Anchoring Wires, p. 87
- Finishing Off, p. 87
- Making Base Rows: Unbeaded Outer Base Rows, p. 87
- Rearranging Rows Upright, p. 88
- Finishing Bezels: Lacing Up Bezels and Tightening Bezels around Cabochons, p. 88

This lavish concoction of gemstones and crystals draws together warm brown and golden hues for a look that's both regal and relaxed.

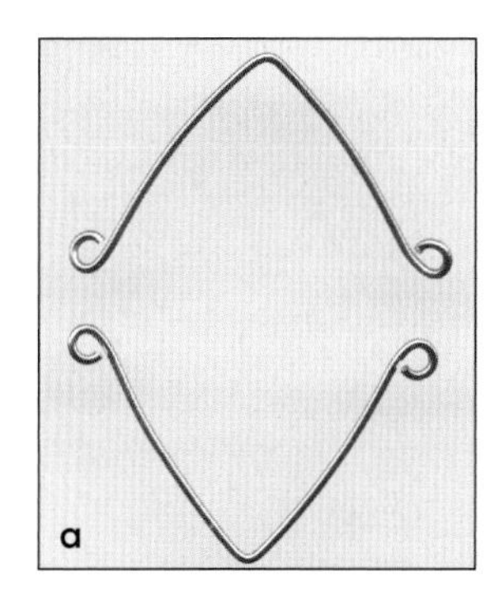
a

Preparation

1 Cut 20-gauge wire into two 3-in. (76 mm) pieces, four 2-in. (51 mm) pieces, and four 1½-in. (38 mm) pieces. Cut 28-gauge wire into 36 3-in. pieces. Cut remaining 28-gauge wire into 2-ft. (91.4 cm) lengths.

2 Using the 3-in. pieces of 20-gauge wire, make a basic ring frame (two frame halves) in a marquise shape *(Inset Ring Bezel Frame)*. Do not join together **(a)**.

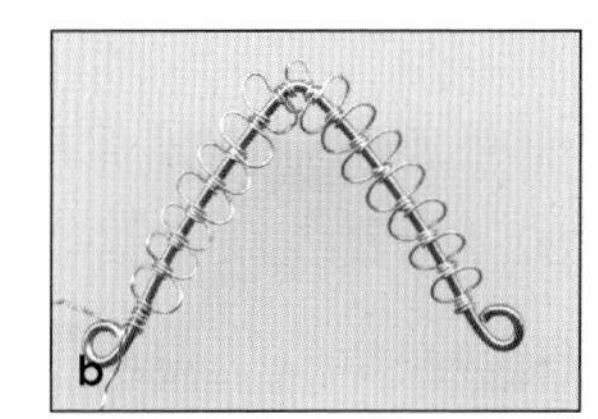
b

3 Using the 2-in. pieces, make two diamond-shaped basic ring frames (four frame halves). Do not join together.

4 Using the 1½-in. pieces, make two teardrop-shaped basic ring frames (four frame halves). Do not join together.

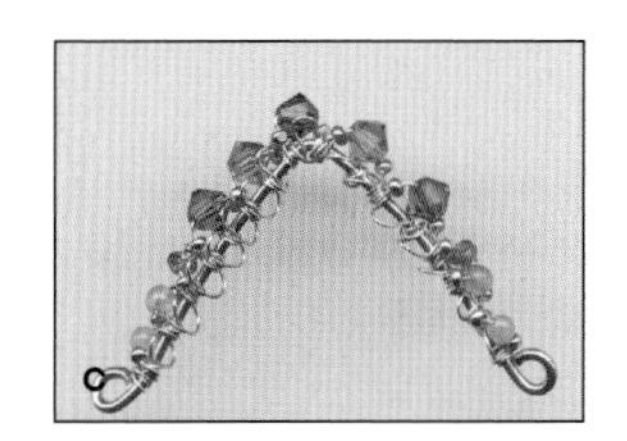
c

Marquise-Shaped Bezel

5 Anchor a piece of 28-gauge wire to a marquise-shaped bezel frame half *(Anchoring Wires)*. Make a 15-arch unbeaded base outer row *(Unbeaded Outer Base Rows)*. Turn frame over and, working back in opposite direction, make a 15-arch unbeaded base inner row *(Unbeaded Inner Base Rows)*. Do not clip tails **(b)**.

6 Rearrange rows of arches *(Rearranging Rows Upright)*. Turn frame over and, working back in opposite direction, make an 11-arch base outer row of 3-bead arches alternating one larger bead with two charlottes as follows: yellow jade, smoky quartz round, citrine, smoky quartz bicone, copper bicone, brown bicone, copper bicone, smoky quartz bicone, citrine, smoky quartz round, and yellow jade.

d

Note: Each of the side arches with the bicones should span two base top and bottom row arches. Finish off *(Finishing Off)* **(c)**.

7 Repeat Steps 5–6 for other frame half.

8 Join frame halves together *(Inset Ring Bezel Frame)*. Anchor a piece of 28-gauge wire in any arch at back of bezel. Lace up back side *(Lacing Up Bezels)*. Finish off **(d)**.

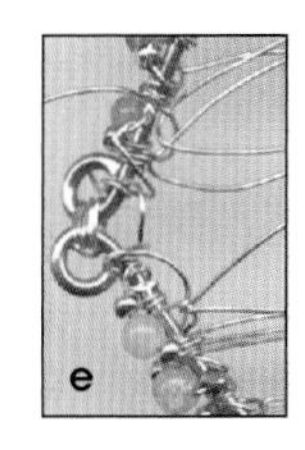
e

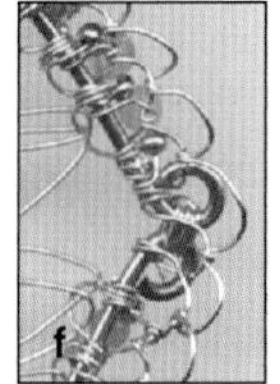
f

9 Anchor a new piece of 28-gauge wire to any front arch and make a 38-arch unbeaded second front row.

Note: Place an extra arch into each frame loop to span the space where the frame halves are joined **(e)**.

10 Bring the wire up through the first arch made and anchor. Repeat Step 9 to make a 38-arch unbeaded third front row **(f)**.

g

11 Repeat Step 10 to make a 38-arch unbeaded fourth front row. Finish off.

12 Insert 30 mm cabochon. Tighten bezel around cabochon *(Tightening Bezels around Cabochons)* **(g)**.

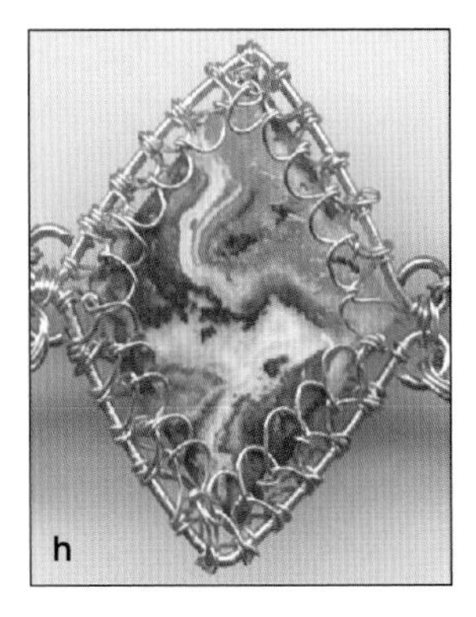

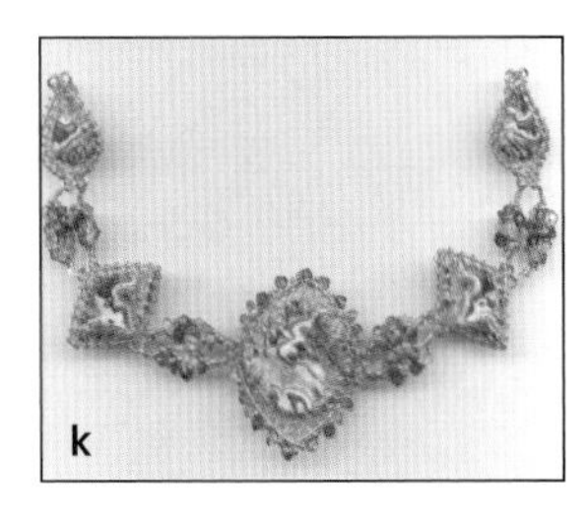

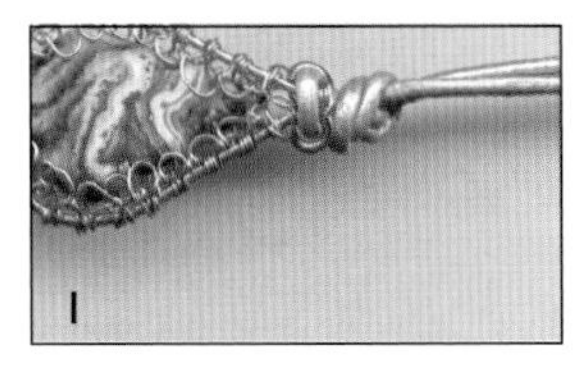

Diamond-Shaped Bezels

13 Anchor a piece of 28-gauge wire to a diamond-shaped bezel frame half. Make an 11-arch unbeaded base outer row. Turn frame over and, working back in opposite direction, make an 11-arch unbeaded base inner row. Finish off. Repeat for other diamond-shaped frame half.

14 Join frame halves together. Anchor a piece of 28-gauge wire in any arch at back of bezel. Lace up back. Finish off.

15 Anchor a new piece of 28-gauge wire to any front arch and make a 26-arch unbeaded second front row.

Note: Place an extra arch into each frame loop to span the space where the frame halves are joined.

16 Insert cabochon. Tighten bezel around cabochon **(h)**.

17 Repeat Steps 13–16 for remaining diamond-shaped bezel.

Teardrop-Shaped Bezels

18 Anchor a piece of 28-gauge wire to a teardrop-shaped bezel frame half. Make a 12-arch unbeaded base outer row. Turn frame over and, working back in opposite direction, make a 12-arch unbeaded base inner row. Finish off. Repeat for other half.

19 Join frame halves together. Anchor a piece of 28-gauge wire in any arch at back of bezel. Lace up back side. Finish off.

20 Anchor a new piece of 28-gauge wire to any front arch and make a 24-arch unbeaded second front row.

Note: Place an extra arch into each frame loop to span the space where the frame halves are joined.

21 Insert cabochon. Tighten bezel around cabochon **(i)**.

22 Repeat Steps 18–21 for remaining teardrop-shaped bezel.

Joining the Links

Note: Set aside two 6 mm round light amber crystal beads.

23 Using four 3-in. pieces of 28-gauge wire as one, make a wire wrap into one of the loops on the marquise-shaped bezel. String 6–7 remaining beads (including charlottes) randomly on each piece. (The beaded portions should all be approximately the same length—about ⅝ in.) Using all four pieces as one again, make a wire wrap into the corresponding loop on one of the diamond-shaped bezels **(j)**.

24 Repeat Step 23 on the other loops of same two bezels, making the beaded sections about ⅛ in. (3 mm) longer.

25 Repeat Steps 23–24 to connect second diamond-shaped bezel to other side of marquise-shaped bezel, and twice to connect teardrop-shaped bezels to diamond-shaped bezels **(k)**.

Finishing

26 Cut leather into two equal pieces. Slide the ends of one leather piece from front to back through the end frame loops of one of the teardrop-shaped bezels. Even out the tails. Make an overhand knot as close to the frame loops as possible **(l)**.

27 Trim leather tails as needed to get desired length. Add fold-over crimps. Using a scrap of wire or a headpin, attach clasp by wire wrapping a 6 mm round amber crystal between loop on crimp and clasp loop. Repeat on other side, using the soldered jump ring **(m)**.

Turquoise Bracelet

Unabashedly opulent, this "linked" bracelet of turquoise, gemstones, glass, and metal is at home at the fanciest of events, yet it's just casual enough to wear with jeans.

Technical Basics Reference

- Making Bezels: Inset Ring Bezel Frame, p. 86
- Anchoring Wires, p. 87
- Making Base Rows: Unbeaded Outer Base Rows and Unbeaded Inner Base Rows, p. 87
- Finishing Off, p. 87
- Rearranging Rows Upright, p. 87
- Making Base Bezel Rows: Beaded Outer Base Bezel Rows, p. 87
- Finishing Bezels: Lacing Up Bezels and Tightening Bezels around Cabochons, p. 88
- Clasps: Hook-and-Bar Clasp, p. 93

Materials

- 3½ ft. (1 m) 20-gauge half-hard wire, gold
- approx. 16 ft. (4.9 m) 28-gauge dead-soft wire, gold
- **2** 7 x 20 mm long oval cabochons, green and brown turquoise
- **3** 22 x 22 mm square cabochons, green and brown turquoise
- **52** 3.5 x 3.5 mm faceted beads, peridot
- **4** 3.5 mm faceted beads, hessonite garnet
- **28** 2 mm rounds, light green chalcedony
- 3 g 15º charlottes or seed beads, gold
- 3 g translucent 11º seed beads, dark amber
- 3 g matte 11º seed beads, dark brown
- 1 g 11º seed beads, dark green
- 3 g opaque 11º seed beads, light green
- **150** 2–4 mm beads in mixed colors and shapes: gemstone, glass, metal; gold, bronze, dark and light green, turquoise, amber, brown; round, rondelle, bicone, barrel, seed beads

Tools

- roundnose pliers
- chainnose pliers
- wire cutters

Dimensions

approx. 8¼ in. (21 cm)

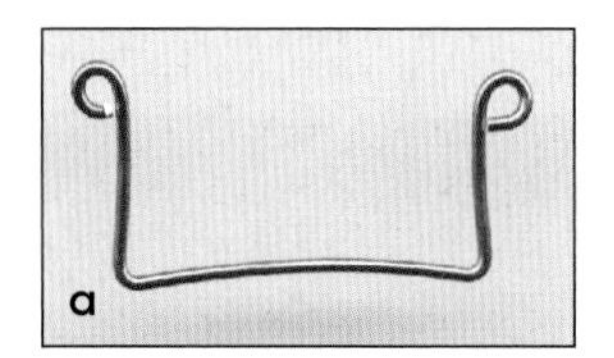
a

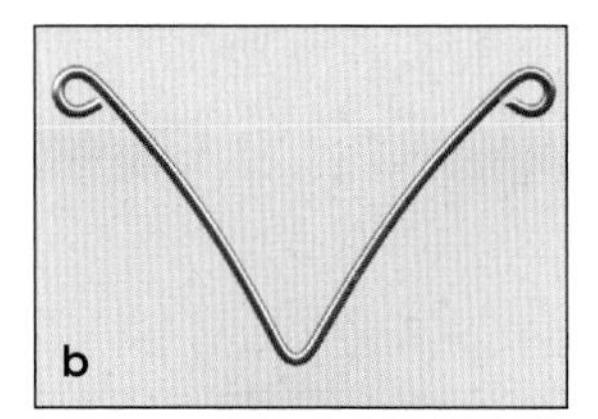
b

Preparation

1 Cut 20-gauge wire into six 2½-in. (64 mm) pieces and four 1¾-in. (44 mm) pieces. Cut 28-gauge wire into 36 3-in. (76 mm) pieces, and then 2-ft. (61 cm) lengths.

2 Using 2½-in. pieces of 20-gauge wire, make three basic ring frames (six frame halves) *(Inset Ring Bezel Frame)*: two for a square bezel **(a)** and one for a diamond-shaped bezel **(b)**. Using 1¾-in. pieces of 20-gauge wire, make two long oval basic ring frames (four frame halves) **(c)**. Do not join frame halves together.

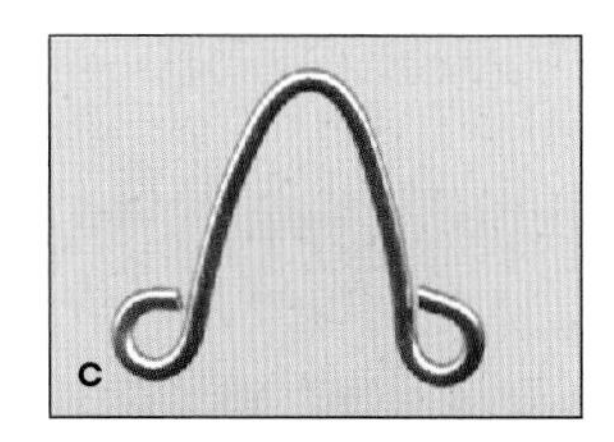
c

Diamond-Shaped Bezel

3 Anchor a piece of 28-gauge wire to a diamond-shaped bezel frame half *(Anchoring Wires)*. Make five more tight coils. Make five unbeaded arches along same side *(Unbeaded Outer Base Rows)*. Turn frame over and, working back in opposite direction, make a 5-arch unbeaded base inner row *(Unbeaded Inner Base Rows)* **(d)**. Finish off *(Finishing Off)*. Repeat for opposite side of same frame half.

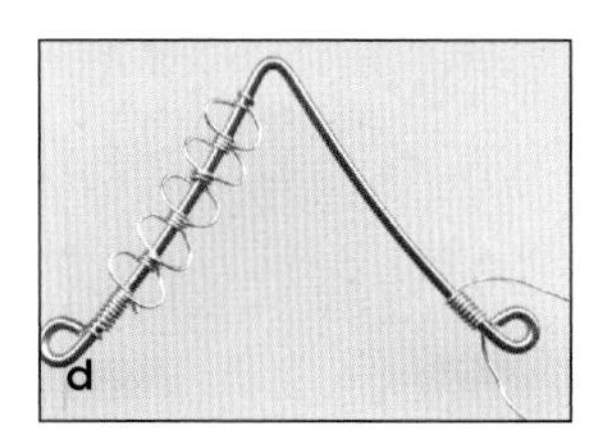
d

4 Rearrange rows of arches *(Rearranging Rows Upright)*. Anchor wire on frame next to frame loop. Make a 13-arch base outer bezel row *(Beaded Outer Base Bezel Rows)* of 3-bead arches as follows: charlotte, brown 11º, charlotte, charlotte, peridot, charlotte. Repeat twice. At corner, make a 4-bead arch using: charlotte, 2 brown 11ºs, charlotte. On the other side, make a 3-bead arch with: charlotte, peridot, charlotte. Make a 3-bead arch with: charlotte, brown 11º, charlotte. Repeat twice. Finish off **(e)**.

5 Repeat Steps 3–4 for second frame half.

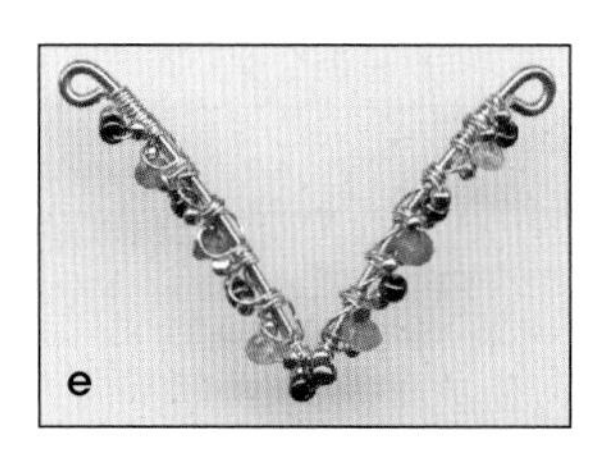
e

6 Anchor a piece of 28-gauge wire in arch of front row of bezel nearest frame corner. Curve wire across corner to corresponding arch on opposite side. Coil around arch once. String: charlotte, hessonite, green 11º. Feed wire between brown 11ºs of corner base outer row **(f)**.

7 Feed wire back through green 11º. String a hessonite and a charlotte. Coil wire around arch where first anchored. Curve wire across corner to corresponding arch on other side again. Finish off **(g)**.

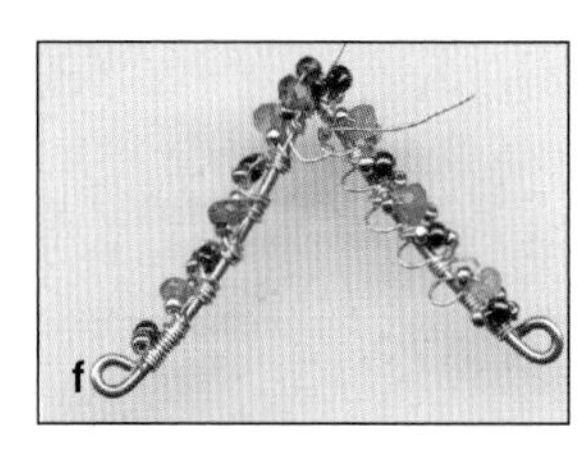
f

8 Repeat Steps 6–7 on second frame half.

9 Join frame halves together *(Inset Ring Bezel Frame)*. Anchor a piece of 28-gauge wire in any arch at back of bezel. Lace up back *(Lacing Up Bezels)*. Finish off.

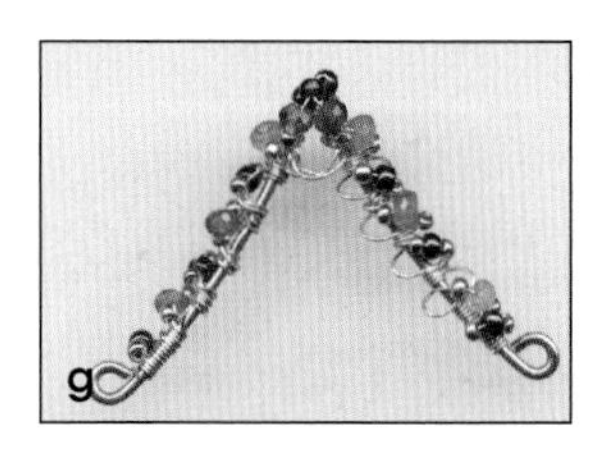
g

10 Anchor a piece of 28-gauge wire in last arch of either front row of bezel (near frame loop). Curve wire across corner to corresponding arch on opposite side of frame loops. Coil around arch twice. Curve wire back to beginning point. Finish off.

11 Insert cabochon. Tighten bezel around cabochon *(Tightening Bezels around Cabochons)*. Repeat Step 10 at opposite side of bezel. Tighten again **(h)**.

h

Square Bezels

12 Anchor a piece of 28-gauge wire to a square-bezel frame half. Make a 13-arch unbeaded base outer row with two arches on short sides, seven arches on long side, and one arch at each corner. Do not clip tails. Turn frame over and, working back in opposite direction, make a 13-arch unbeaded base inner row. Do not clip tails **(i)**.

13 Rearrange rows of arches upright. Turn. Working back in opposite direction, make a 13-arch base outer base bezel row of 3-bead arches as follows: charlotte, brown 11º, charlotte; charlotte, peridot, charlotte; charlotte, 2 brown 11ºs, charlotte (at corner). On long side **(j)**, alternate charlotte, peridot, charlotte with charlotte, brown 11º, charlotte. End with charlotte, 2 brown 11ºs, charlotte at corner. Finish short side with charlotte, peridot, charlotte; charlotte, brown 11º, charlotte. Finish off.

14 Repeat Steps 12–13 for other square frame halves.

15 Join together. Anchor a piece of 28-gauge wire in an arch at back of bezel. Lace up back of bezel. Finish off.

16 Anchor a piece of 28-gauge wire to first arch of what is now front row of either bezel frame. Curve wire across corner to second arch on long side. Coil around arch once. String: charlotte, chalcedony, 2 amber 11ºs. Feed wire between brown 11ºs of corner base outer row **(k)**.

17 String: two amber 11ºs, chalcedony, charlotte. Coil wire around arch where wire was first anchored. Curve wire across corner to second arch on long side. Finish off **(l)**.

18 Repeat Steps 16–17 at two more corners of bezel. Insert cabochon. Tighten bezel around cabochon. Repeat Steps 16–17 at fourth corner. Tighten again **(m)**. Repeat Steps 12–18 for remaining square bezel.

Long Oval Bezels

19 Anchor a piece of 28-gauge wire to a frame half. Make a 7-arch unbeaded base outer row. Turn frame over and, working back in opposite direction, make a 7-arch unbeaded base inner row. Do not clip tails **(n)**.

20 Rearrange rows of arches upright. Turn. Working in opposite direction, make a 7-arch base outer bezel row with one-bead arches of brown 11º, peridot, brown 11º; a 3-bead arch of peridot, brown 11º, peridot; and one-bead arches of brown 11º, peridot, brown 11º. Finish off **(o)**.

21 Anchor wire in second front-row arch on either side of bezel. String a chalcedony and 2 amber 11ºs. Go through brown 11º at tip of beaded outer row of arches **(p)**.

22 String two amber 11ºs and a chalcedony. Coil around second-to-last front-row arch on other side. Finish off **(q)**.

23 Repeat Steps 19–22 for another frame half. Join frame halves together. Anchor a piece of 28-gauge wire in any arch at back of bezel. Lace up back side. Finish off.

24 Insert cabochon. Tighten bezel around cabochon **(r)**.

25 Repeat Steps 19–22 at other end of bezel. Tighten.

26 Repeat Steps 19–25 for remaining long oval bezel.

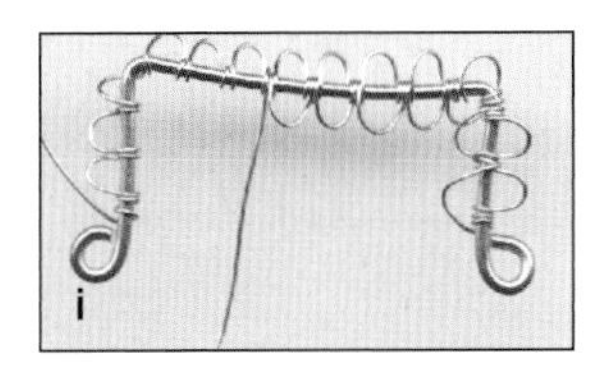

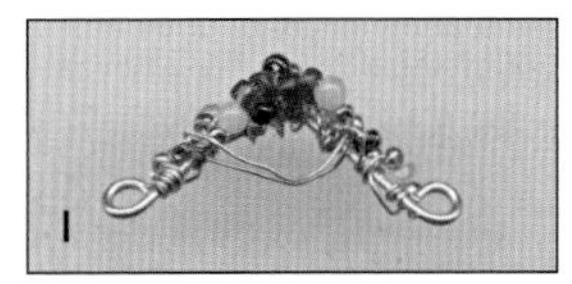

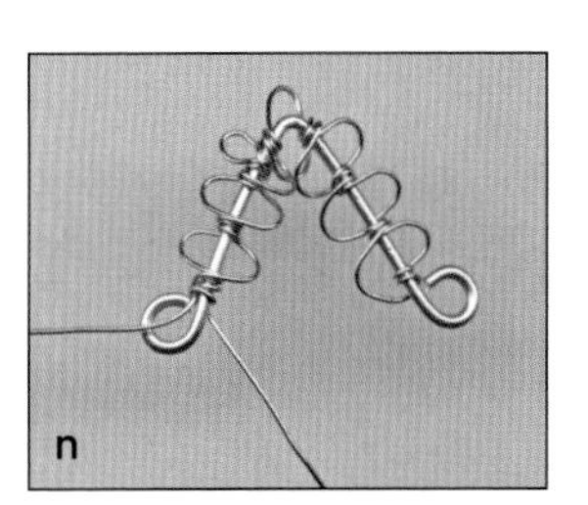

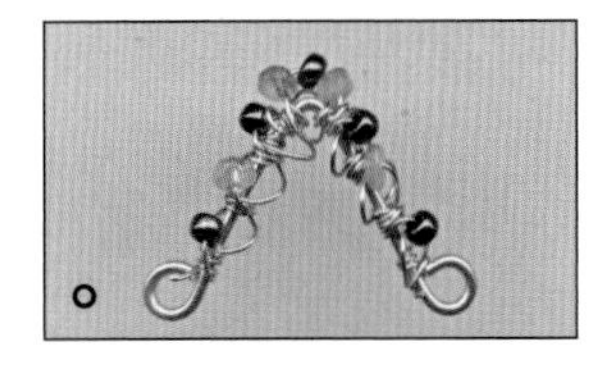

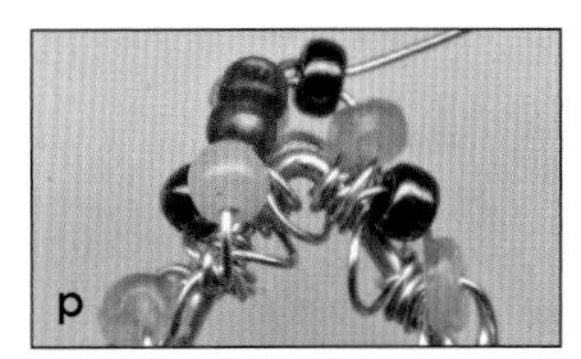

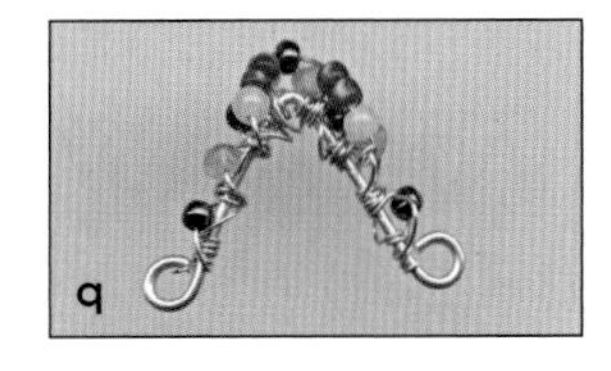

Joining the Links

27 Using four 3-in. pieces of 28-gauge wire as one, make a wire wrap into one loop on the diamond-shaped bezel. String 5–7 of the remaining beads randomly on each piece, so the beaded portions are all approximately the same. Using all four pieces of wire as one, make a wire wrap into the corresponding loop on one of the square bezels **(s)**.

28 Repeat Step 27 on other loops of same two bezels. Repeat Step 27 twice to connect second square bezel to other side of diamond-shaped bezel.

29 Repeat Step 28 four times to connect long oval bezels to square bezels.

Clasp

30 Using a scrap of 20-gauge wire, make a clasp (*Hook-and-Bar Clasp*). Open clasp loops and insert into long oval frame loops at ends of bracelet. Close clasp loops.

Turquoise Ring

The sky-blue color of turquoise from certain mines works beautifully with both light and dark apatite beads. A little hematite picks up the dark gray color of the veins in the stone for a harmonious yet exotic look.

Materials

- 5 in. (12.7 cm) 18-gauge half-hard wire, silver
- 8 in. (20.3 cm) 20-gauge half-hard wire, silver
- approx. 3 ft. (91.4 cm) 26-gauge dead-soft wire, silver
- 8–10 ft. (2.4–3.1 m) 28-gauge dead-soft wire, silver
- 10 x 13–15 x 20 mm cabochon, turquoise
- **20** 2 x 3 mm faceted rondelles, electric blue apatite
- **9** 3 mm round beads, light blue apatite or aventurine
- **44** 2 mm round beads, turquoise
- **8** 2 mm round beads, hematite
- 4 g 15º charlottes or seed beads, silver
- epoxy glue (optional)

Tools

- roundnose pliers
- chainnose pliers
- wire cutters
- ring mandrel

Dimensions of Beaded Bezel

approx. 1¼ in. x ⅞ in. (32 x 22 mm)

Technical Basics Reference

- Making Frames: Basic Frame, p. 86
- Anchoring Wires, p. 87
- Making Base Rows: Unbeaded Outer Base Rows and Unbeaded Inner Base Rows, p. 87
- Rearranging Rows Upright, p. 87
- Making Base Bezel Rows: Unbeaded Outer Base Bezel Rows, p. 88
- Finishing Off, p. 87
- Finishing Bezels: Lacing Up Bezels, p. 88
- Building onto Base Rows: Beaded Arches, p. 88

Preparation

1 Cut 28-gauge wire into 2-ft. (61 cm) lengths.

2 Using 20-gauge wire, make a basic frame in a marquise shape *(Basic Frame)* **(a)**.

3 Using roundnose pliers, make loops at top of frame toward back side **(b)**.

Bezel Frame

4 Anchor a piece of 28-gauge wire to frame next to a frame loop *(Anchoring Wires)*. Make a 19-arch unbeaded base outer row *(Unbeaded Outer Base Rows)*. Turn frame over and, working back in opposite direction, make a 19-arch unbeaded base inner row *(Unbeaded Inner Base Rows)*. Do not clip tails **(c)**.

5 Rearrange rows of arches *(Rearranging Rows Upright)*. Turn frame over and, working back in opposite direction, make a 19-arch unbeaded outer base bezel row *(Unbeaded Outer Base Bezel Rows)*. Do not clip tails **(d)**.

6 Bring wire through first arch of back base row and anchor. Lace up back of bezel *(Lacing Up Bezels)*. Finish off *(Finishing Off)*.

7 Anchor a piece of 28-gauge wire in first arch of outer row. Make an 18-arch second outer row of 3-bead arches *(Beaded Arches)* using: turquoise, dark blue apatite rondelle, turquoise. Finish off **(e)**.

Insert Cabochon

8 Join a piece of 28-gauge wire on frame between frame loop and last arch on what is now front row.

String a hematite round. Carry wire across top of bezel and coil twice around frame between first front arch and other frame loop, pulling tightly to close top end of bezel.

With charlottes, make a one-bead arch in each of next seven front-row arches, tipping the front row of arches inward a bit and pulling the one-bead arches tightly to close up front side of bezel.

With two charlottes, a light blue apatite round, and a dark blue apatite rondelle, skip one arch and make a 4-bead arch into the next arch (last arch on current side of frame).

With a hematite round, make a one-bead arch across to first arch on other side of bezel.

With a dark blue apatite rondelle, a light blue apatite round, and two charlottes, skip one arch and make a 4-bead arch into next arch.

Insert cabochon. With charlottes, make a one-bead arch in each of next 6 top-row arches and one more anchored on frame where wire for this row was first anchored. Bring wire up through nearest frame loop and coil tightly three times **(f)**.

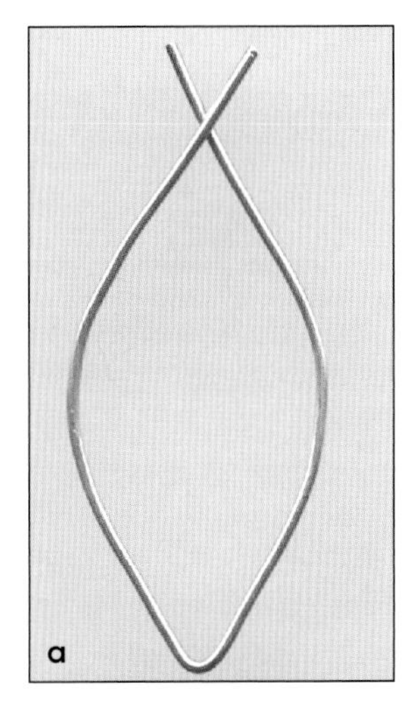
a

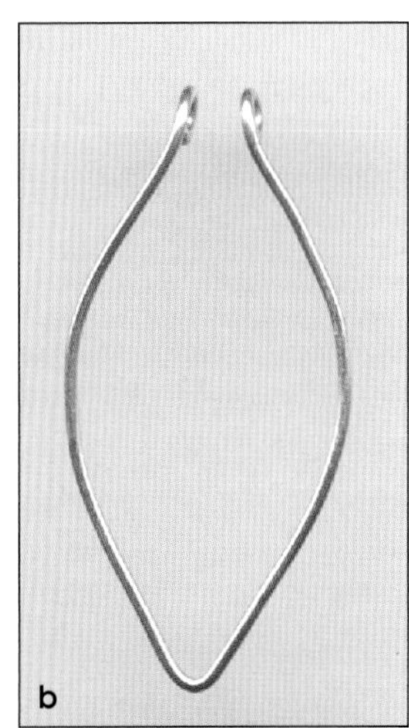
b

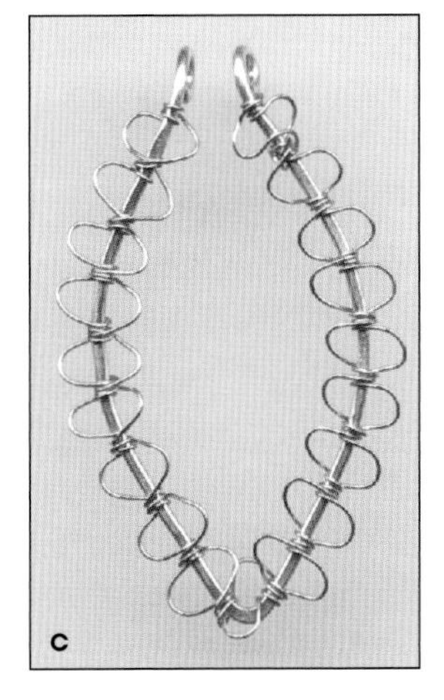
c

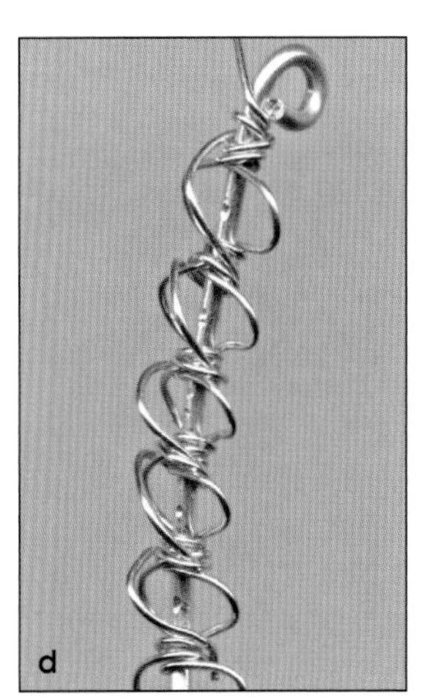
d

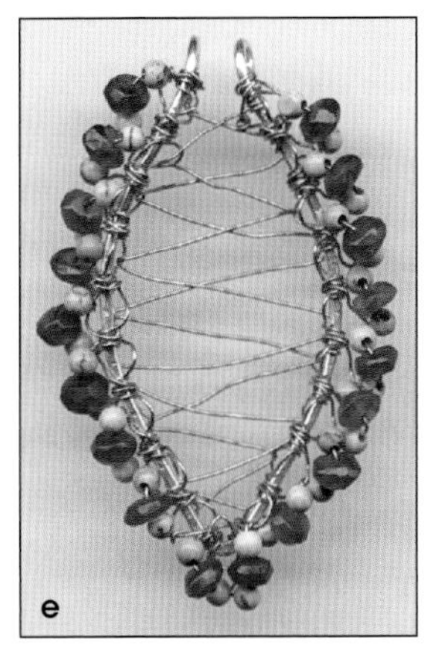
e

f

g

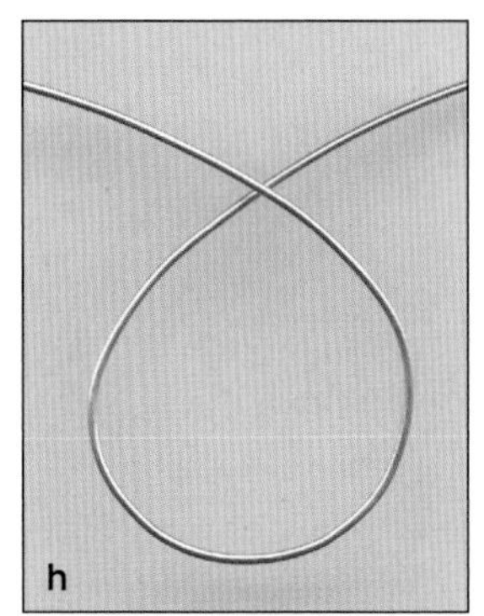
h

i

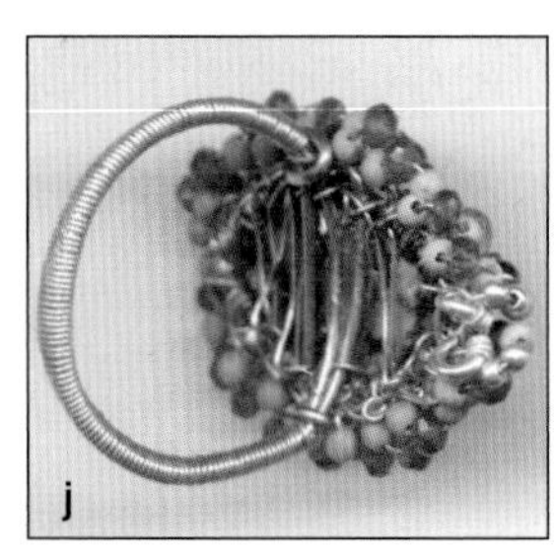
j

9 String: two charlottes, a turquoise, a charlotte, a hematite round, a charlotte, a light blue apatite round, and a charlotte. Bring wire down through bezel between top and outer rows of beaded arches after second arch. Bring wire up under bezel on other side of frame wire.

10 Repeat Step 9, omitting final charlotte and skipping two arches this time, bringing wire down through bezel after third arch.

11 Repeat Step 10.

12 Make an unbeaded arch above hematite round at top end of bezel.

13 String a light blue apatite round, a charlotte, a hematite round, a charlotte, a turquoise round, and two charlottes. Bring wire down through bezel between top and outer rows of beaded arches directly across from corresponding place on opposite side of bezel. Bring wire up from under bezel on other side of frame wire.

14 Repeat Step 13.

15 Repeat Step 13 again, stringing a charlotte at beginning of sequence and ending by coiling several times in top frame loop. Finish off **(g)**.

Complete the Ring

16 Using 18-gauge wire, shape as in photo **(h)**.

17 Gently bring ends of wire through back arches closest to center point of bezel. Use mandrel to size ring. Bend wires at points where they begin to cross the back of bezel so that they are flat **(i)**.

Note: Cabochon may pop out during this process. Just gently reinsert it after ring band is finished. If cabochon is not completely secure, use epoxy glue to secure it.

18 Coil each tail around ring portion of wire as close to bezel as possible.

19 Using 26-gauge wire, anchor to ring portion as close to bezel as possible and coil tightly all the way around ring portion. Clip tails **(j)**.

ch.5 Twisted Wire

Crystal Comb

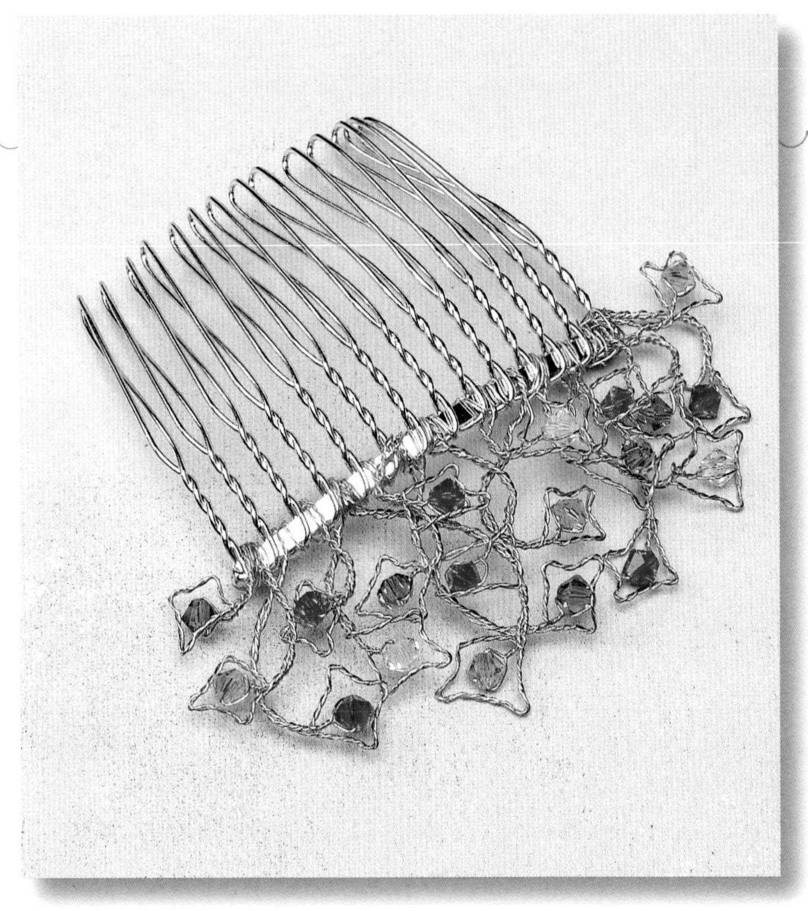

This sprinkling of ultra-bright crystals outlined in twists of gold was designed to stand out against blonde and brunette hair alike.

Materials
- 20 ft. (6 m) 28-gauge dead-soft wire
- **20** 4 mm bicone cystals in **5** bright colors
- 2-in. (51 mm) metal comb

Tools
- roundnose pliers
- chainnose pliers
- wire cutters

Dimensions
approx. 2½ x 3 in. (64 x 76 mm)

Technical Basics Reference
- Twisting Wire: Twisting a Main Stem, Twisting Branches, Tweaking, and Shaping, p. 89
- Finishing Off, p. 87

1 Center wire over comb at one end.

2 Twist about ½ in. (13 mm) of main stem *(Twisting a Main Stem)* **(a)**. String bead.

3 Make a very short branch. Twist three times back to main stem *(Twisting Branches)* **(b)**.

4 Twist both wires together for about 1 in. (25.5 mm). Using chainnose pliers, bend wire in a diamond shape around bead. Bring one wire over one side of main stem and the other wire over the other side at base of branch **(c)**.

5 Twist a section the same length as main stem **(d)**. Holding main stem and newly twisted section together at comb, twist them together down to comb base **(e)**. Wrap both wires around comb twice to anchor.

6 Repeat Steps 2–5 18 times, making main stems between ½ in. and 1½ in. (13 and 38 mm) and spreading colors out to get a nice balance. Finish off *(Finishing Off)* **(f)**.

7 Using chainnose pliers, tweak the diamond shapes to make the corners more pointed *(Tweaking)*. Shape the main stems to make shapes graceful and to distribute beads evenly throughout *(Shaping)*.

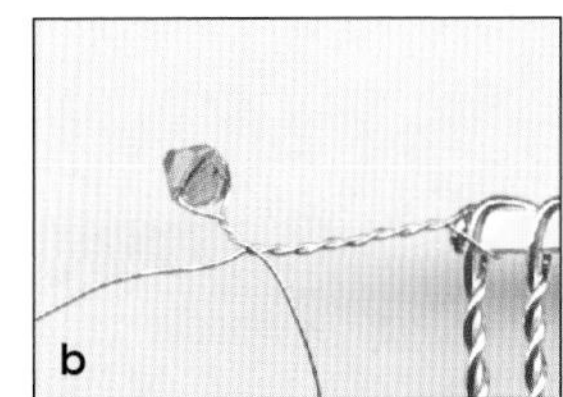

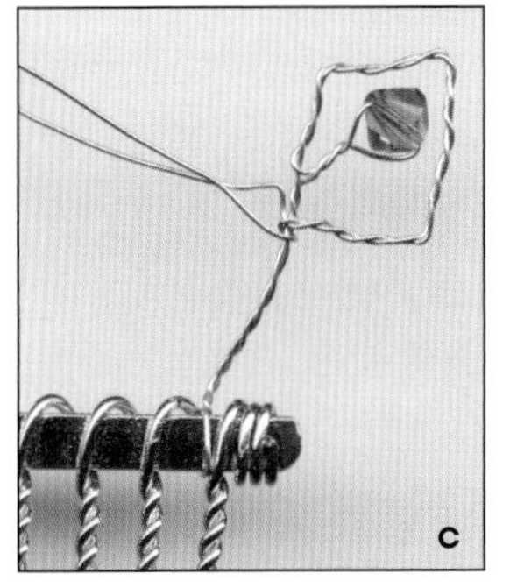

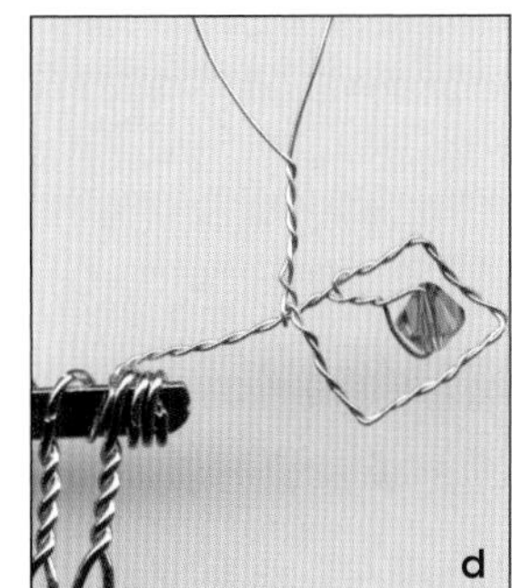

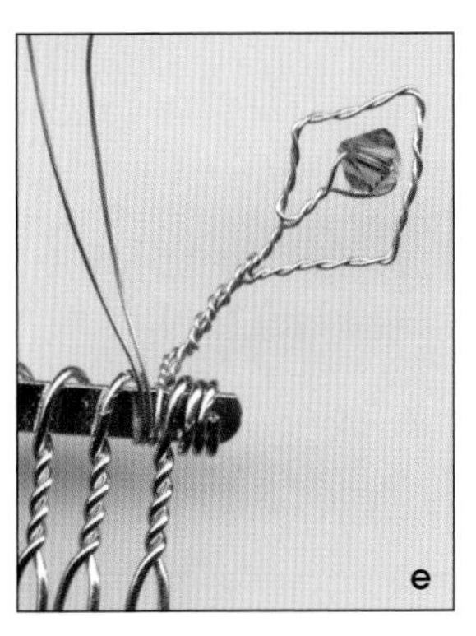

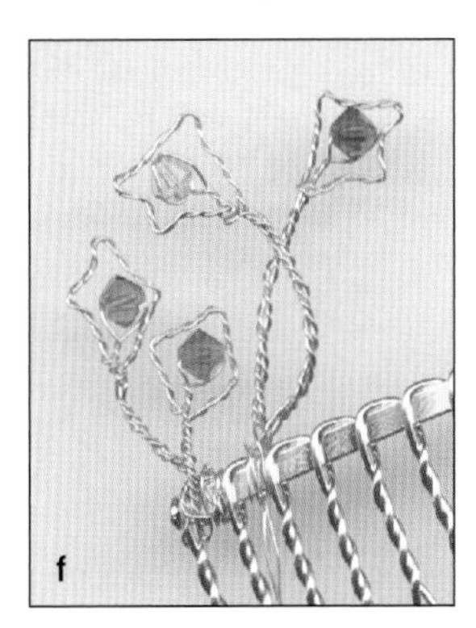

Silver, Crystal, & Pearl Pin

This riot of rhinestones, crystals, and pearls in a tangle of silvery wires is stunning with a cocktail gown or against a solid-colored coat or suit jacket.

Materials

- 6 in. (15.2 cm) 18-gauge dead-soft wire, silver
- 50–60 ft. (15.2–18.2 m) 28-gauge dead-soft wire, silver (26-gauge wire for a less delicate pin)
- ¾-in. (19 mm) rhinestone button with back loop
- **150** (approx.) 4 mm fire-polished beads, crystal AB
- **135–150** (approx.) 4 mm pearls, white
- **10–20** 6 mm bicones, crystal AB (optional)
- **13–14** 6 mm pearls, white
- 2-in. (51 mm) pinback, silver
- epoxy glue (optional)

Tools

- roundnose pliers
- chainnose pliers
- wire cutters

Dimensions

approx. 3½ in. (89 mm)

Technical Basics Reference

- Twisting Wires: Twisting a Main Stem, Twisting Branches, and Adding a Bead to a Main Stem, p. 89
- Anchoring Wires, p. 87
- Finishing Off, p. 87

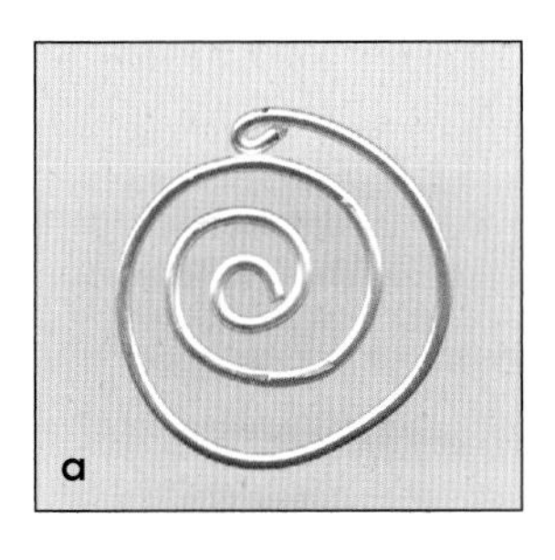

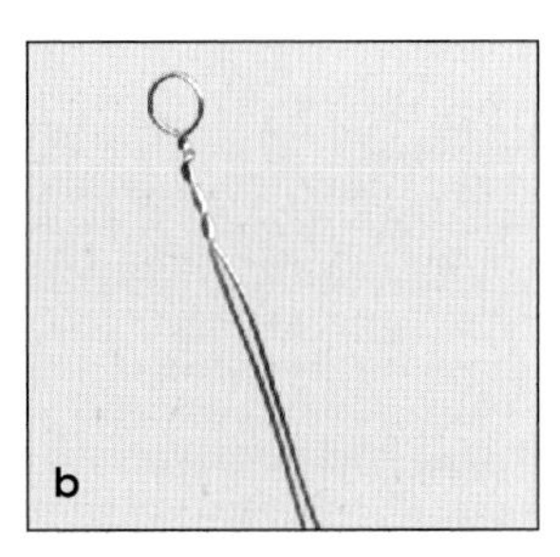

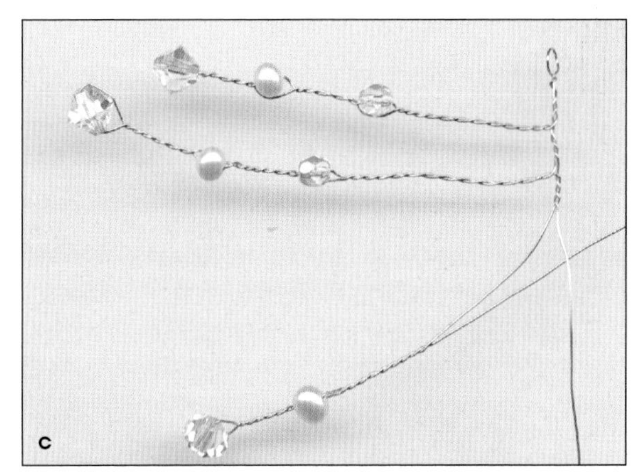

Preparation

Note: 28- and 26-gauge wires are interchangeable for this pattern.

1 Cut 28-gauge (or 26-gauge) wire into 4-ft. (1.2 m) lengths.

2 Using 18-gauge wire, make a spiral. Curl a loop at the end **(a)** and pinch to close.

3 Using roundnose pliers and a piece of 28-gauge wire, curl a loop at center point and give wires three half-twists *(Twisting a Main Stem)* **(b)**.

Shape the Pin

Note: Use beads randomly (except for 6 mm pearls).

4 Make a long branch (about 2½ in./64 mm) *(Twisting Branches)* with one bead at end point and two others at various points along the way back to main stem *(Adding a Bead to a Main Stem)*. Give both wires a few half-twists to extend main stem.

5 Continue adding branches **(c)** until main stem measures about 6 in. (15.2 cm) and has 21 branches. Using a new piece of 28-gauge wire, anchor on coil at beginning loop *(Anchoring Wires)* **(d)**.

6 Attach main stem to base coil by coiling around it and main stem at same time to end. Finish off *(Finishing Off)* **(e–i)**.

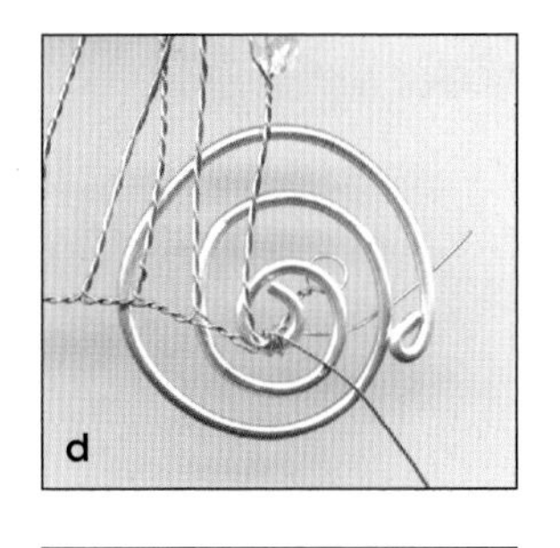

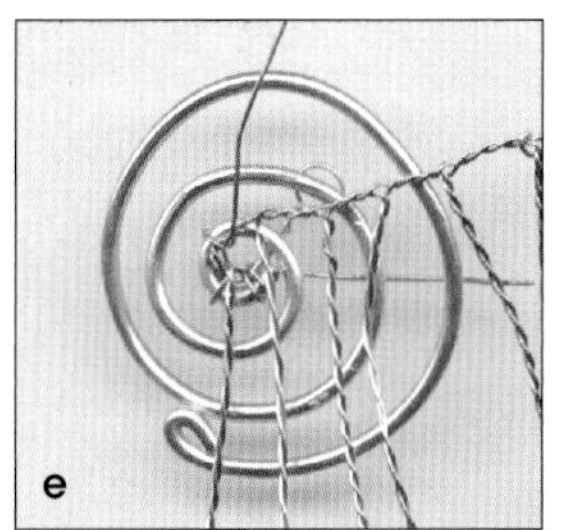

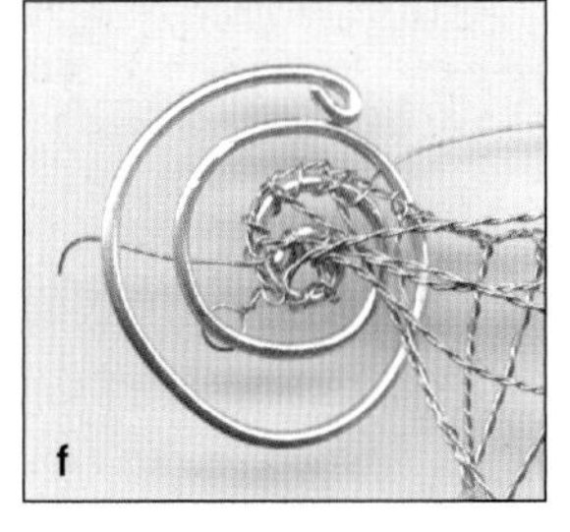

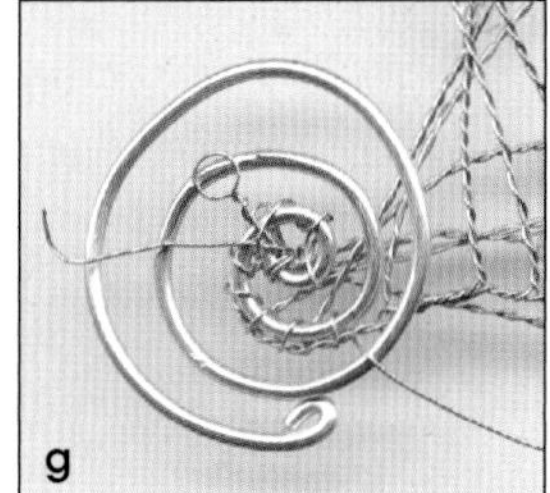

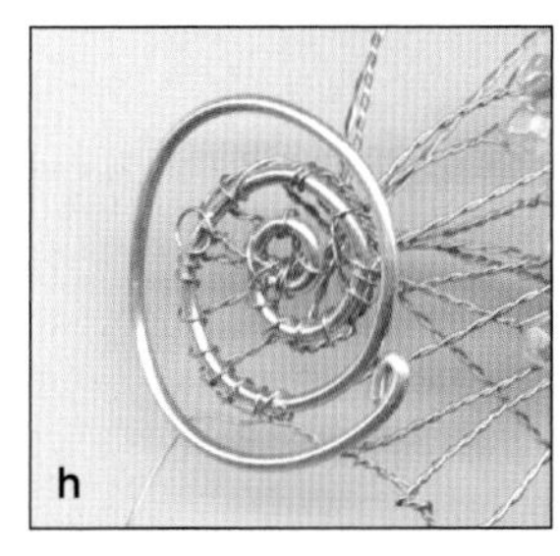

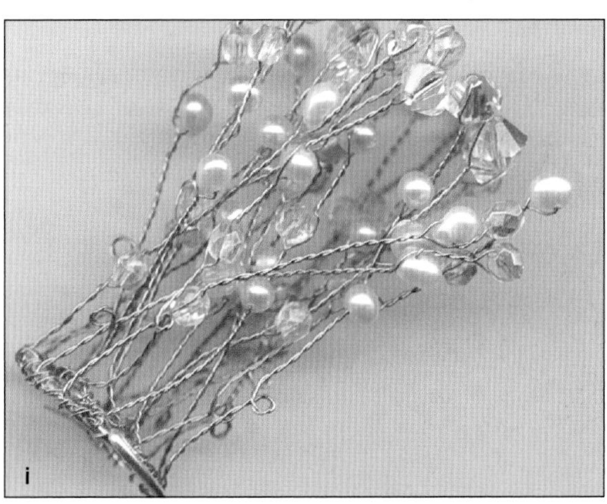

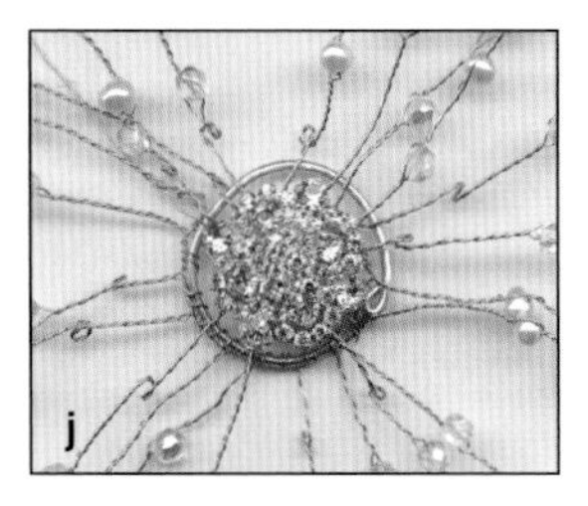
j

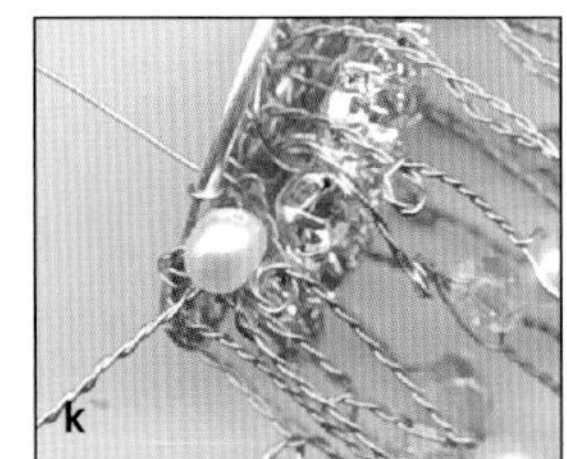
k

l

m

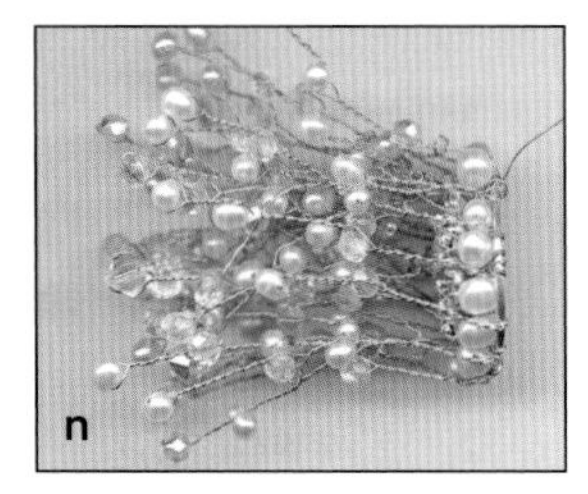
n

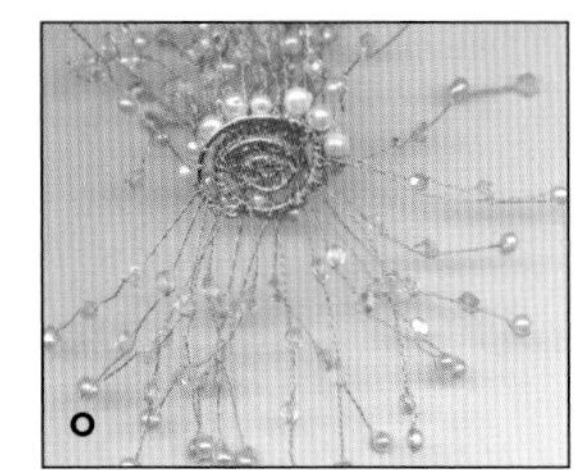
o

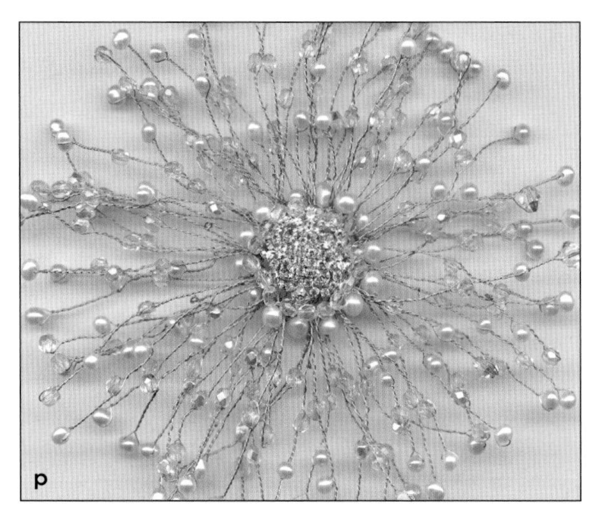
p

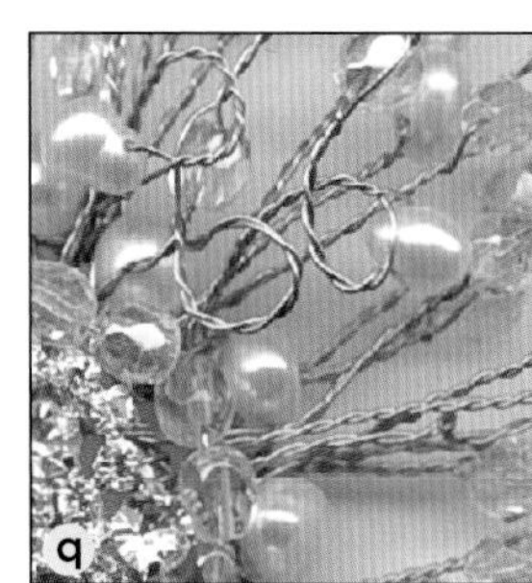
q

r

s

7 Using 28-gauge wire, wire button firmly onto center coil. Finish off **(j)**.

8 Anchor a new piece of 28-gauge wire to outer coil.

9 String a 6 mm pearl and coil twice around center coil just after next branch **(k)**.

10 Repeat Step 9 all the way around outside of center coil **(l-n)**.

11 Working off of the outer center coil, make branches as before, placing three between each of the 6 mm pearls. Finish off **(o, p)**.

12 Tweak each branch by making a loop somewhere along its length.

Note: Work from right to left, bringing each branch to front as you make loop so that branches layer and tangle with each other. This helps stabilize the branches **(q-s)**.

13 Glue or wire pinback onto center back.

ch.6 Sculpted Wire

Floral Pin

This pin is lightweight, yet large enough to make a statement. Its blend of three metals guarantees that it will go with almost any outfit.

Materials
- approx. 15 ft. (4.6 m) 28-gauge dead-soft wire, copper
- approx. 6 ft. (1.8 m) 28-gauge dead-soft wire, gold
- approx. 9 ft. (2.7 m) 28-gauge dead-soft wire, silver
- 8 in. (20.3 cm) 20-gauge half-hard wire, copper
- 10 mm round cabochon
- 1¼ in. (32 mm) pinback
- epoxy glue

Tools
- roundnose pliers
- chainnose pliers
- wire cutters

Dimensions
approx. 3 x 3 in. (76 x 76 mm)

Technical Basics Reference
- Jump Rings: Double Jump Rings, p. 92
- Anchoring Wires, p. 87
- Making Triple-Layer Arches, p. 90
- Finishing Off, p. 87
- Sculpting Wire: Crinkling Triple-Layer Arches, p. 90, Making Sculpted Points, p. 91

1 Using 20-gauge wire, make four 8 mm double jump rings *(Double Jump Rings)*. Cut all 28-gauge wire into 3-ft. (91.4 cm) pieces.

2 Anchor a piece of copper wire onto a double-coil jump ring *(Anchoring Wires)*. Make an outer base row of eight ¾-in. (19 mm) triple-layer arches **(a)** *(Making Triple-Layer Arches)*. Finish off *(Finishing Off)*.

3 Using roundnose pliers, crinkle the arches *(Crinkling Triple-Layer Arches)*. Finish off **(b)**.

4 Using gold wire, repeat Steps 2–3, making seven 1-in. (25.5 mm) arches.

5 Using silver wire, repeat Steps 2–3, making 10 1¼-in. (32 mm) arches **(c)**.

6 Using copper wire, repeat Step 2, making nine 1¾-in. (44 mm) arches.

7 Using chainnose pliers, make a point at top of each arch *(Making Sculpted Points)* **(d)**.

8 Crinkle the arches **(e)**.

9 Stack four flower motifs in attractive arrangement with largest on bottom and smallest on top. Bring a 6-in. (15.2 cm) scrap of copper wire up through all four motifs, over several copper wires on top motif, and then down through all four motifs to back. Repeat several times until motifs are secure **(f)**.

10 Nudge, curl, and tweak petals as needed to create balanced look. Finish off.

11 Glue on pinback and cabochon.

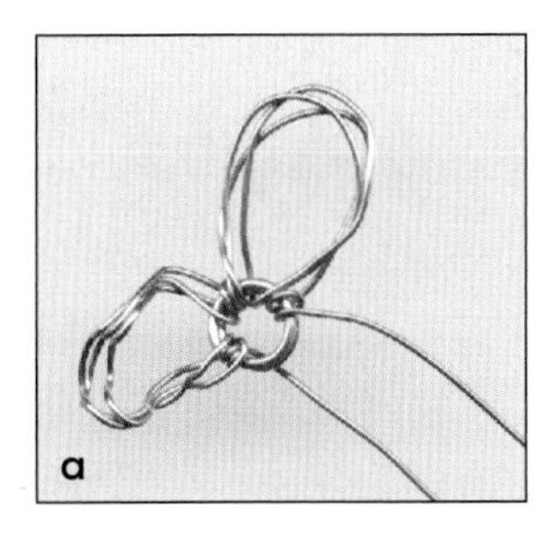
a

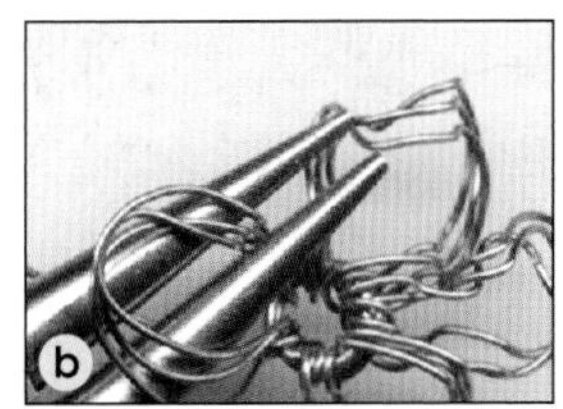
b

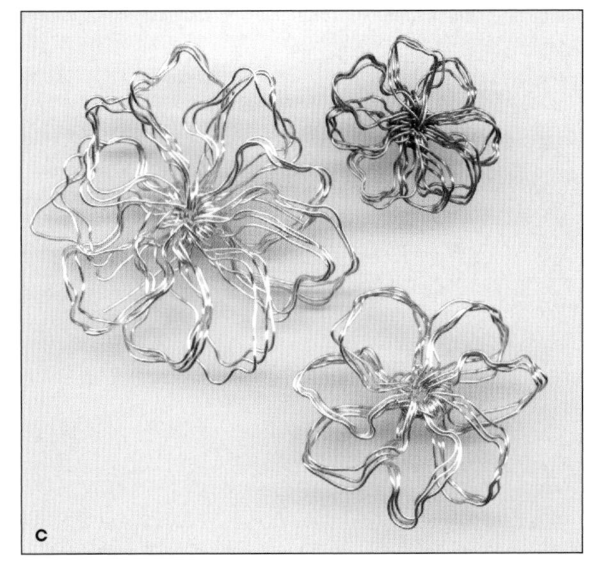
c

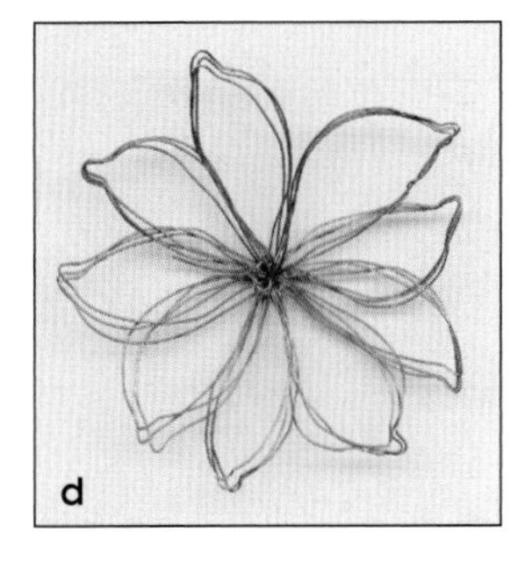
d

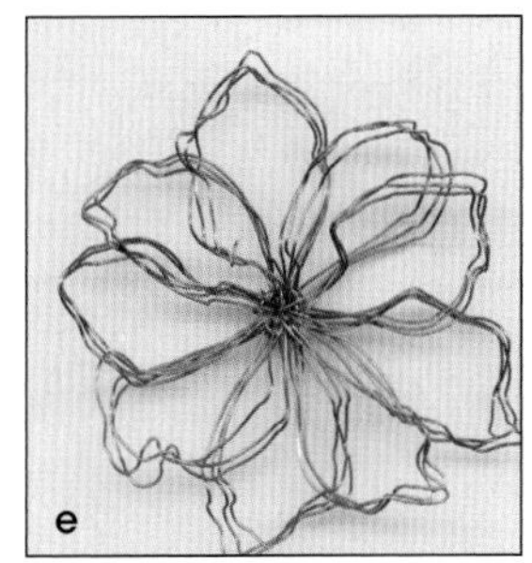
e

f

Spiky Earrings

With spiky points like shooting golden flames and the crystalline shimmer of icicles, these earrings are all fire and ice. Dramatic and dynamic, they will steal the show at even the dressiest occasions.

Materials
- 10 in. (25.4 cm) 20-gauge half-hard wire, gold
- 3 ft. (91.4 cm) 26-gauge half-hard wire, gold
- approx. 8 ft. (2.43 m) 28-gauge dead-soft wire, gold
- **2** 5 x 9 mm briolette crystals, crystal AB
- **2** 12 x 17 mm baroque crystals, crystal AB
- **10** 6 mm bicone crystals, crystal AB
- **10** 4 mm bicone crystals, crystal AB
- **10** 3 mm bicone crystals, crystal AB
- **8** headpins, gold
- pair of earring wires, gold

Tools
- roundnose pliers
- chainnose pliers
- wire cutters

Dimensions
dangle is approx. 3 in. (76 mm)

Technical Basics Reference:

- Making Frames: Basic Frame, p. 86
- Anchoring Wires, p. 87
- Sculpting Wire: Making Triple-Layer Arches, p. 90
- Making Sculpted Points, p. 91
- Finishing Off, p. 87

1 Cut 20-gauge wire into two 5-in. (12.7 mm) lengths. Cut 28-gauge wires into 2-ft. (61 cm) lengths.

2 Using 20-gauge wire, make basic frames in a marquise shape *(Basic Frame)* **(a)**. Using roundnose pliers, curl loops at top of frame towards back side of frame.

3 Anchor a piece of 28-gauge wire near top of the frame *(Anchoring Wires)*.

4 Make a 5 mm triple-layer arch *(Making Triple-Layer Arches)*. Coil wire around frame once more tightly. Repeat **(b)**.

5 Bring wire halfway around frame and, working down inside of frame, repeat Step 4 **(c)**.

6 Make a 6 mm triple-layer arch. Doubling back, make a double-layer 4 mm arch inside the 6 mm triple arch. Coil wire around frame once more tightly. Repeat **(d)**.

7 Make a 7 mm triple-layer arch. Doubling back, make a double-layer 4 mm arch inside the 7 mm triple arch. Coil wire around frame once more tightly and make a 4 mm double-layered arch on outside of frame at tip **(e)**.

8 Working up opposite side of frame, make a 7 mm triple-layered arch on inside of frame. Doubling back, make a 4 mm double-layered arch inside triple one. Coil wire around frame once more tightly.

9 Repeat Step 8 twice, making the larger arches 6 mm.

10 Repeat Step 4.

11 Bring wire halfway around frame and, working up outside of frame, repeat Step 4. Finish off *(Finishing Off)*.

12 Anchor a new piece of wire to frame inside fourth inner arch from top. Make a 4 mm double arch on outside of frame for hanging drops later. Coil down to next 4 mm arch and repeat. Finish off.

13 Repeat Step 12 at corresponding points on opposite side of frame.

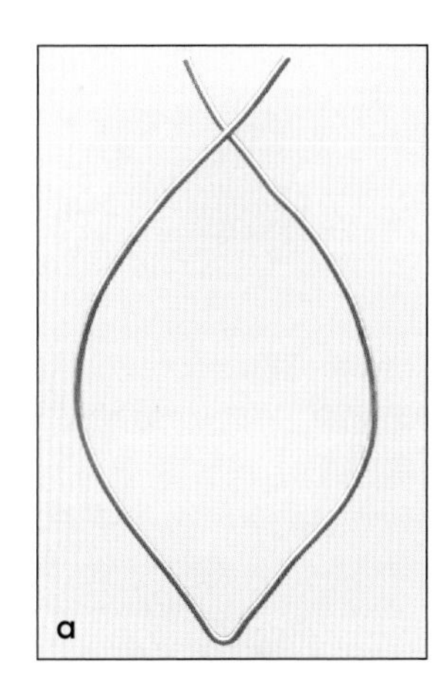

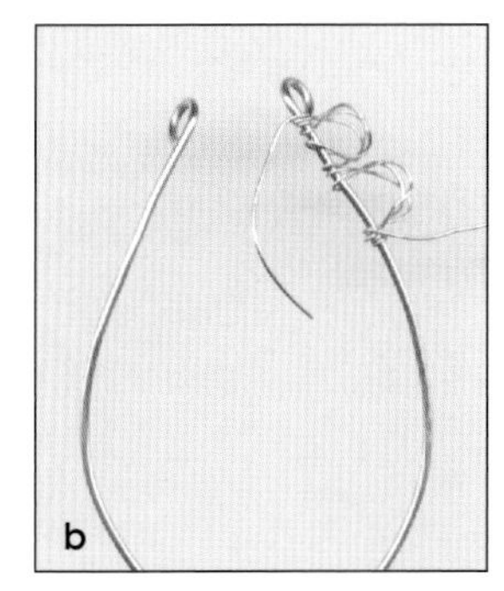

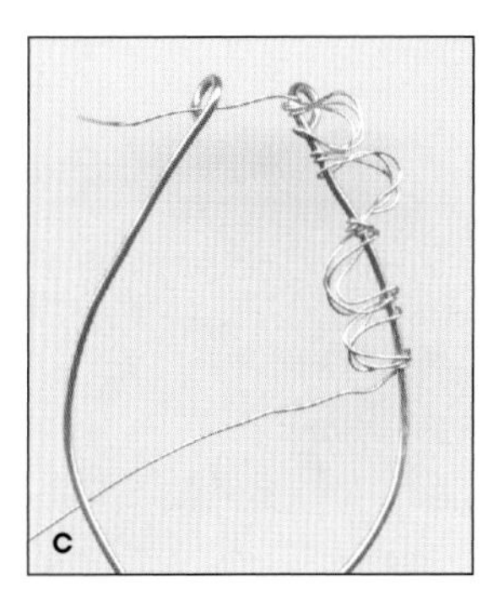

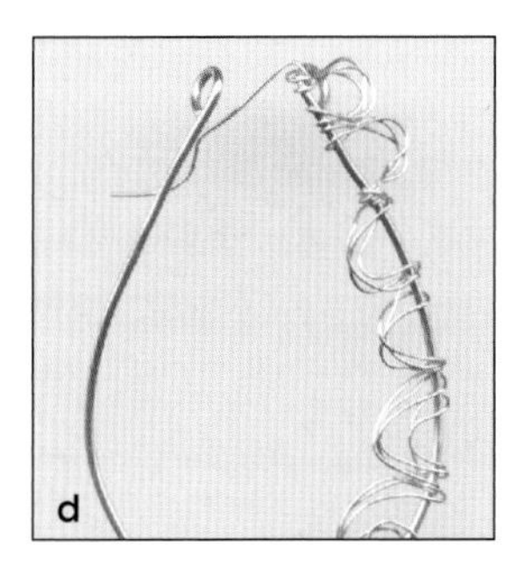

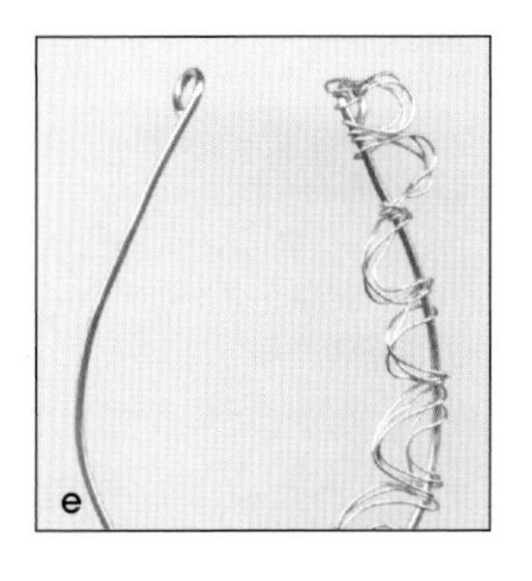

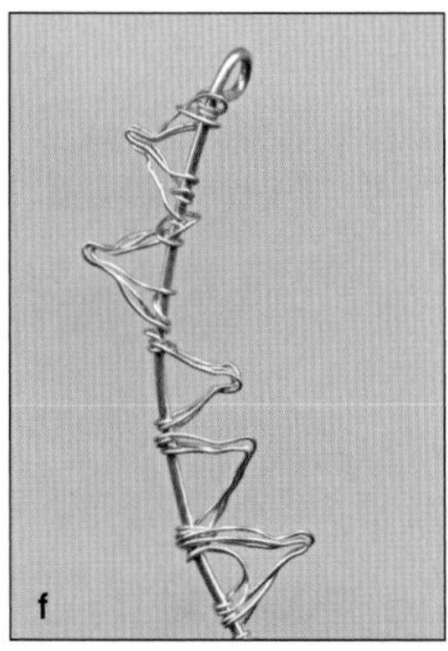

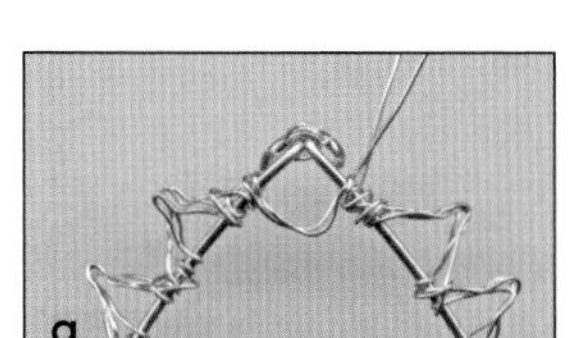

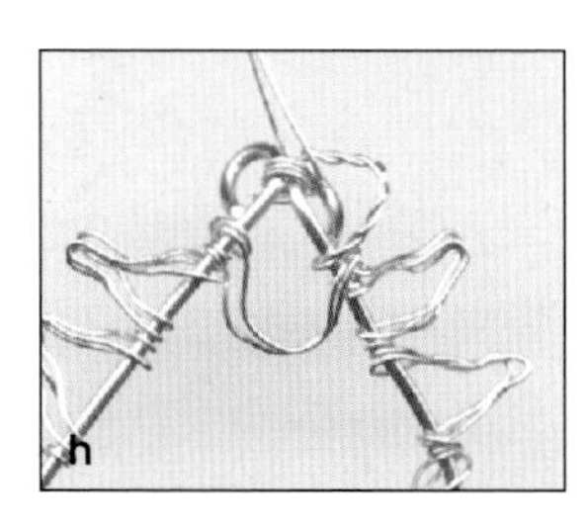

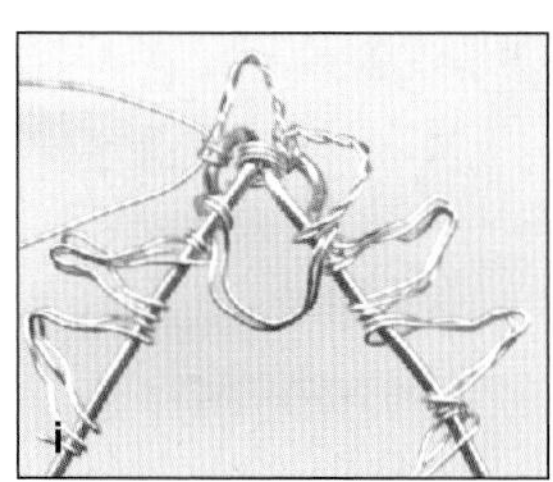

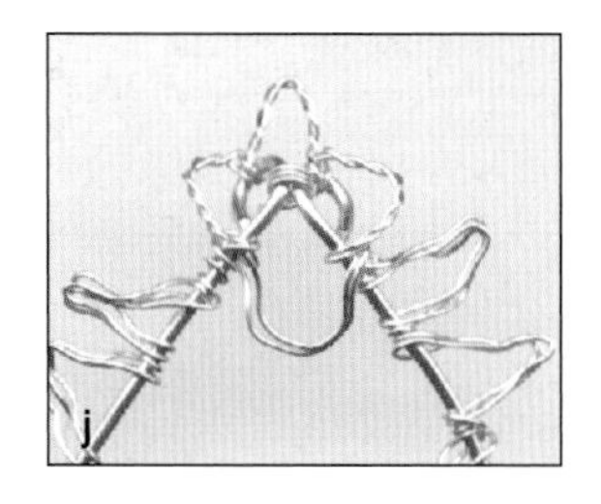

14 Using chainnose pliers, sculpt points on all four 4 mm outer arches at top of frame and on all 6 mm and 7 mm arches (*Making Sculpted Points*) **(f)**.

15 Bring top frame loops together. Using a scrap of 28-gauge wire, make several coils around the point where they touch. Finish off.

16 Fold a piece of 28-gauge wire in half and place fold over spot where previous wire was just finished off. Coil once tightly around frame over previous coils. Using both wires as one, carry across to corresponding spot on opposite side of frame, leaving loose enough to curve downwards for hanging center drop from later. Coil tightly twice **(g)**.

17 Twist wires together for about ½ in. (13 mm). Curve the twisted portion up to mimic frame loop. Coil both wires tightly around top of frame loop **(h)**.

18 Twist another section about ¾ in. (19 mm). Bend downward at halfway point of section and coil tightly around top of other frame loop **(i)**.

19 Twist another ½-in. section. Curve it down to mimic frame loop and finish off where wire was originally anchored to frame **(j)**.

20 Attach an earring wire.

21 Using 26-gauge wire, wire-wrap crystals to bottom loops and center top loop as shown in project photo.

22 Make a second earring to match the first.

Floral Necklace

A stunning centerpiece of dainty golden flowers with pearl centers creates a sweet yet sophisticated look that is perfect for a wedding or a 50th wedding anniversary celebration.

Materials

- 1 ft. (30.5 cm) 20-gauge half-hard wire, gold
- approx. 7 ft. (2.1 m) 26-gauge half-hard wire, gold
- approx. 16 ft. (4.9 m) 28-gauge dead-soft wire, gold
- **40** 4 mm pearls, white
- **13** 2.5 mm pearls, white
- lobster-claw clasp and 4 mm soldered jump ring, gold

Tools

- roundnose pliers
- chainnose pliers
- wire cutters

Dimensions of Floral Portion

approx. 3½ in. (89 mm) wide

Necklace Length

19 in. (48.3 cm)

Technical Basics Reference:

- Making a 5-petal Flower, p. 90
- Making Sculpted Points, p. 91
- Finishing Off, p. 87

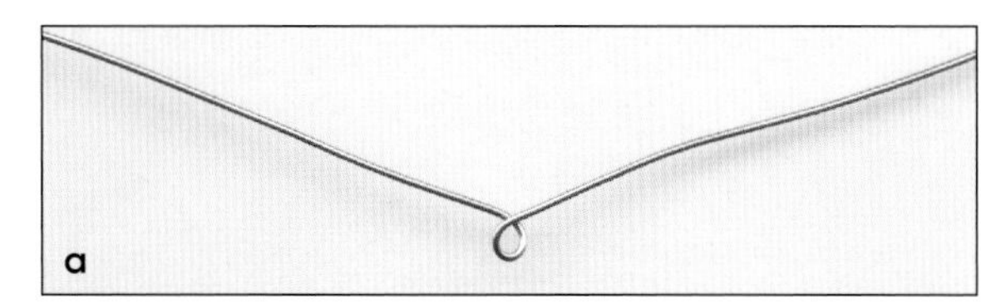
a

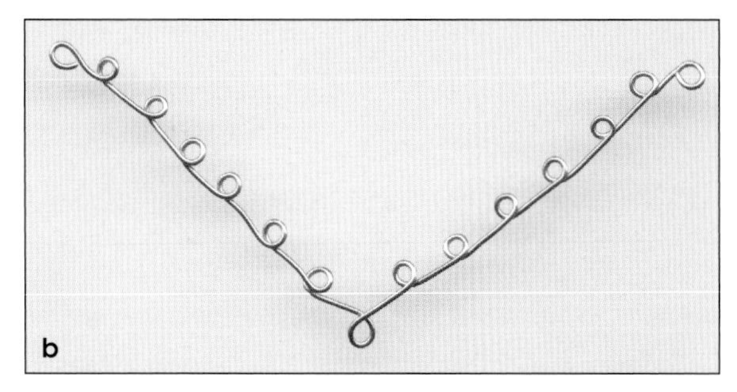
b

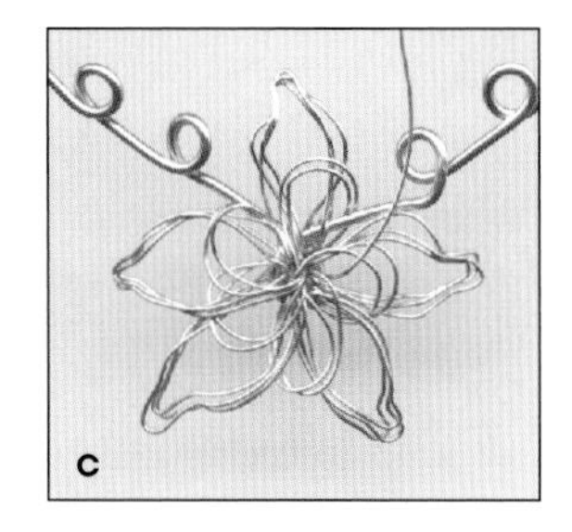
c

d

e

f

g

1 Cut 26- and 28-gauge wire into 2-ft. (61 cm) lengths.

2 Using 20-gauge wire and roundnose pliers, make a 4 mm loop in the center **(a)**.

3 Curl 4 mm loops at ¾ in. (19 mm) intervals along top of frame, making six loops on each side of center. Curl a final loop downward on each side and clip excess wire **(b)**.

4 Using center loop on frame as base, make a 5-petaled flower *(Making a 5-Petal Flower)* consisting of five 6 mm triple-layered arches with 4 mm double-layered arches inside them. Sculpt points at the tops of the 6 mm arches *(Making Sculpted Points)* **(c)**.

5 Feed wire up through center of any petal to front of flower, string a 2.5 mm pearl, and feed wire back down to back of flower through center of petal on other side. Wrap wire several times around part of any nearby petal at back of flower to secure it. Finish off *(Finishing Off)* **(d)**.

6 On each frame loop at either side of center flower, make smaller, three-petal flowers with only triple-layer 4 mm petals **(e)**. String 2.5 mm pearl as in Step 5. Finish off **(f)**.

7 On next pair of loops, repeat Steps 4–5.

8 On next pair of loops, repeat Step 6.

9 On each of next three pairs of loops, repeat Steps 4–5 **(g)**.

10 Using 26-gauge wire, wire wrap a chain of 20 4 mm pearls, attaching it to the final frame loop at one end and to the lobster-claw clasp at other. Repeat on the other side, substituting a jump ring for the clasp.

ch.7

Curlicue Lace

Purple Necklace

Make an entirely different kind of setting for a knock-out centerpiece using a druzy stone, curlicue lace techniques with sturdy wire, and a few crystals and rhinestones for a little extra sparkle.

Materials
- 35 x 42 mm purple druzy centerpiece bead with hole large enough for 20-gauge wire to pass through twice, amethyst, sugelite, or charoite
- 7 ft. (2.1 m) 20-gauge dead-soft wire, silver
- 6 in. (15.2 cm)18-gauge dead-soft wire, silver
- **4** 4 mm pavé rhinestone rounds
- **6** 6 mm rhinestone spacers, crystal AB
- **12** 4 mm bicone crystals, crystal AB
- 10 in. (25.4 cm) gemstone chips (coordinate with centerpiece bead)

Tools
- roundnose pliers
- chainnose pliers
- wire cutters

Note: No two stones are exactly alike. These instructions are only guidelines. Let the stone you choose determine the path your lace will follow and the shapes it will take.

Technical Basics Reference:
- Making Curlicue Lace, p. 91
- Clasps: Spiral Point Clasp, p. 92

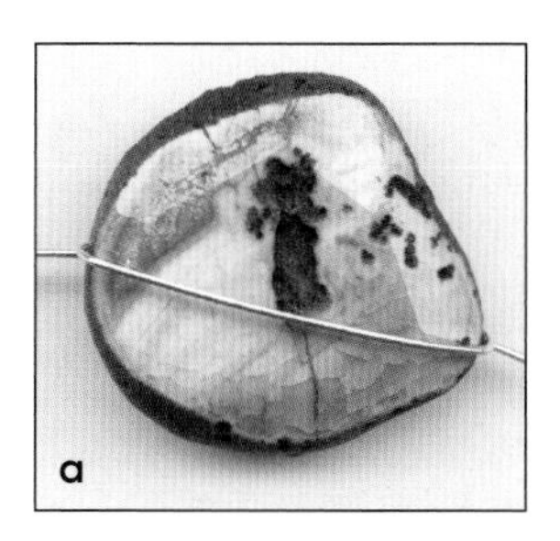

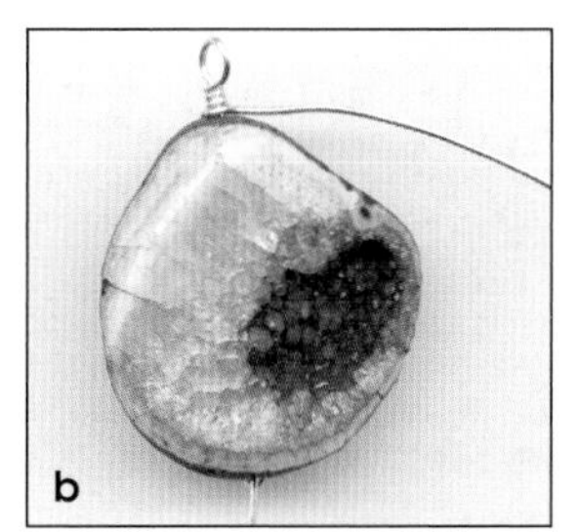

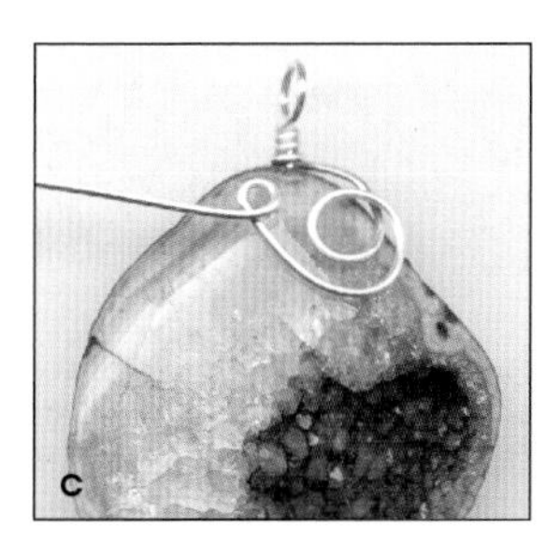

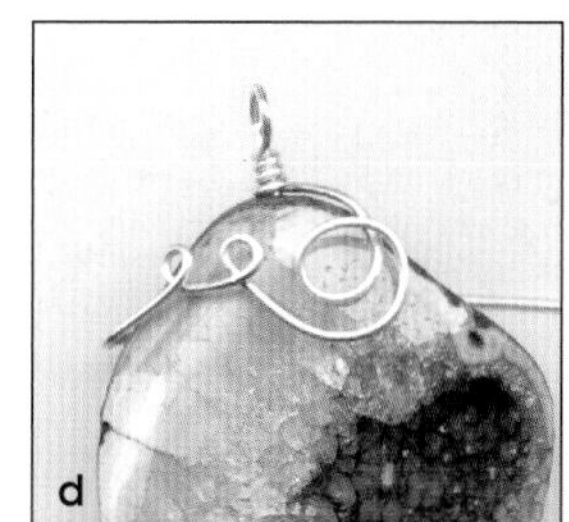

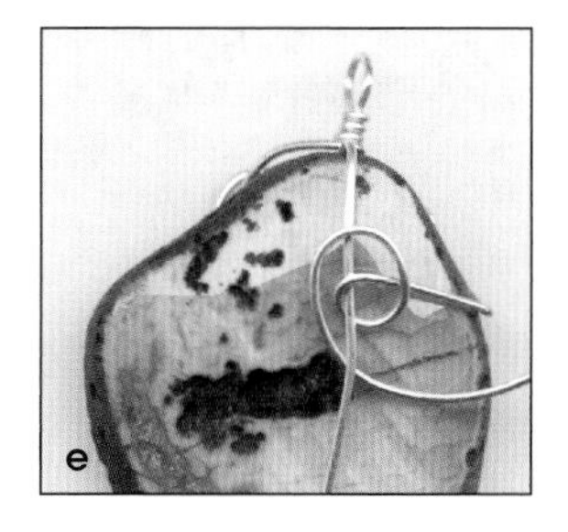

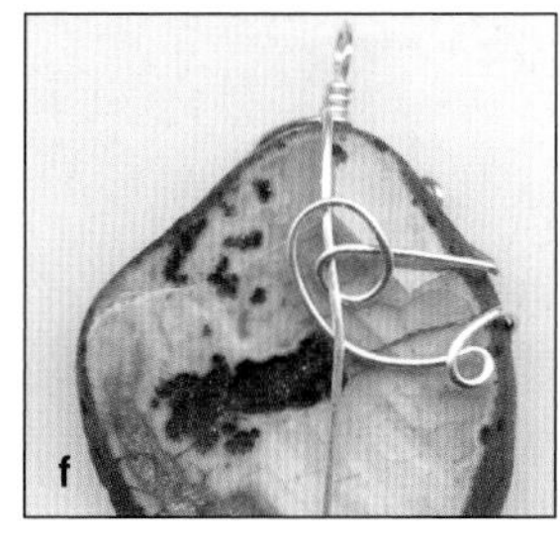

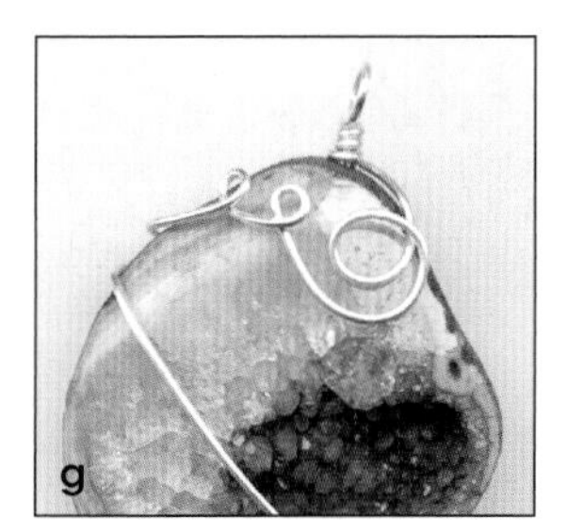

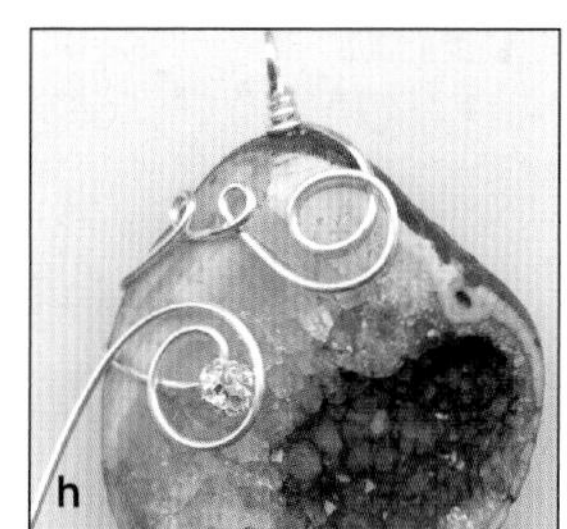

Preparation

1 Cut 20-gauge wire into one 3-ft. (91.4 cm) piece and two 2-ft. (61 cm) pieces.

Pendant

2 Place the 3-ft. wire across the back of the centerpiece stone, and bring the ends around and through the center hole from opposite directions **(a)**. Leaving a 3-in. (76 mm) tail at bottom end, draw other end through, tightening it across back side of bead. Wire wrap a loop at top end of bead **(b)**. Do not trim the tail.

3 Bring wire tail from the loop to front of bead and make a few curlicues across its face *(Making Curlicue Lace)* **(c, d)**.

Note: Where bends in wire are required to make lace lie flat against face of bead, grasp wire with chainnose pliers just prior to place where bend will be and bend wire with fingers against the pliers.

4 Bring wire around to back of bead, bending as necessary at edges to make front lace lie flat. Carry wire across vertical wire in back and make a curlicue around it in such a way that it pulls the front lace down tightly against front of bead **(e, f)**.

Note: This is to stabilize the front lace while making the back side of bead look attractive.

5 Bring wire back towards same side of bead as before and around to front of bead. Make a few curlicues, stringing bead(s) as desired **(g, h)**

6 Repeat Step 4 **(i, j)**.

7 Repeat Step 5 **(k)**.

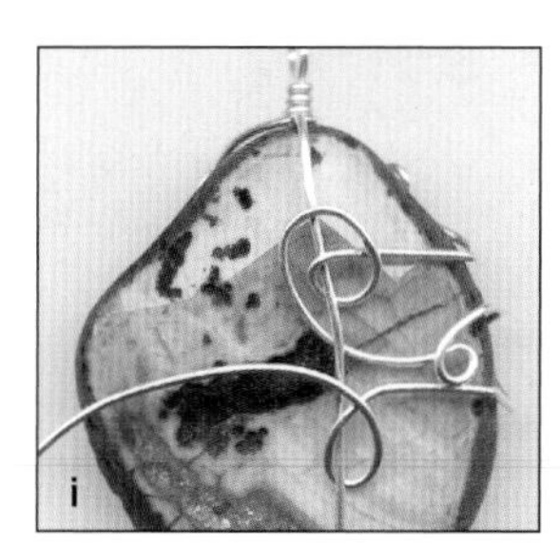

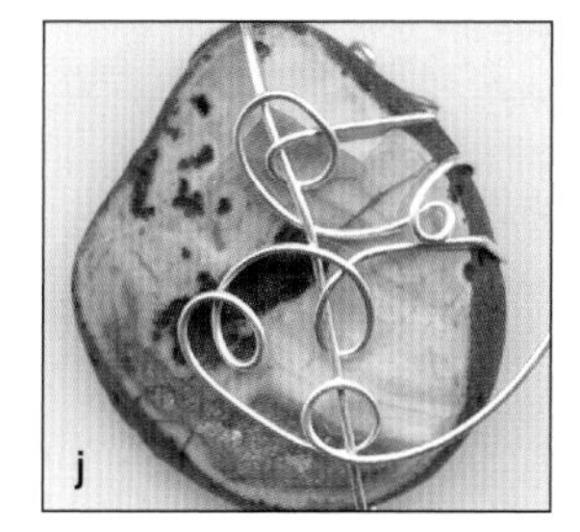

l

m

8 Bring wire to bottom tail and coil it twice tightly as close to bead as possible **(l)**.

9 Make a few curlicues in tail, ending with a curl on face of bead. Trim excess wire **(m)**.

Chain

Note: Use 20-gauge wire for all components and embellishments.

10 Cut a 1-in. (25.5 mm) piece of 20-gauge wire. Make a "V" at its center point and curl two loops toward center **(n)**.

11 Using a piece of 20-gauge wire, curl a loop and string about ¾ in. (19 mm) of amethyst chip beads. Clip excess wire and curl another loop. Attach to one loop on "V" **(o)**.

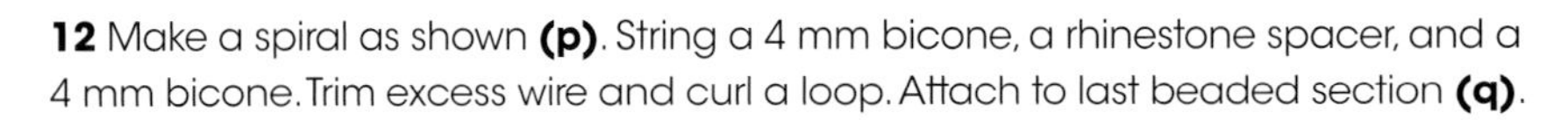
12 Make a spiral as shown **(p)**. String a 4 mm bicone, a rhinestone spacer, and a 4 mm bicone. Trim excess wire and curl a loop. Attach to last beaded section **(q)**.

13 Make a spiral and string about ½ in. (13 mm) amethyst chip beads. Clip excess wire and curl a loop. Attach to last beaded section.

14 Make a spiral and string a pavé ball. Clip excess wire and curl a loop. Attach to last beaded section **(r)**.

15 Make a spiral and string about 1 in. amethyst chip beads. Clip excess wire and curl a loop. Attach to last beaded section.

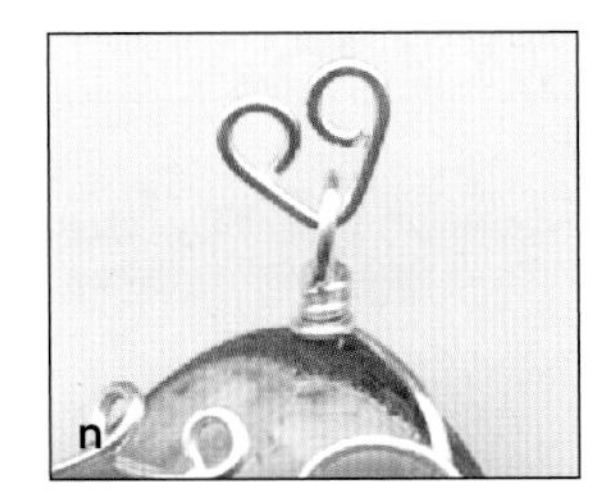
n

16 Repeat Step 13.

17 Make a spiral and string about 1½ in. (38 mm) amethyst chip beads. Clip excess wire and curl a loop. Attach to last beaded section.

18 Repeat Step 13.

19 Make a spiral and string about 1¼ in. (32 mm) amethyst chip beads. Clip excess wire and curl a loop. Attach to last beaded section.

20 Repeat Steps 11–19 on other end of necklace.

Clasp

21 Make a spiral point clasp *(Spiral Point Clasp)*. Attach to last beaded section.

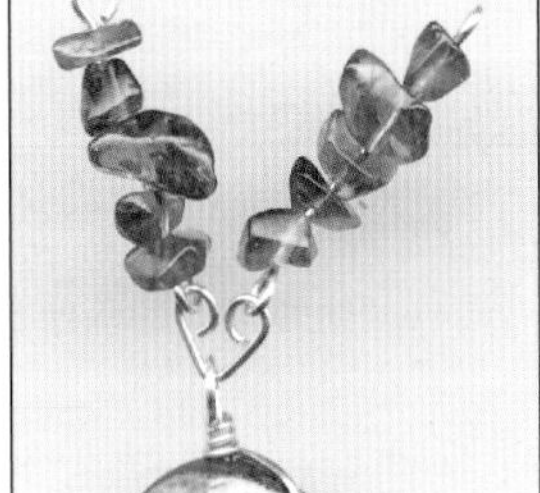
o

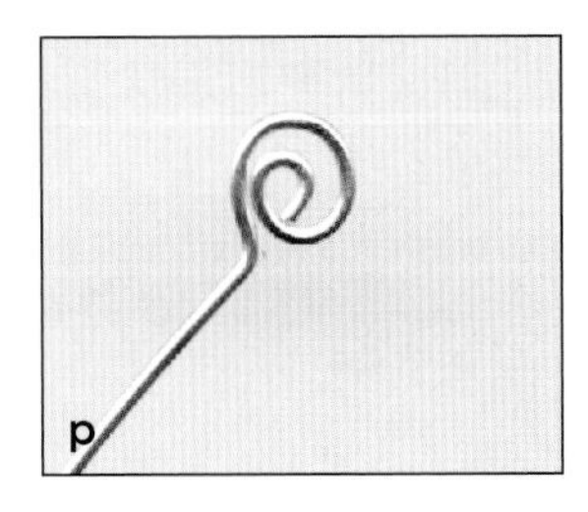
p

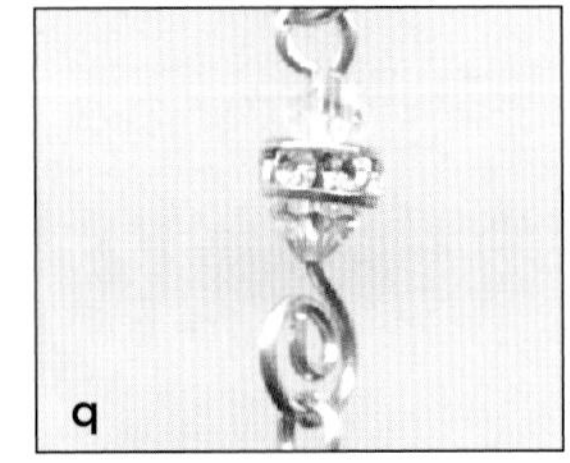
q

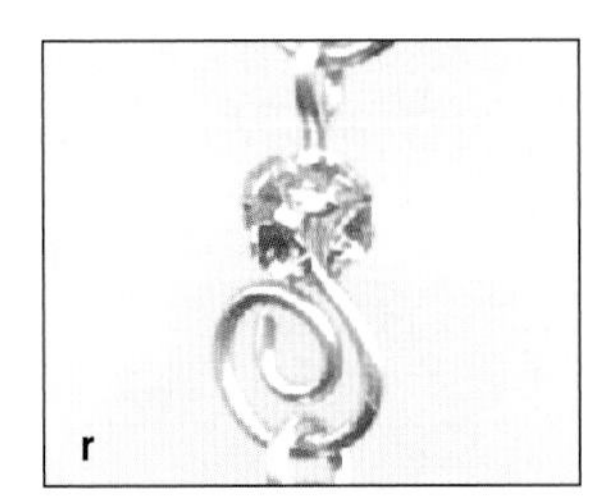
r

Sophisticated Headband

This chic headband is especially nice because it's reversible. Turn it one way and it sits somewhat upright, almost like a tiara. Turn it over and it lies flat against the head. Either way, you'll feel like a princess.

Materials
- double headband, gold
- 40–50 ft. (12.2–15.2 m) 24-gauge dead-soft wire, gold

Tools
- roundnose pliers
- chainnose pliers
- wire cutters

Technical Basics Reference:
- Making Curlicue Lace, p. 91
- Finishing Off, p. 87

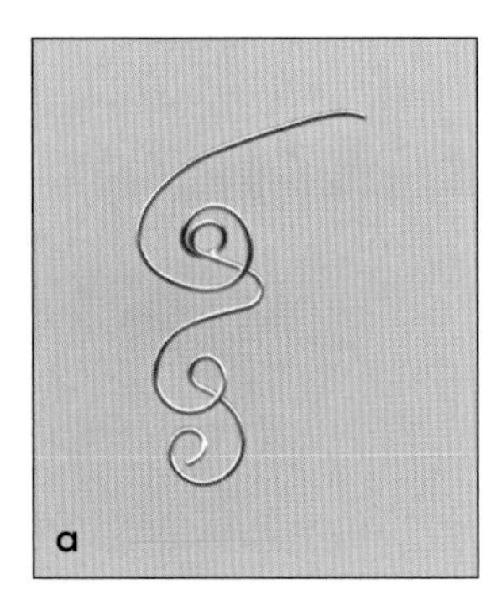

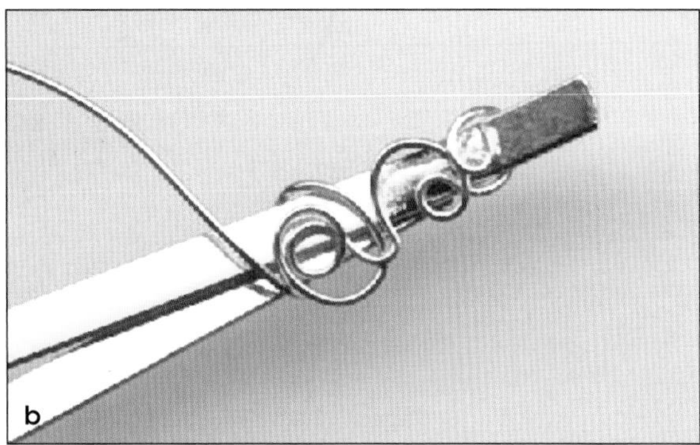

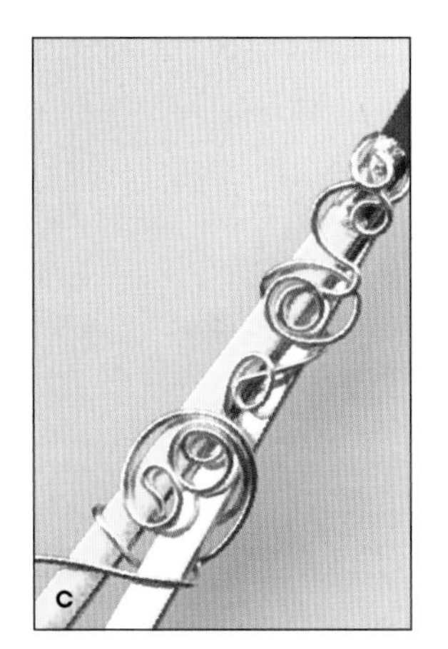

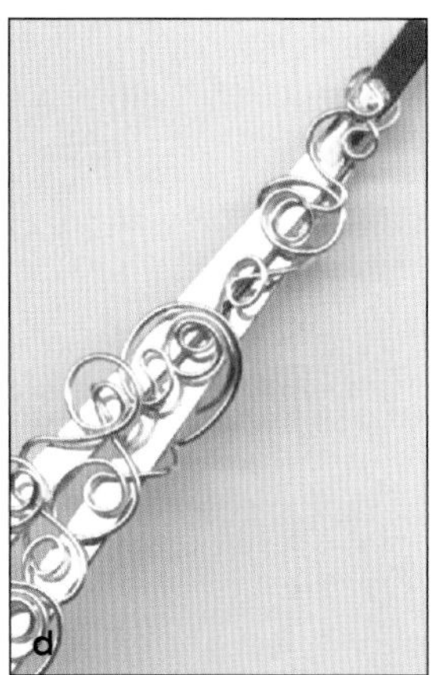

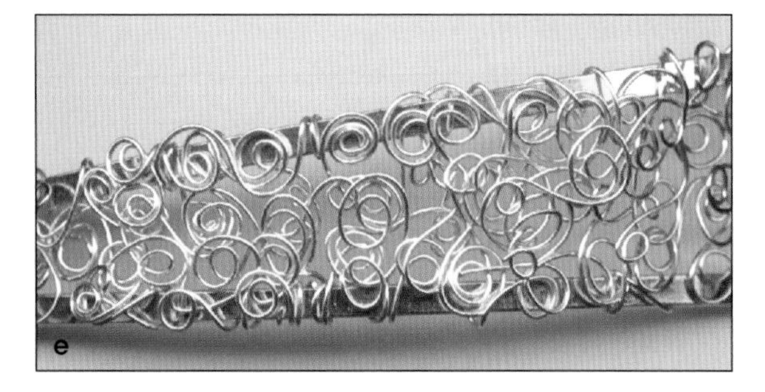

1 Cut wire into 4-ft. (1.2 m) lengths.

2 Begin lace strip with a spiral. Make several more curlicues *(Making Curlicue Lace)* **(a)**.

3 Using chainnose pliers as needed, curl original spiral around double headband near end **(b)**.

4 Make a few more curlicues. Coil wire once or twice around one side of headband **(c)**.

5 Make a few more curlicues. Coil wire once or twice around other side of headband.

6 Repeat Steps 4–5 to end of headband. Finish off *(Finishing Off)* **(d, e)**.

Strawberry Quartz Earrings

These large strawberry quartz briolettes take on a more light-hearted personality when accented by a frivolous outline of silvery curlicue lace.

Materials

- 5 ft. (1.5 m) 28-gauge dead-soft wire, silver
- 1 ft. (30.5 cm) 20-gauge half-hard wire, silver
- **2** 17 x 25 mm briolettes
- 2 g 15º silver metallic charlottes or seed beads
- pair of earring wires, silver

Tools

- roundnose pliers
- chainnose pliers
- wire cutters

Dimensions

approx. 3 x 5¼ in. (76 x 127 mm)

Technical Basics Reference

- Making Frames: Basic Frame, p. 86
- Making Base Rows: Beaded Outer Base Rows, p. 87
- Attaching Laces to Frames: Attaching Lace Directly to Frame with Beaded Arches, p. 91

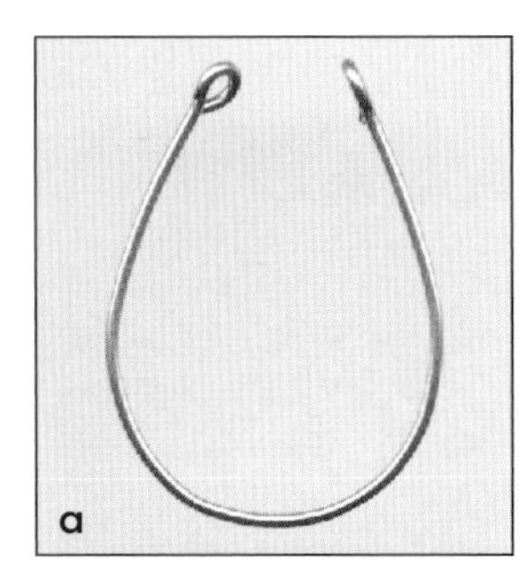
a

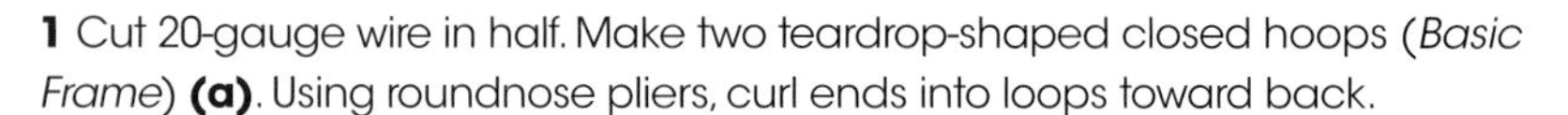

1 Cut 20-gauge wire in half. Make two teardrop-shaped closed hoops (*Basic Frame*) **(a)**. Using roundnose pliers, curl ends into loops toward back.

2 Cut 28-gauge wire into 2 ft. (61 cm) pieces. Make two narrow (¼-in./6.5 mm wide) strips of curlicue lace about 4 in. (10.2 cm) long (or the length needed to fit around the inside edge of the frame) **(b)**. Gently shape them so that they fit around insides of frames.

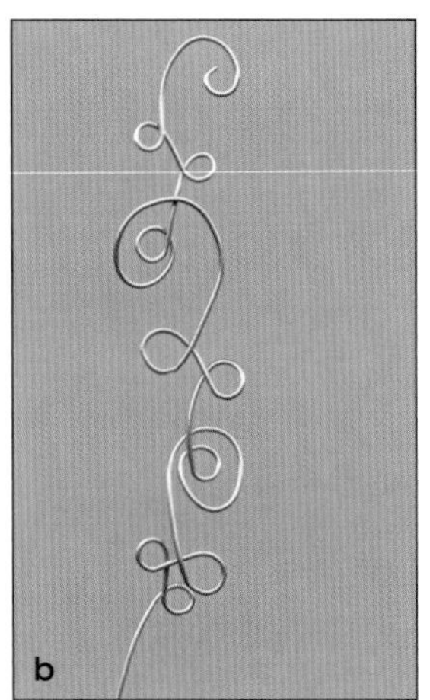
b

3 Using charlottes, begin at top of frame on one side to make an outer base row of one-bead arches all the way around outside of the frame (*Beaded Outer Base Rows*), attaching lace to frame along the way (*Attaching Lace Directly to Frame with Beaded Arches*) **(c)**.

4 Anchor a new piece of 28-gauge wire to one side of frame at the point that will allow the briolette to hang at desired height, threading wire through the lace as needed and coiling around frame to secure **(d, e)**.

5 String briolette and coil the wire around corresponding place on opposite side of frame, making sure briolette is hanging straight inside the lace.

6 Attach an earring wire.

7 Make a second earring to match the first.

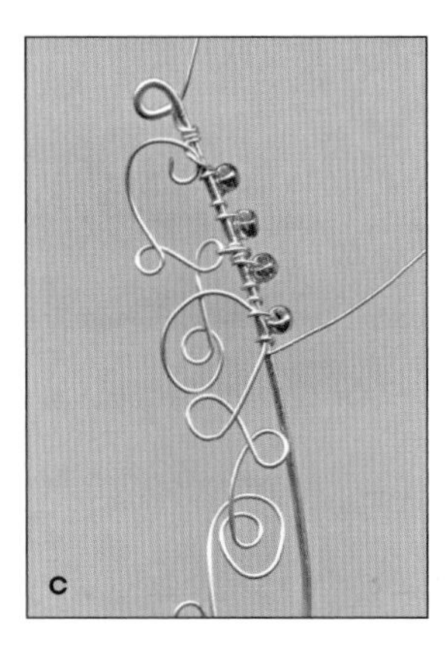
c

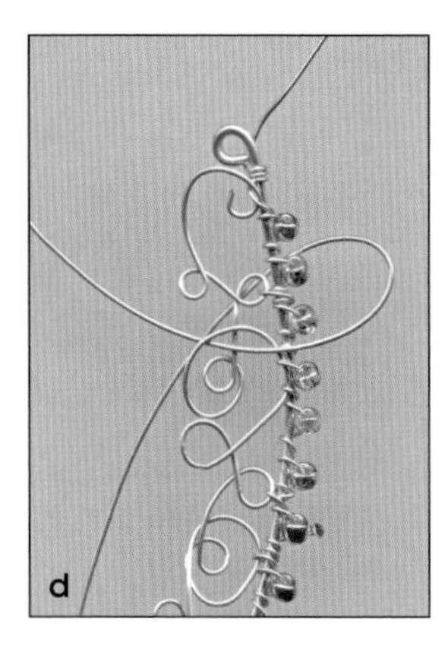
d

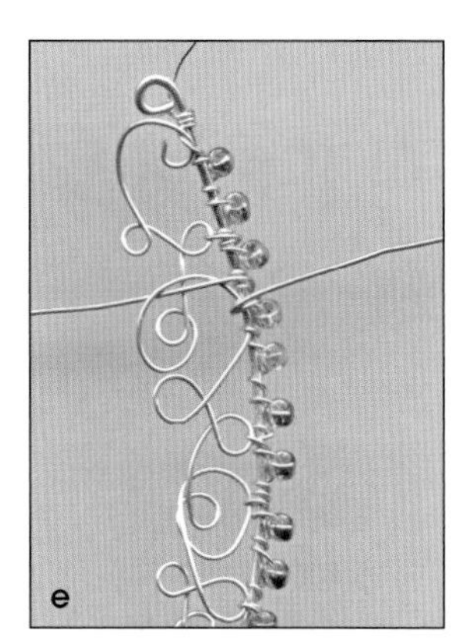
e

ch.8 Combination Projects

Orange Crazy Lace Agate Necklace

Not all lace is light and airy. This sturdy yet intricate version consists of 16-gauge wire flourishes connected by bauxite beads from central Ghana and handmade wire beads produced by young Krobo jewelry artisans.

Technical Basics Reference:

- Making Frames: Basic Frame, p. 86
- Anchoring Wires, p. 87
- Making Base Rows: Unbeaded Outer Base Rows, p. 87
- Finishing Off, p. 87
- Building onto Base Rows: Anchoring and Unbeaded Arches, p. 88
- Rearranging Rows Upright, p. 87
- Finishing Bezels: Lacing Up Bezels and Tightening Bezels around Cabochons, p. 88
- Jump Rings: Single Jump Rings, p. 92
- Clasps: Basic Hook-and-Eye Clasp, p. 92

Materials

- approx. 3 ft. (91 cm) 24-gauge dead-soft wire, copper
- 3 ft. 20-gauge dead-soft wire, copper
- 3 ft. 16-gauge dead-soft wire, copper
- 22 x 30 mm oval crazy lace agate cabochon
- **12** 5 x 5 mm tube-shaped bauxite beads
- **2** 10 x 10 mm handmade copper beads

Tools

- roundnose pliers
- chainnose pliers
- wire cutters
- flush cutters

Pendant Dimensions

approx. 1¾ x 1¼ in. (44 x 32 mm)

Bezel

1 Using 20-gauge wire, make basic inset bezel frame *(Basic Frame)*. Coil one tail around other at top of frame to secure frame closed. Turn a loop on other tail close to frame, clipping any excess length **(a, b)**.

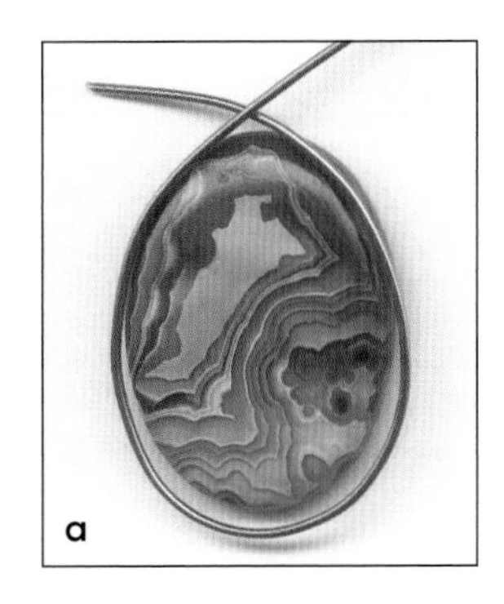

a

b

Note: All arches are unbeaded.

2 Anchor 24-gauge wire to frame *(Anchoring Wires)* and make a 25-arch base outer row *(Unbeaded Outer Base Rows)*. Finish off *(Finishing Off)* **(c)**.

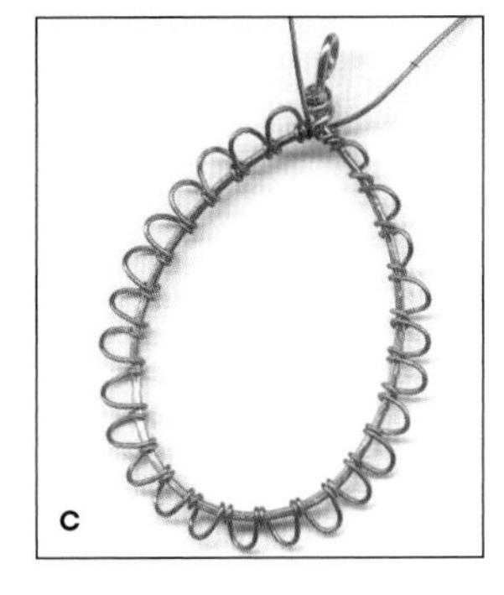

c

3 Turn frame over. Anchor wire in last arch made and, working in opposite direction, make a 24-arch second outer row *(Anchoring Wires* and *Unbeaded Arches)* **(d)**. Finish off.

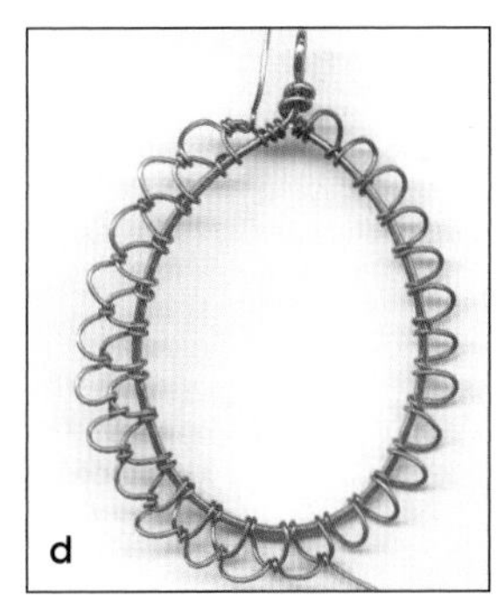

d

4 Rearrange rows *(Rearranging Rows Upright)*. Lace up back *(Lacing Up Bezels)*, working around the bezel frame under the arches rather than on the arches themselves **(e)**. Finish off.

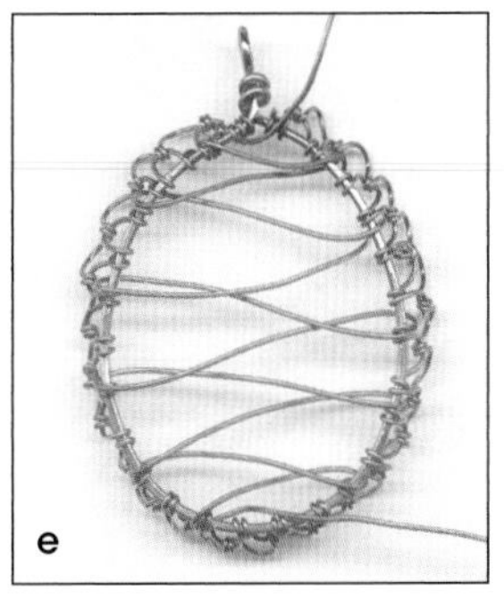

e

5 Insert cabochon. Tighten bezel around cabochon *(Tightening Bezels around Cabochons)* **(f, g)**.

f

g

Note: If cabochon is not secure, remove it, work an unbeaded outer row onto what is now top row of bezel, reinsert cabochon, and repeat tightening process.

Beaded Links (make 12)

6 Using a short length of 20-gauge wire, make a loop on one end, string a bauxite bead, and make a loop on the other end **(h)**.

h

Lacy Wire Chain Sections (make eight)

7 Using 16-gauge wire and roundnose pliers, turn a loop at one end of wire **(i)**.

i

8 Move pliers to point just behind first loop and form a loop in opposite direction **(j)**.

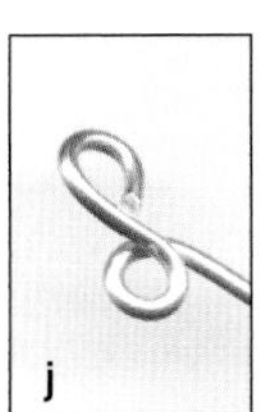

j

9 Move pliers to point just behind second loop and make loop in opposite directions and so on until all five loops are completed **(k, l)**.

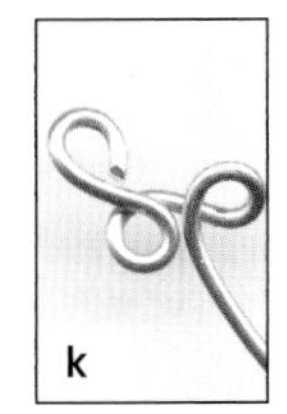

k

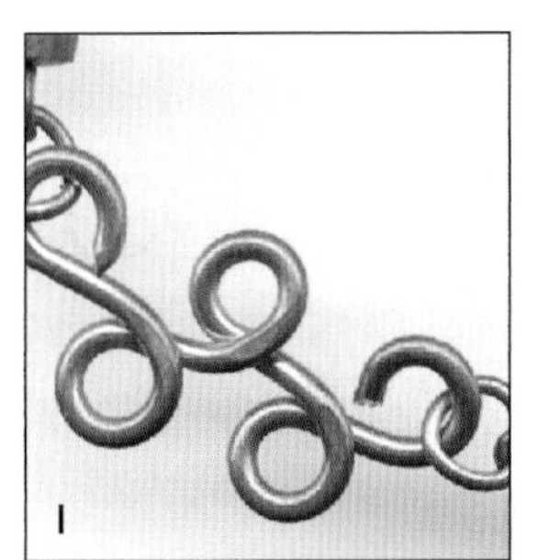

l

Assemble the Necklace

10 Using 20-gauge wire, make 24 jump rings *(Single Jump Rings)*.

11 Use jump rings to attach lacy wire sections and bead links as shown. Add jump ring to pendant and attach sides of necklace with last two jump rings.

12 Make hook-and-eye clasp *(Basic Hook-and-Eye Clasp)*. Attach to chain with jump rings.

Sunburst Pin

Concentric rounds of flame-shaped arches in copper, silver, and gold create a wonderful sunburst effect. By gluing a different finding on the back, you can turn this pin into a pendant, a comb, or a barrette.

Materials
- 4 in. (10.2 cm) 20-gauge half-hard wire, gold
- approx. 14 ft. (3 m) 28-gauge dead-soft wire, gold
- approx. 4 ft. (1.2 m) 28-gauge dead-soft wire, copper
- approx. 6 ft. (1.8 m) 28-gauge dead-soft wire, silver
- 10 x 20 mm oval amazonite cabochon
- 2 g 15º charlottes or seed beads, gold
- pin back, gold
- epoxy glue

Tools
- roundnose pliers
- chainnose pliers
- wire cutters

Pendant Dimensions

approx. 1¾ x 2 in. (44 x 51 mm)

Technical Basics Reference:
- Making Frames: Inset Bezel Frame, p. 86
- Anchoring Wires, p. 87
- Making Base Rows: Unbeaded Outer Base Rows, Unbeaded Inner Base Rows, p. 87
- Rearranging Rows Upright, p. 87
- Making Base Bezel Rows: Unbeaded Outer Base Bezel Rows, p. 88
- Finishing Bezels: Lacing Up Bezels, Tightening Bezels around Cabochons, p. 88
- Building onto Base Bezel Rows, p. 88
- Sculpting Wire: Making Triple-Layer Arches, p. 90, Making Sculpted Points, p. 91

Preparation

1 Cut 28-gauge wire into 2-ft. (61 cm) pieces.

Frame

2 Using 20-gauge wire, make basic inset bezel frame *(Inset Bezel Frame)*. Turn loops towards outside **(a)**.

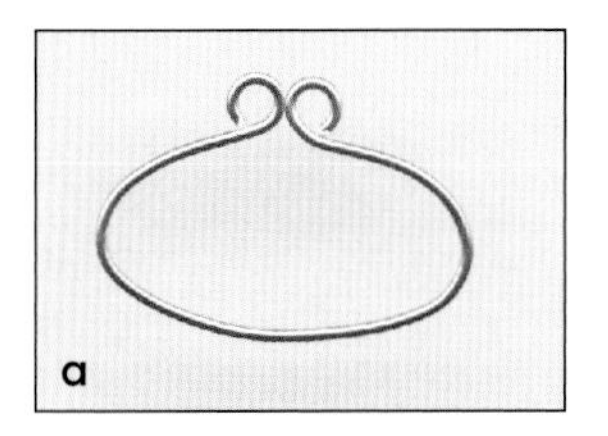

a

Outer Base Row

3 Anchor a piece of 28-gauge gold wire to frame *(Anchoring Wires)* and make a 28-arch outer base row *(Unbeaded Outer Base Rows)*. Do not clip tails **(b)**.

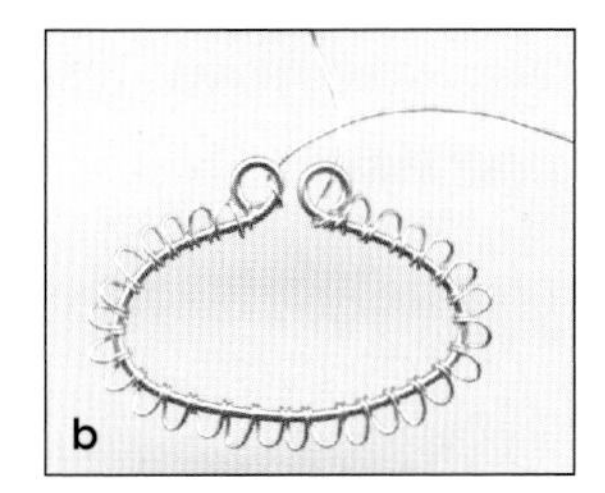

b

Inner Base Row

4 Turn frame over and, working back in opposite direction, make a 28-arch inner base row *(Unbeaded Inner Base Rows)*. Do not clip tails.

Outer Base Bezel Row

5 Rearrange rows upright *(Rearranging Rows Upright)*. Turn frame over and, working back in the other direction, make a 28-arch outer base bezel row *(Unbeaded Outer Base Bezel Rows)*. Finish off.

6 Anchor a piece of gold wire to first arch of what is now back row of arches. Lace up back side of bezel *(Lacing Up Bezels)*. Finish off **(c)**. Using a scrap of 28-gauge gold wire, coil top frame loops together.

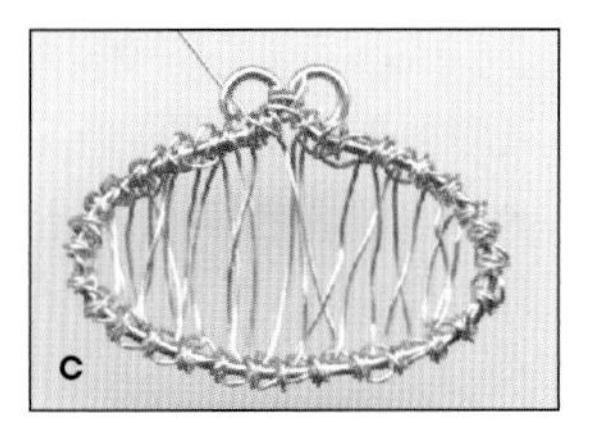

c

Second Front Row

7 Anchor a piece of 28-gauge gold wire in first arch of what is now top row. Make an unbeaded arch into each unbeaded arch all the way around frame. Insert cabochon **(d)**.

d

8 Tighten bezel around cabochon *(Tightening Bezels around Cabochons)*. Finish off **(e)**.

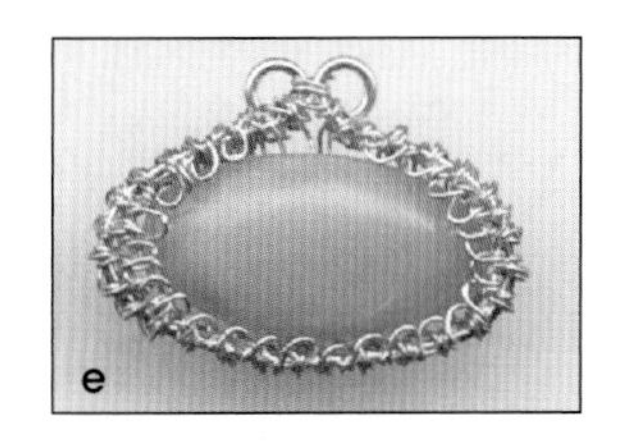

e

Note: If cabochon is not secure in bezel, remove the cabochon, anchor wire in first arch made, and add another unbeaded row of arches on row just made. Reinsert cabochon, and repeat tightening process. Finish off.

f

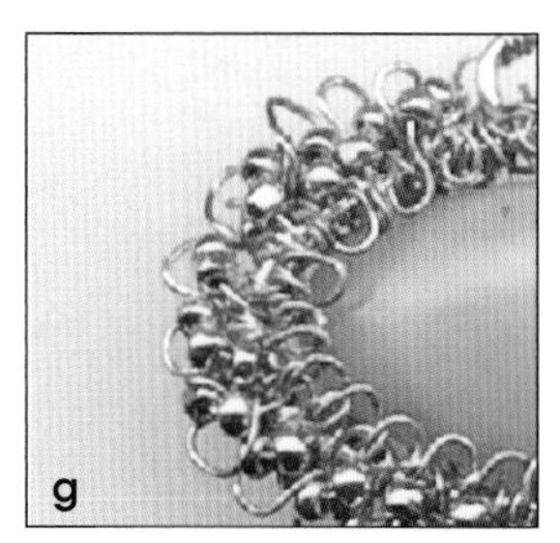
g

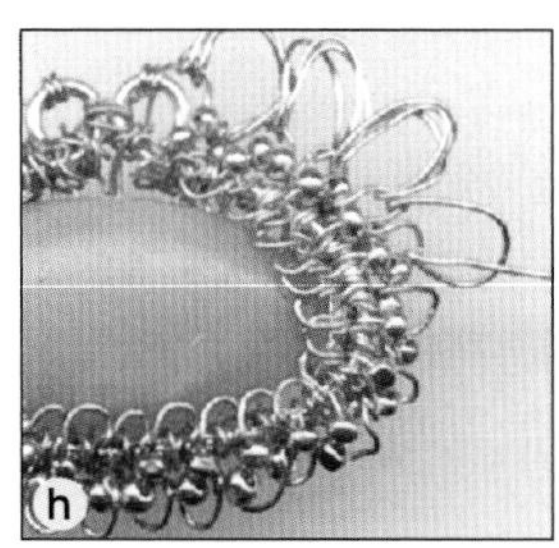
h

i

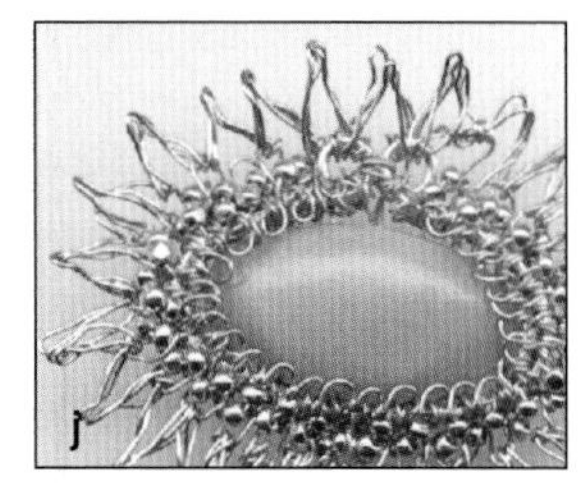
j

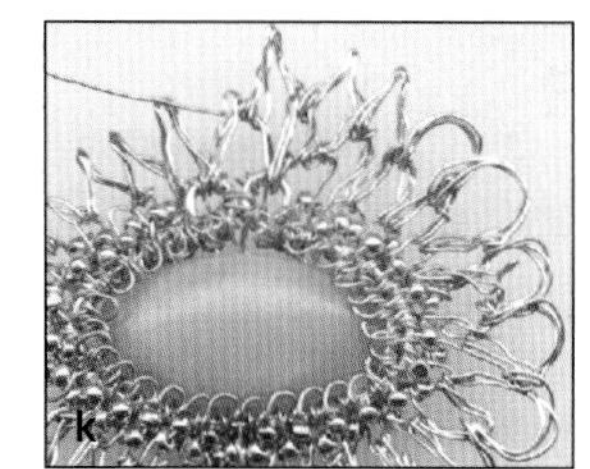
k

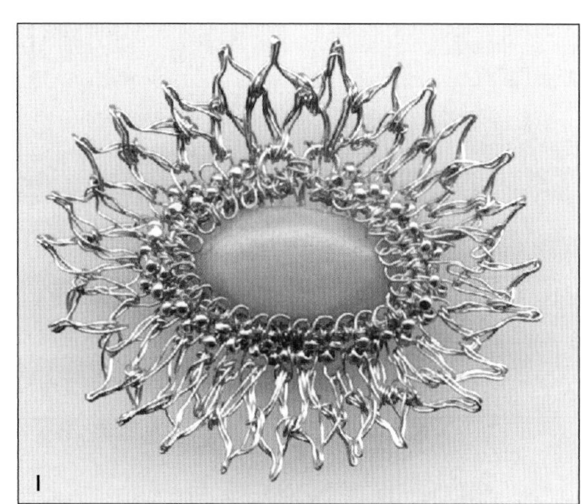
l

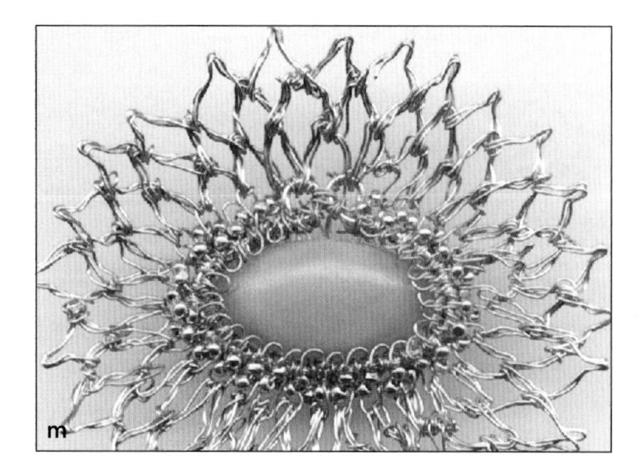
m

Second Outer Bezel Row

9 Anchor a piece of 28-gauge wire in first arch of outer base bezel row. Using 15º seed beads, make a 3-bead arch into each arch all the way around frame *(Building onto Base Bezel Rows)*. Finish off **(f)**.

Third Outer Bezel Row

10 Anchor a piece of 28-gauge gold wire in right-hand frame loop. Make an unbeaded arch into the spaces between the beaded arches all the way around frame, placing coils over previous coils **(g)**. End with arch into left-hand frame loop. Finish off.

Fourth Outer Bezel Row

11 Anchor a piece of copper wire into first unbeaded arch of last row made. Make a 4 mm triple-layer arch into each unbeaded arch **(h)** all the way around the frame *(Making Triple-Layer Arches)*. Finish off.

12 Using chainnose pliers, sculpt a point at the top of each arch *(Making Sculpted Points)* **(i)**.

Fifth Outer Bezel Row

13 Using silver wire and making 5 mm arches, repeat Steps 11–12 **(j–l)**.

Sixth Outer Bezel Row

14 Using gold wire and making 6 mm arches, repeat Steps 11–12 **(m)**.

15 Glue pin back in place.

Blue & Copper Krobo Bracelet

An example of lusciously heavy lace, this ultra-feminine bracelet is made of four gauges of copper wire and four different kinds of traditional hand-made recycled-glass beads from the Krobo region of Ghana.

Materials

- 8 in. (20.3 cm) 14-gauge dead-soft wire, copper
- 4 ft. (1.2 m) 18-gauge dead-soft wire, copper
- 3 ft. (91.4 cm) 20-gauge dead-soft wire, copper
- approx. 6 ft. (1.8 m) 24-gauge dead-soft wire, copper
- 20 mm Krobo recycled glass round bead
- **6** 11 x 13 mm painted Krobo recycled glass tube-shaped beads
- **36** Krobo recycled glass E-beads, turquoise
- **4** 3 x 10 mm Krobo recycled glass rondelles

Tools

- roundnose pliers
- chainnose pliers
- wire cutters
- hammer
- anvil

Dimensions

approx. 1¼ x 8 in. (32 x 203 mm)

Technical Basics Reference:

- Anchoring Wires, p. 87
- Finishing Off, p. 87
- Making Base Rows: Unbeaded Outer Base Rows, p. 87
- Building onto Base Bezel Rows: Anchoring and Unbeaded Arches, p. 88
- Making Curlicue Lace, p. 91
- Clasps: Basic Hook-and-Eye Clasp, p. 92
- Jump Rings: Single Jump Rings, p. 92

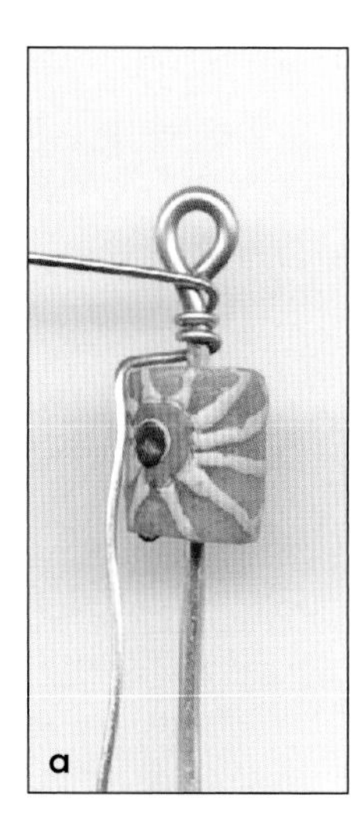

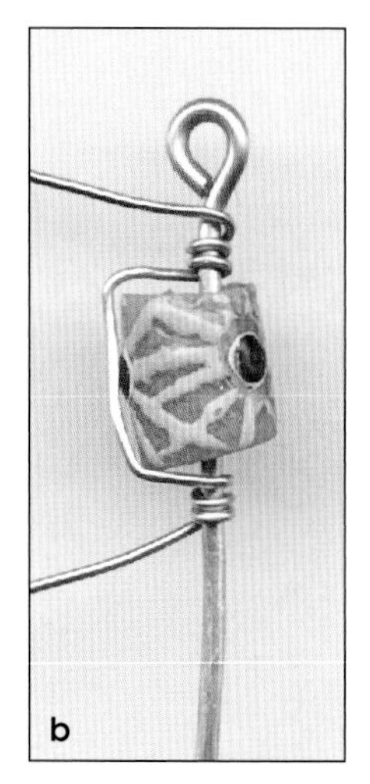

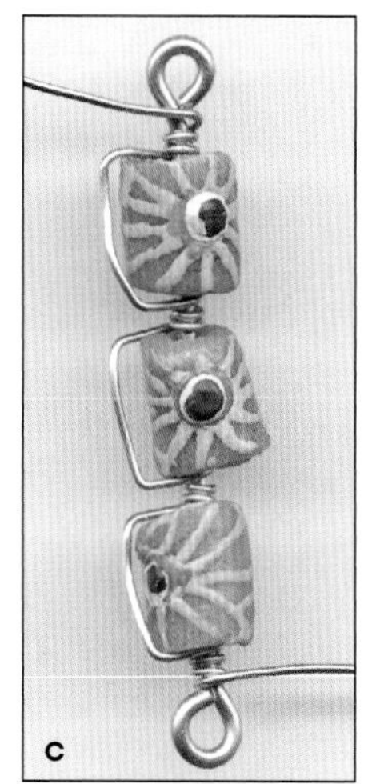

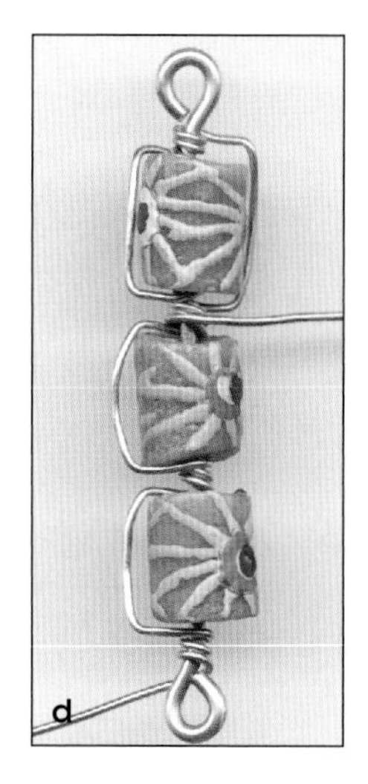

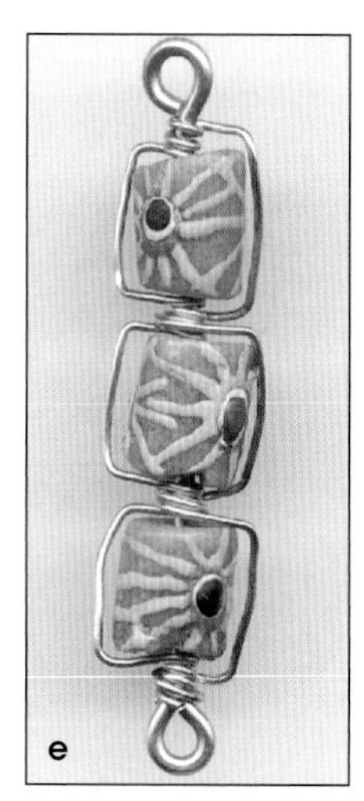

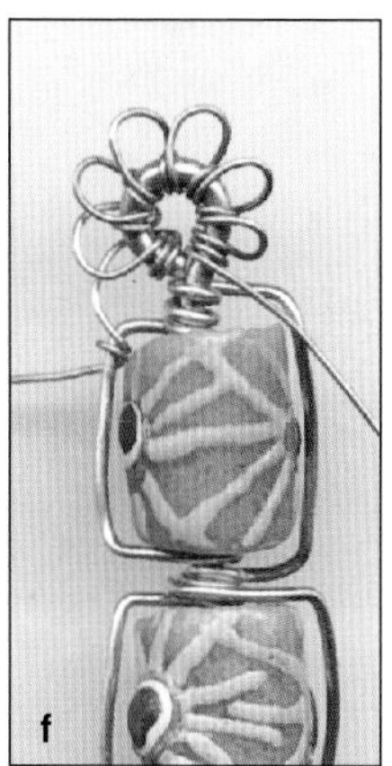

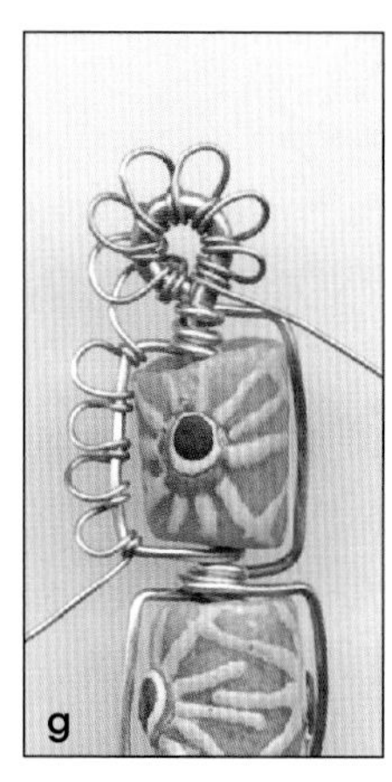

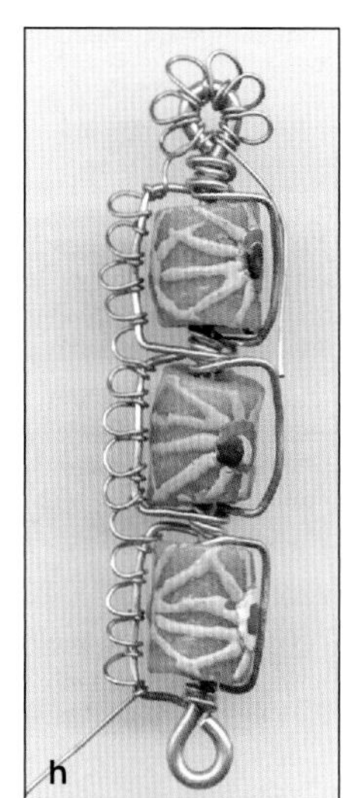

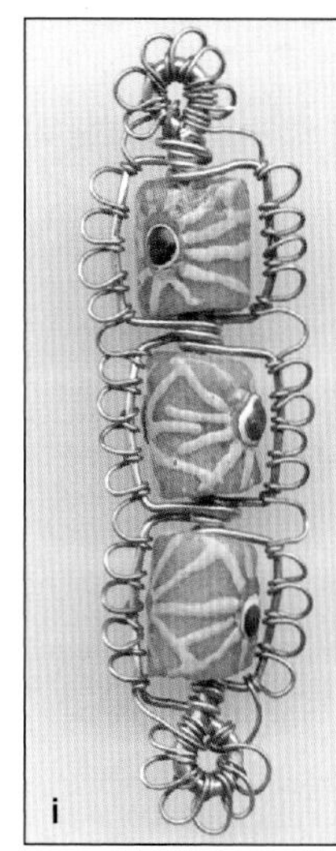

Preparation

1 Cut 14-gauge and 18-gauge wires in half. Cut 24-gauge wire into 3-ft. (91.4 cm) lengths. Turn a loop at one end of each piece of 14-gauge wire.

Center Frame

2 Anchor a piece of 18-gauge wire to one of the frames next to loop *(Anchoring Wires)*.

3 String a painted bead. Using chainnose pliers, bend 18-gauge wire 45° so it lies parallel to long side of bead **(a)**. Bend it again at other end of bead and coil twice around 14-gauge wire **(b)**.

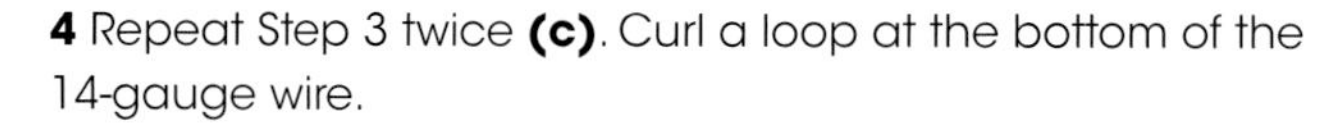

4 Repeat Step 3 twice **(c)**. Curl a loop at the bottom of the 14-gauge wire.

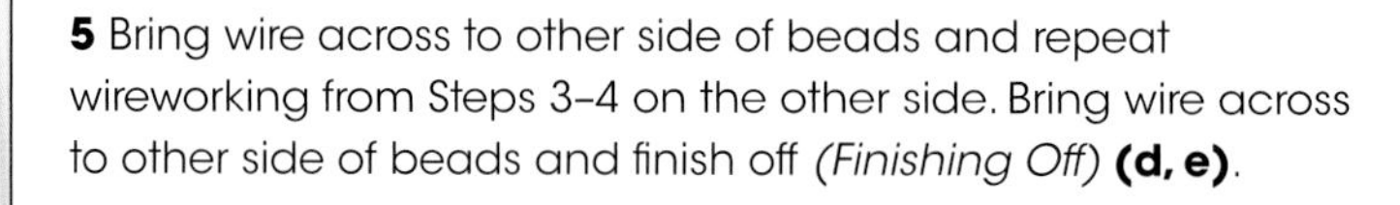

5 Bring wire across to other side of beads and repeat wireworking from Steps 3–4 on the other side. Bring wire across to other side of beads and finish off *(Finishing Off)* **(d, e)**.

Base Outer Row

6 Anchor a piece of 24-gauge wire in 14-gauge frame loop. Make six unbeaded arches into loop *(Unbeaded Outer Base Rows)*.

7 Make an unbeaded arch into first corner of first 18-gauge frame section on side of bracelet **(f)**.

8 Make four unbeaded arches in first frame section **(g)**. Make an unbeaded arch into next frame section.

Note: You will not have room to insert your pliers under the 18-gauge frame wire without bending it, so make the arches as explained in (*Anchoring* and *Unbeaded Arches*).

9 Repeat Step 8 twice, working final unbeaded arch into 14-gauge end loop **(h)**. Make six unbeaded arches around end loop.

10 Repeat Steps 7–9 on the other side. Coil wire twice around frame over previous coil. Do not clip tail **(i)**.

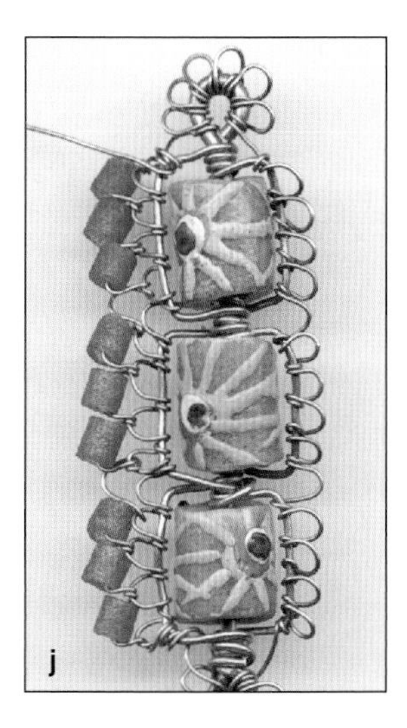

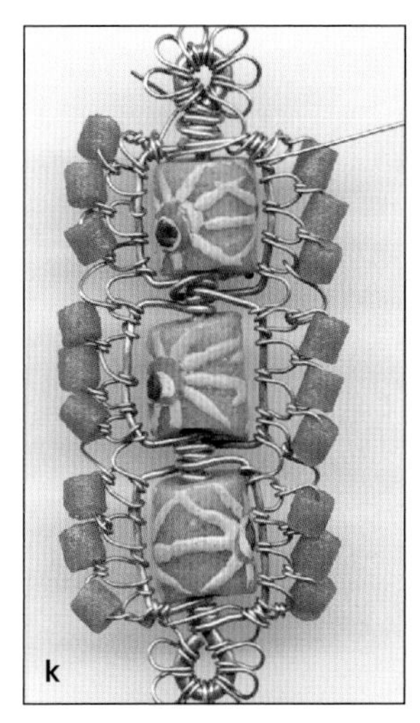

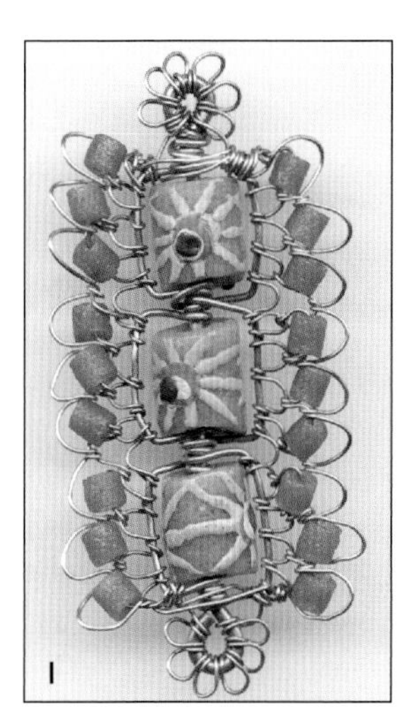

Second Outer Row

11 Anchor wire into first arch of base outer row.

12 Using E-beads, make a one-bead arch into each of next three arches.

Note: To get these cylindrical beads to sit more or less straight, bend the wire at a 45° angle ¼ in. (6.5 mm) from base prior to adding each bead.

13 Skip one arch. Make an unbeaded arch into next arch.

14 Repeat Steps 12–13.

15 Repeat Step 12 **(j)**.

16 Bring wire across to other side of frame and repeat Steps 12–15 **(k)**.

17 Bring wire across to other side of frame and coil twice around frame over previous coil. Finish off.

Third Outer Row

18 Anchor wire in first one-bead arch just prior to bead.

19 Make an unbeaded arch into each of next two one-bead arches just prior to bead. Make an unbeaded arch into next unbeaded arch.

20 Repeat Step 19 twice, working last arch into final arch on base outer row.

21 Bring wire across to other side of frame and Repeat Steps 19–20. Bring wire across to other side of frame and coil twice around frame over previous coil. Finish off **(l)**.

22 Repeat Steps 2–21 for second beaded section of bracelet. Gently curl each section into a "U" shape.

Centerpiece Bead

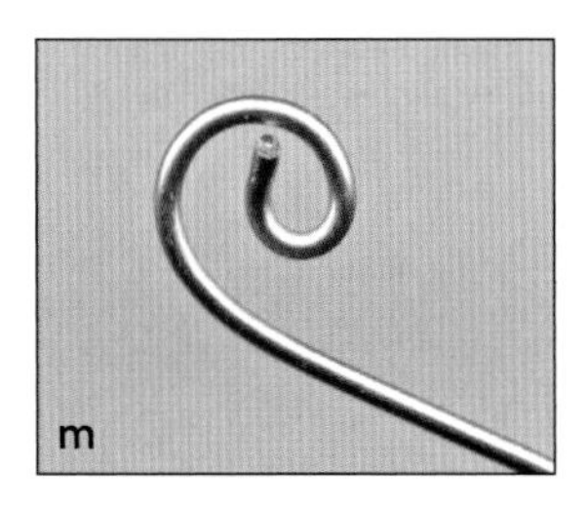
m

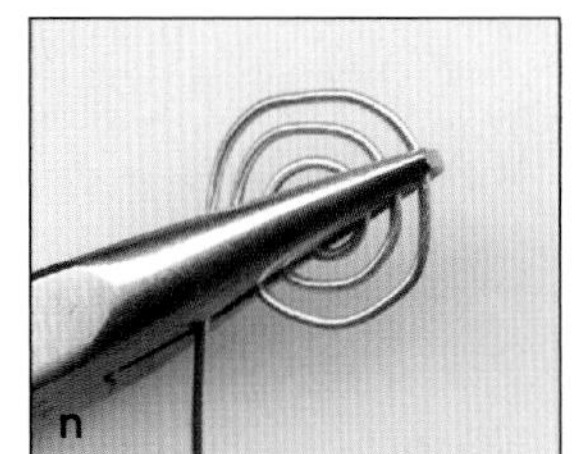
n

23 Using 20-gauge wire, curl a loop at one end **(m)**. Using chainnose pliers, nudge wire into a spiral almost as big as 20 mm round bead. (This gives you something to press against top of bead as you shape your wire cage.) **(n)**.

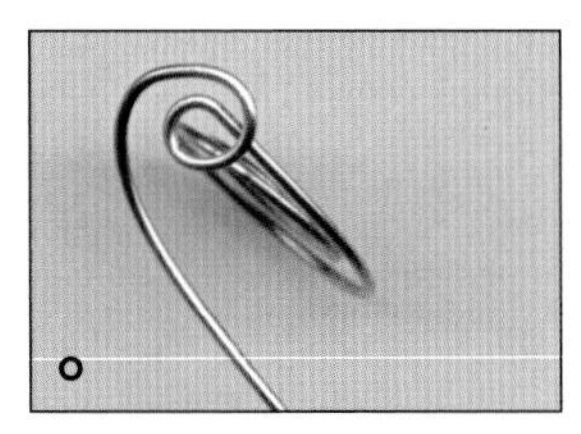
o

p

q

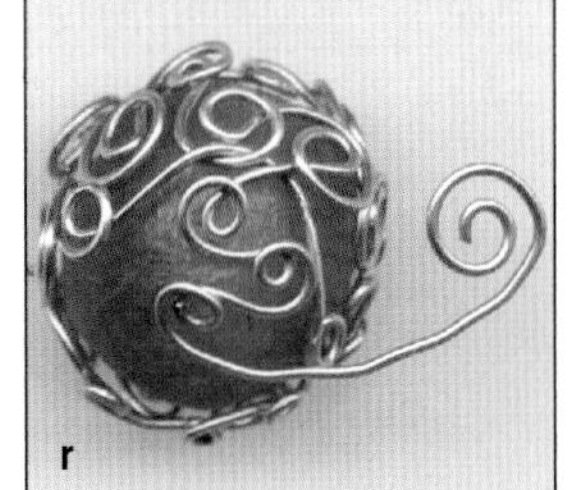
r

s

24 Using roundnose and chainnose pliers, make a curlicue lace cage for 20 mm bead, stopping often to shape the lace around bead so that it fits snugly and securely (*Making Curlicue Lace*). Once sides of cage meet, insert bead and lace the two sides together by bringing wire through at several points and/or by hooking curlicues around each other **(o–s)**. Play out the wire in the original spiral, making curlicues over the space it covered.

Assembling the Bracelet

25 Cut two 2-in. (51 mm) pieces of 18-gauge wire from leftover scraps. Turn a loop at one end of each piece. Insert both wires through large lacy bead and turn loops in other end of each wire as close to bead as possible.

t

26 Open loops just enough to attach to third and fourth unbeaded arches surrounding 14-gauge frame loops at one end of each beaded section **(t)**.

27 Using an 18-gauge scrap of wire, make a basic hook clasp *(Basic Hook-and-Eye Clasp)* and a jump ring *(Single Jump Rings)*.

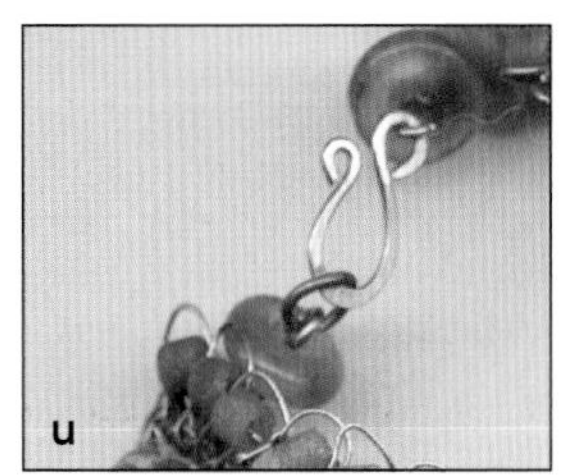
u

28 Using 18-gauge scraps, make a rondelle chain by turning loops on either side of beads and hooking together as needed to add length to bracelet. Attach clasp to one end and ring to the other **(u)**.

Curlicue Lace Earrings

Jewelry just doesn't get much lacier than this! These earrings combine a bright turquoise cabochon set in an inset bezel and surrounded by a dense double layer of silvery curlicue lace. Yum!

Technical Basics Reference:

- Making Frames: Inset Bezel Frame, p. 86
- Making Base Rows: Unbeaded Outer Base Rows, Unbeaded Inner Base Rows, p. 87
- Rearranging Rows Upright, p. 87
- Making Base Bezel Rows: Unbeaded Outer Base Bezel Rows, p. 88
- Finishing a Bezel: Lacing Up a Bezel, Tightening Bezels around Cabochons, p. 88
- Making Curlicue Lace, p. 91
- Attaching Laces to Frames: Tacking Laces in Place, p. 91, Attaching Lace to Base Row of Arches, p. 92

Materials

- 10 in. (25.4 cm) 20-gauge half-hard wire
- approx. 22 ft. (6.7 m) 28-gauge dead-soft wire
- 12 x 24 mm elongated diamond cabochon (turquoise or fossil coral)
- pair of earring wires
- **2** 5 mm jump rings

Tools

- roundnose pliers
- chainnose pliers
- wire cutters

Dimensions

approx. 1½ in. (38 mm)

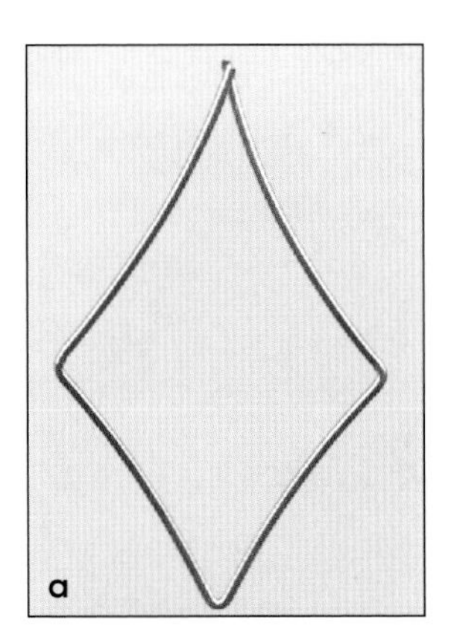
a

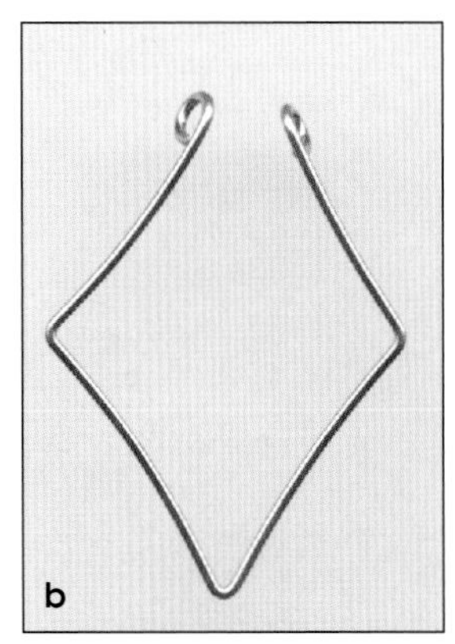
b

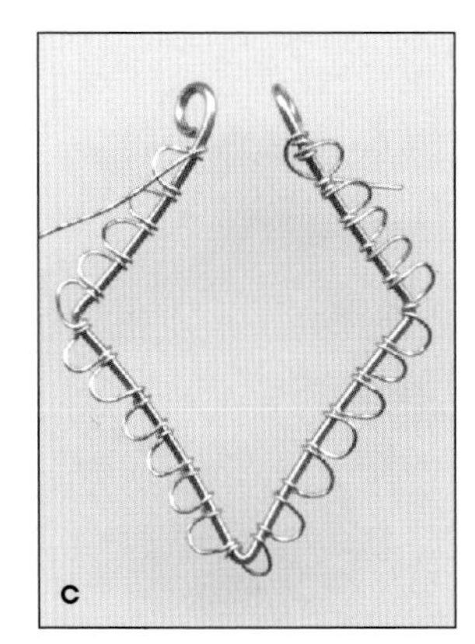
c

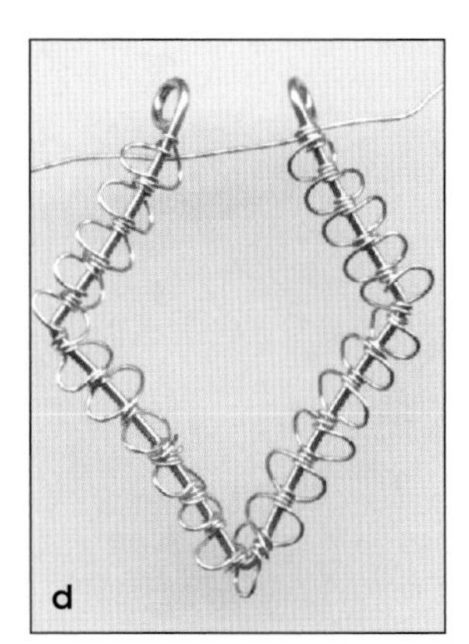
d

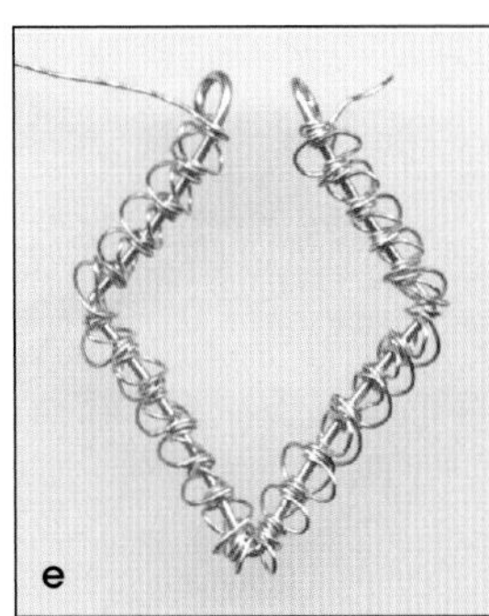
e

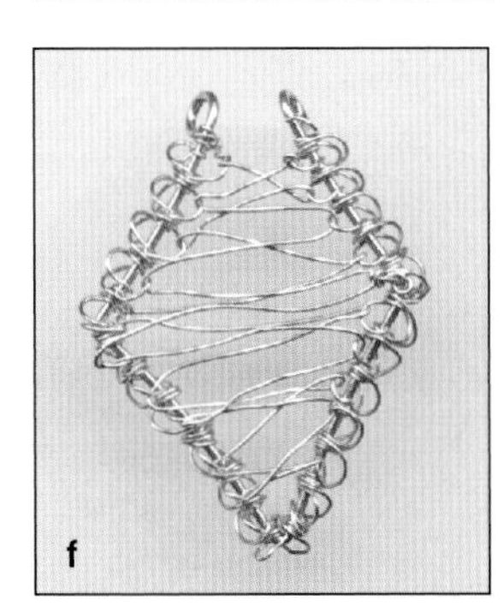
f

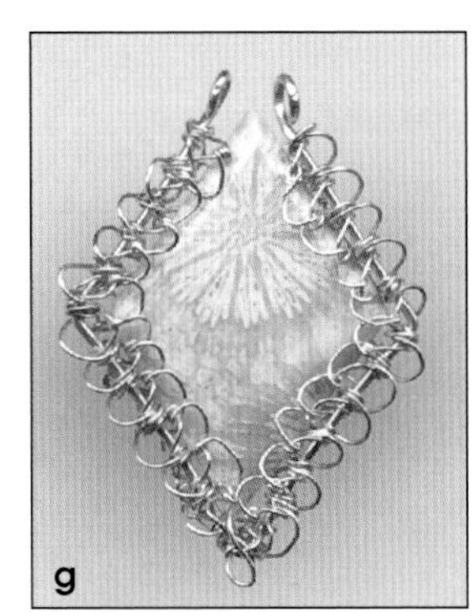
g

Preparation

1 Cut 28-gauge wire into 2-ft. (61 cm) pieces.

Frame

2 Using 20-gauge wire, make two basic inset bezel frames in shape of cabochon *(Inset Bezel Frame)* **(a)**. Turn loops at top of frames towards back and tip them towards the front to center them above frames **(b)**.

Outer Base Row

3 Anchor a piece of 28-gauge gold wire to frame and make 23-arch outer base row *(Unbeaded Outer Base Rows)*. Do not clip tails **(c)**.

Inner Base Row

4 Turn frame over and, working back in opposite direction, make 23-arch inner base row *(Unbeaded Inner Base Rows)*. Do not clip tails **(d)**.

Outer Base Bezel Row

5 Rearrange rows upright *(Rearranging Rows Upright)*. Turn frame over and, working back in opposite direction, make 23-arch outer base bezel row *(Unbeaded Outer Base Bezel Rows)*. Do not clip tails **(e)**.

6 Anchor a piece of wire to first arch of what is now back row. Lace up back side of bezel *(Lacing Up a Bezel)*. Finish off *(Finishing Off)* **(f)**.

Second Front Row

7 Anchor a piece of wire in second arch of what is now front row of arches. Make a second front row of 22 unbeaded arches. Insert cabochon **(g)**. Tighten bezel around cabochon *(Tightening Bezels around Cabochons)*.

Note: If cabochon is not secure in bezel, remove the cabochon, anchor wire in first arch made, and add another unbeaded row to row just made. Reinsert cabochon, and repeat tightening process. Finish off.

8 Repeat Steps 3–7 for second earring.

9 Make two pieces of curlicue lace to fit around frames *(Making Curlicue Lace)*.

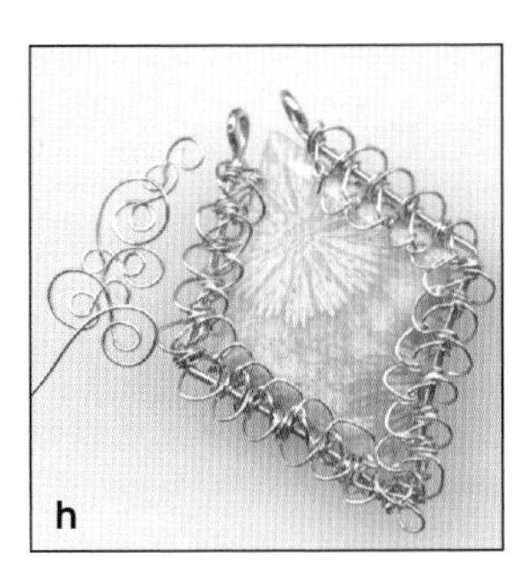

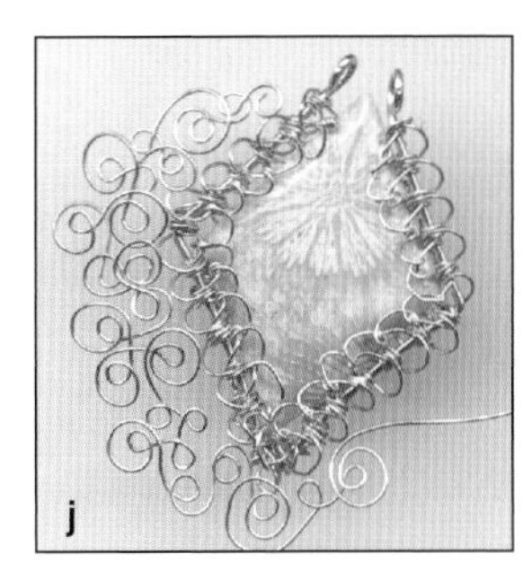

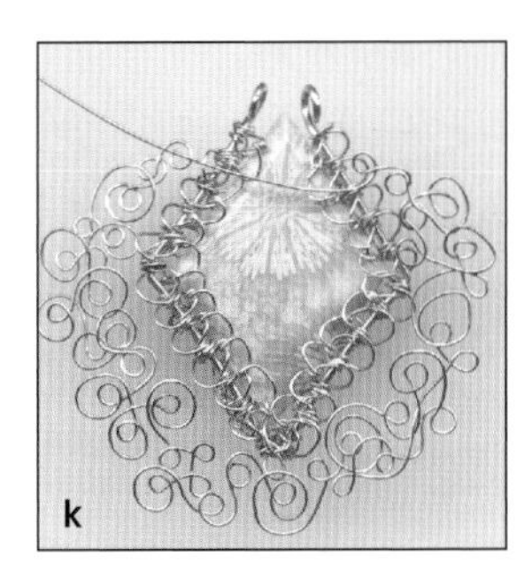

Note: The laces need only approximate the shape. They can be shaped and patched later if necessary **(h-k)**.

10 Layer any two lace pieces and tack them to frame if desired *(Tacking Laces in Place)*. Attach them to base outer bezel row of arches *(Attaching Lace to Base Row of Arches)*. Do not clip tails **(l-q)**.

Note: While it is best to take wire through both pieces of lace when possible, it's fine to skip one layer, or even a base arch, as needed to get the lace to sit nicely. Any irregularities will hide in the busyness of the laces.

11 Shape the laces as needed to make them more or less symmetrical and also consistent with each other. If a section of doubled lace is sparse, take the tail behind the lace to that point (or anchor a new wire to nearest frame loop) and make a few more curlicues as necessary to get a consistent look. Anchor the new curlicues to other curlicues as needed for strength and stability **(r)**.

12 If frame loops are too far apart for a jump ring to fit through them easily, use a scrap of 28-gauge wire to wrap tightly around them, pulling them in towards center **(s)**.

13 Repeat Steps 9–12 for the second earring.

14 Attach the earring wires with jump rings.

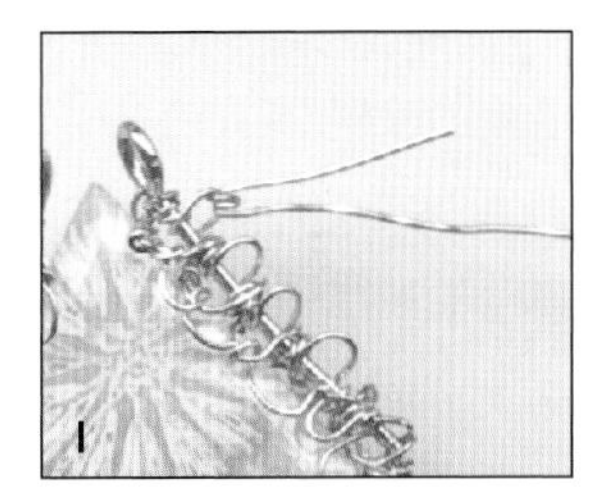

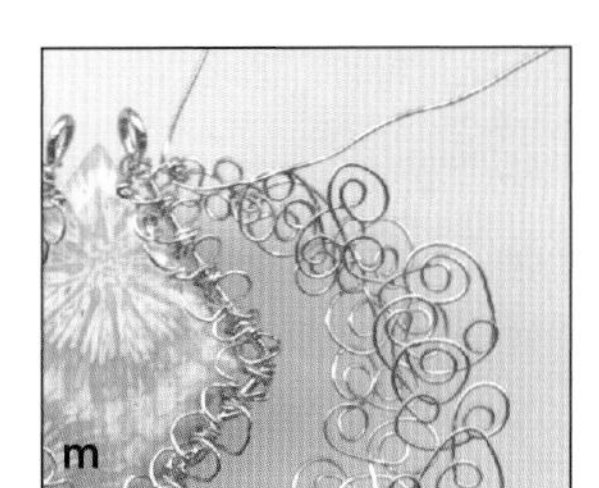

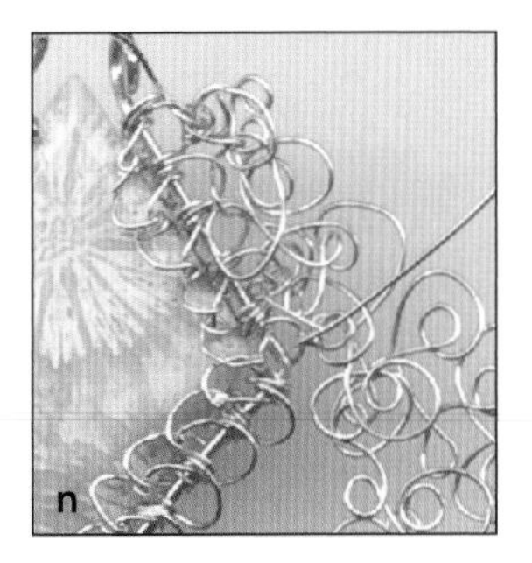

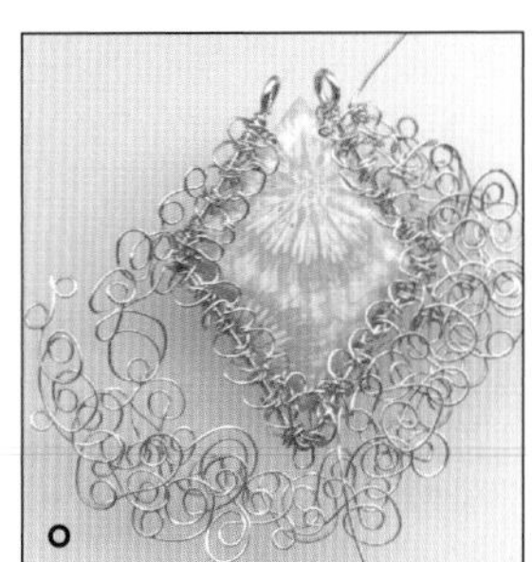

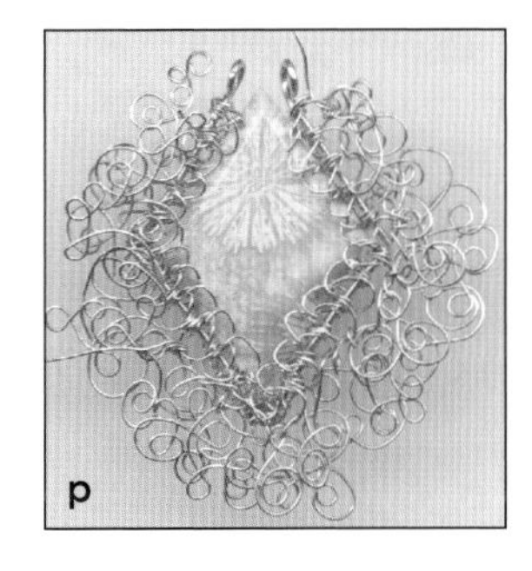

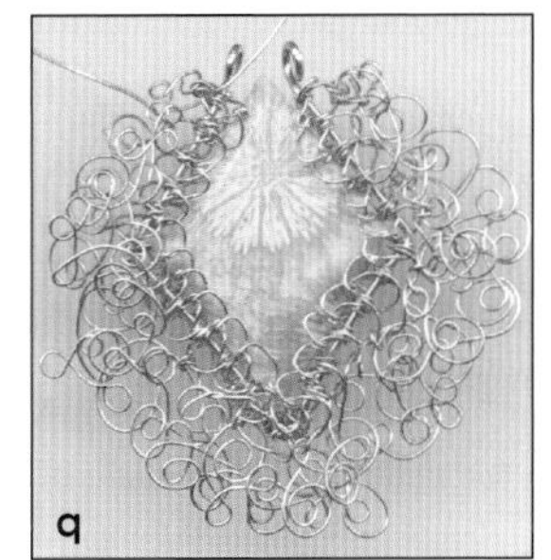

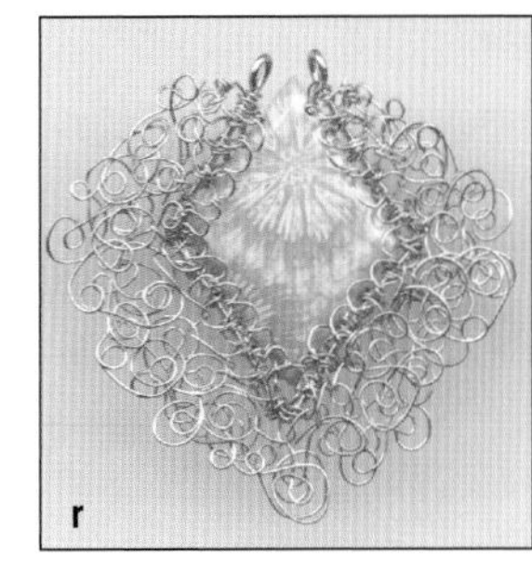

Paua Shell Necklace

It's time to get really fancy! This pendant combines a basic inset bezel with a froth of twisted wire randomly curved and curled to give the shell a lacy frame. The twisted wire is studded with crystals in all the same colors that glimmer out from the paua shell.

Technical Basics Reference:
- Making Frames: Inset Bezel Frame, p. 86
- Anchoring Wires, p. 87
- Making Base Rows: Unbeaded Outer Base Rows, Unbeaded Inner Base Rows, p. 87
- Finishing Off, p. 87
- Rearranging Rows Upright, p. 87
- Making Base Bezel Rows: Unbeaded Outer Base Bezel Rows, p. 88
- Finishing a Bezel: Lacing Up a Bezel, Tightening Bezels around Cabochons, p. 88
- Twisting Wires: Twisting a Main Stem, p. 89

Materials
- 5 in. (12.7 cm) 20-gauge half-hard wire, gold
- approx. 9 ft. (2.7 m) 28-gauge half-hard wire, gold
- 20 x 30 mm oval paua shell cabochon
- 4 mm bicone crystal beads:
  6 bright turquoise
  7 bright pink
  7 lime green
  4 light blue
  4 light purple
- 12 in. (30.5 cm) chain, gold
- small lobster claw clasp and 5 mm soldered jump ring, gold
- 3 mm jump ring, gold
- 3 headpins, gold

Tools
- roundnose pliers
- chainnose pliers
- wire cutters

Pendant Dimensions
approx. 1⅜ in. x 2½ in. (3.5 x 6.4 cm)

Preparation

1 Cut 28-gauge wire into 2-ft. (61 cm) pieces. Cut chain into 1-in. (25.5 mm)pieces.

Frame

2 Using 20-gauge wire, make basic inset bezel frame *(Inset Bezel Frame)*. Turn loops at top towards outsides of frame **(a)**.

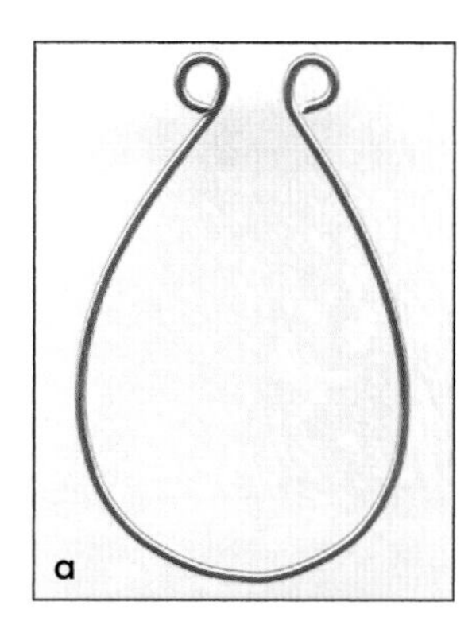
a

Note: All arches are unbeaded.

Outer Base Row

3 Anchor 24-gauge wire to frame *(Anchoring Wires)* and make 36-arch outer base row *(Unbeaded Outer Base Rows)*. Do not clip tails.

Inner Base Row

4 Turn frame over and, working back in the other direction, make 36-arch inner base row (*Unbeaded Inner Base Rows*). Do not clip tails.

b

Second Inner Base Row

5 Bring wire back through last arch made and anchor with 2 coils. Make a 35-arch second inner row (*Building onto Base Rows*). Finish off (*Finishing Off*).

Second Outer Base Row

6 Anchor a new wire to first arch on outer base row. Make a 35-arch second outer row. Finish off.

7 Rearrange rows upright (*Rearranging Rows Upright*).

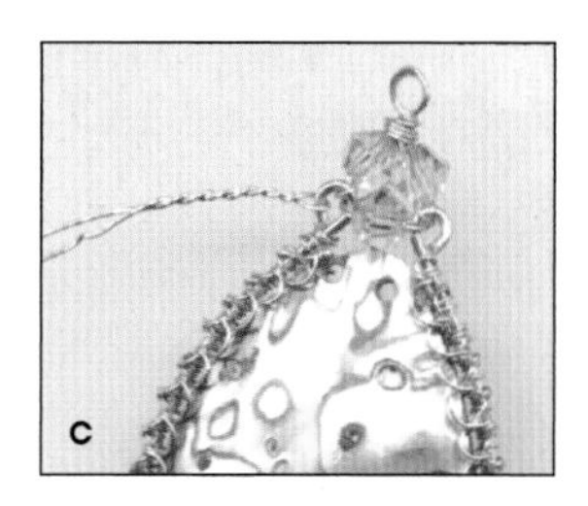
c

8 Insert cabochon. Tighten bezel around cabochon (*Tightening Bezels Around Cabochons*).

Note: If cabochon is not secure in bezel, remove the cabochon, add an unbeaded outer row onto what is now the top row of the bezel, reinsert cabochon, and repeat tightening process.

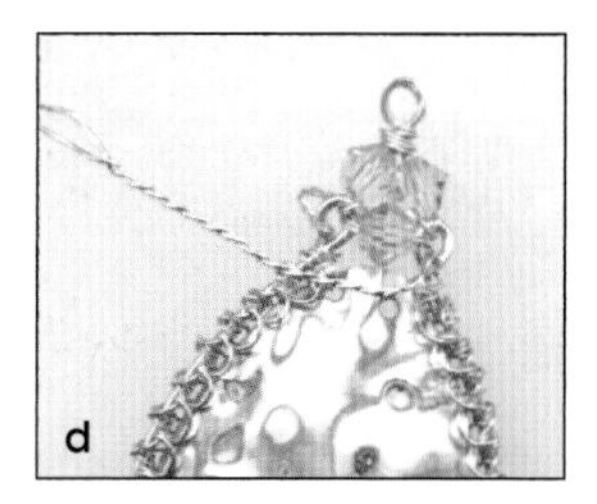
d

9 String a pink crystal on a scrap of 28-gauge wire. Bring wire through one top frame loop from back to front, leaving a 2-in. (51 mm) tail. Coil wire around frame loop twice. String a green crystal. Bring wire through other top frame loop from front to back. Coil wire around frame loop twice. String a pink crystal. Using both tails of wire as one, wire wrap a loop at top of bezel **(b)**.

Twisted Portion

10 String a 24-gauge wire through the left top frame loop and center. Twist about 2 in. (*Twisting a Main Stem*) **(c)**.

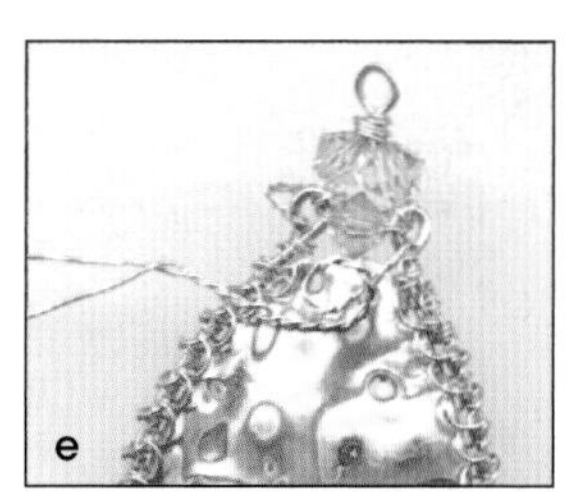
e

11 Bring wire in a graceful curve around behind top of bezel and through other frame loop **(d)**.

12 Bring wire across face of cabochon, curling a loop as shown in photo **(e)**. Carry wire back up and behind bezel again and on around towards front.

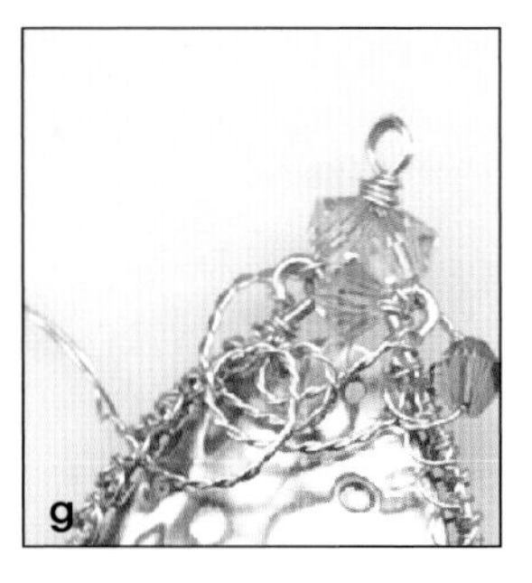

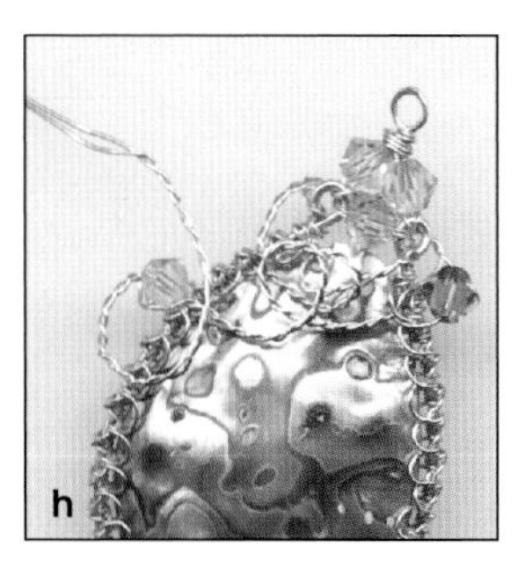

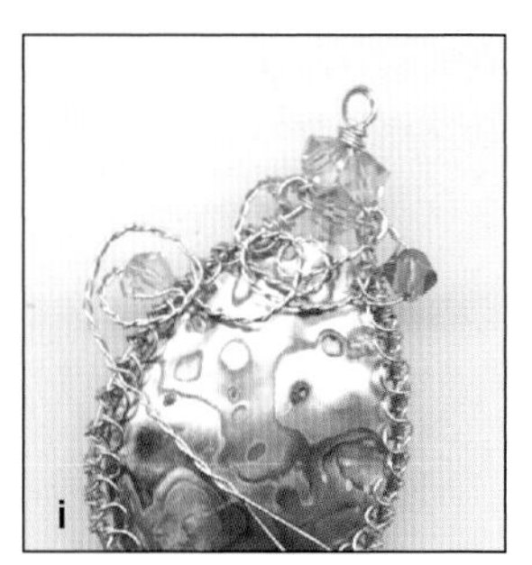

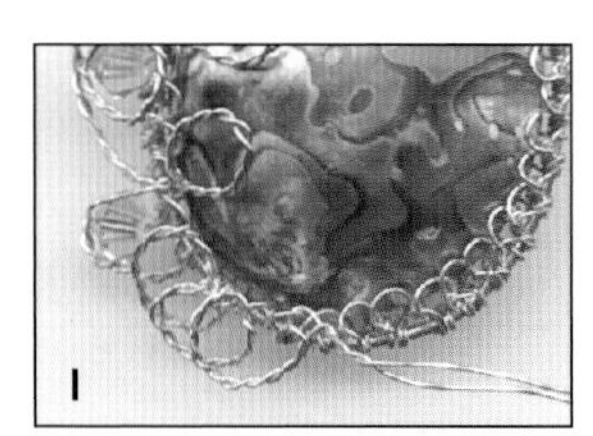

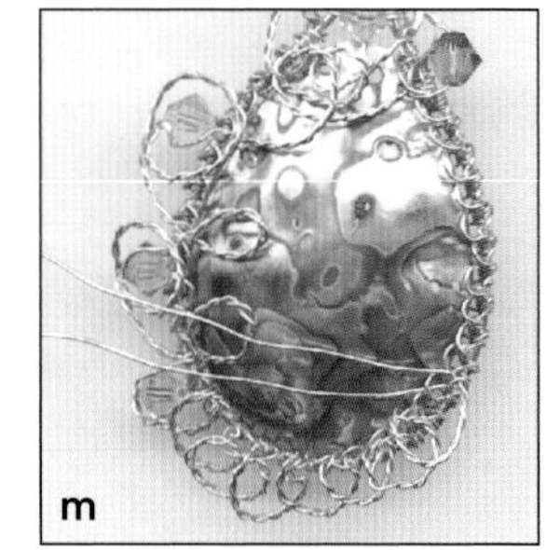

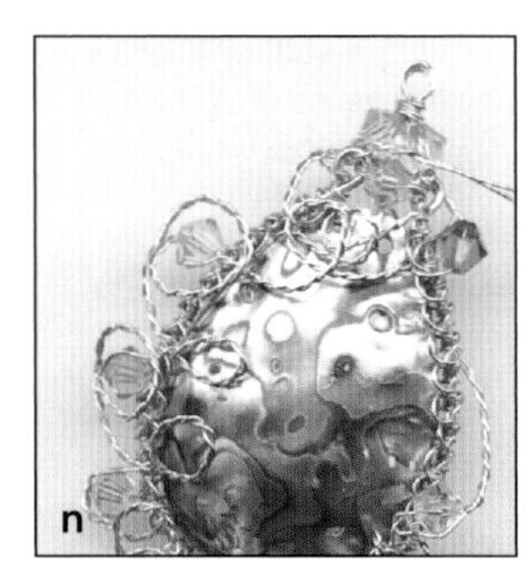

13 String a turquoise crystal on one wire and thread same wire through first arch. Twist another inch or so **(f)**.

14 Make a loop in twisted section. Bring one wire through third or fourth arch on other side of bezel **(g)**.

15 String a light blue crystal. Twist about 1 in. and make a loop **(h)**.

16 Bring one wire through arch about halfway down on same side of bezel. Twist about ¾ in. (19 mm) **(i)**.

17 Make a loop. String a purple crystal. Twist about an inch and make a loop **(j)**.

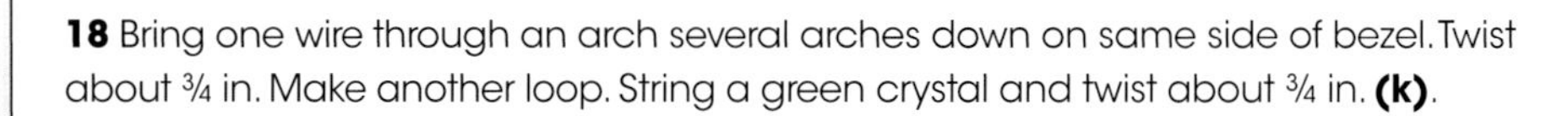

18 Bring one wire through an arch several arches down on same side of bezel. Twist about ¾ in. Make another loop. String a green crystal and twist about ¾ in. **(k)**.

19 Make a loop. Bring one wire through next arch **(l)**.

20 Repeat Step 14 six times **(m)**.

21 Twist about 2 in. Bring wire up in a graceful curve behind bezel and back around front just under two top pink beads. Carry wire behind bezel and finish off in top frame loop **(n–p)**.

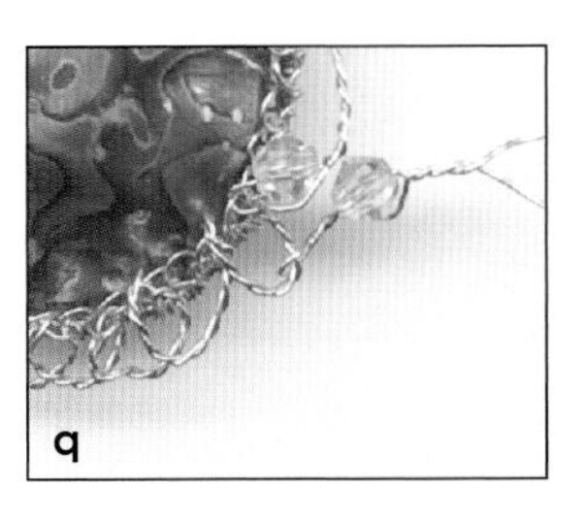
q

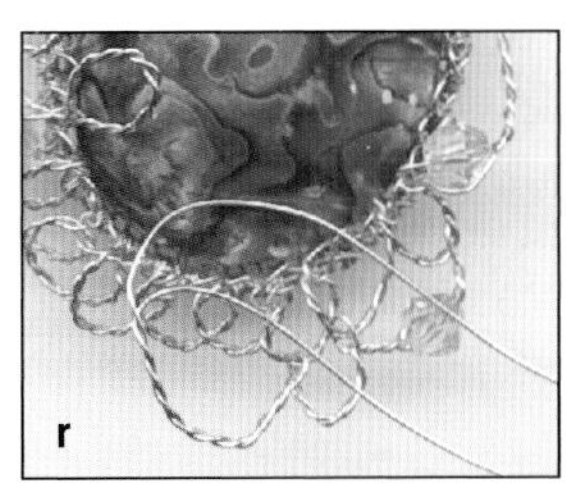
r

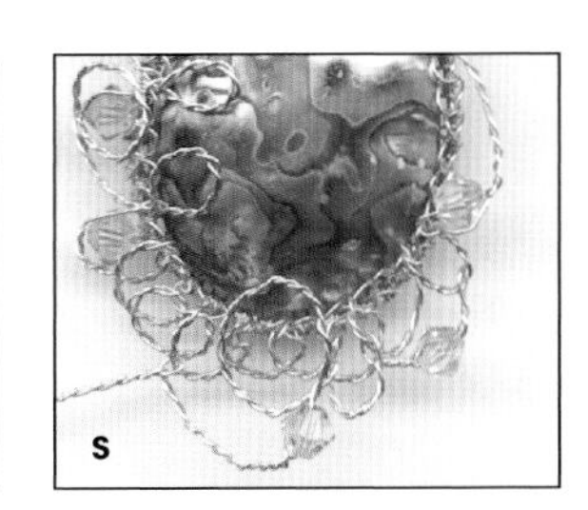
s

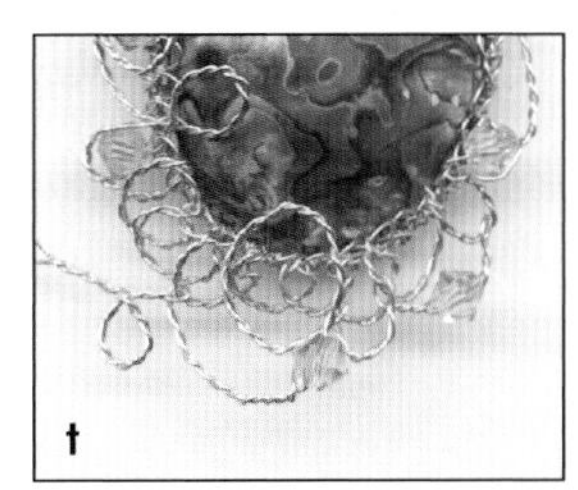
t

22 Join a new piece of 28-gauge wire to last lower twisted loop made. Twist ¼ in. (6.5 mm). String a light blue bead. Twist another ¼ in. **(q)**.

23 Bring one wire through next twisted loop. Twist about ½ in. (13 mm). Bring one wire through next twisted loop. Twist about an inch. Make a loop **(r)**.

24 String a green bead. Twist about ¾ in. Skip three twisted loops. Bring one wire through next twisted loop **(s)**.

25 Twist about 2½ in. (64 mm). Make three loops, rolling final loop up from bottom and doubling it, with clipped ends in back **(t, u)**.

26 Using headpins, wire wrap a purple crystal, a pink crystal and a turquoise crystal to dangle as shown **(v)**.

27 Attach pendant to middle link of a section of chain with a jump ring. Wire wrap crystals to chain sections and to clasp **(w)**.

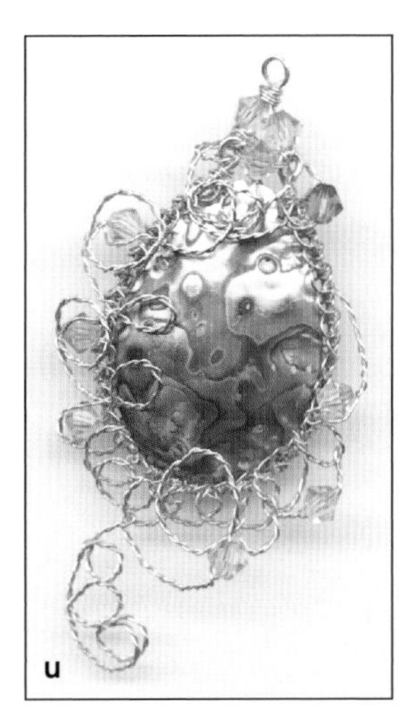
u

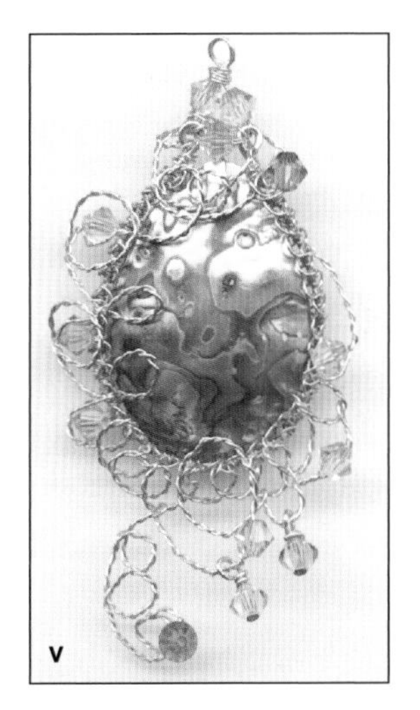
v

w

Technical Basics

Here are the building blocks for every project in this book. Before you start a project, look over the Technical Basics Reference next to the supply list. This guide gives page references to this section for each technique used in the project. Anything that's unique to a project (adding specific beads, or curling loops in a particular direction) is mentioned in the project directions. Practice with some inexpensive copper wire. If you're more confident, choose a project and then refer back to the techniques that apply.

MAKING FRAMES

Basic Frame

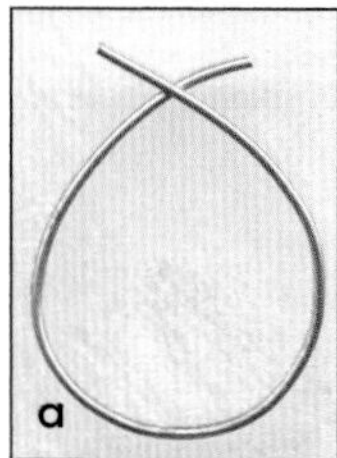

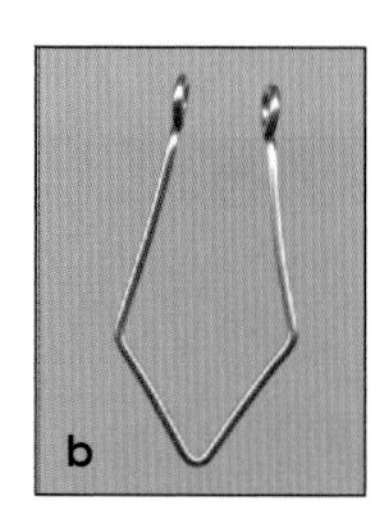

Cut 20-gauge half-hard wire to length and shape as specified in pattern. You may choose to use a mandrel to shape curved sections, or you may simply nudge wire with fingers of one hand against forefinger of other hand bit by bit along its length, shaping it very gradually **(a)**. For corners and other sharp angles, hold wire with chainnose pliers and bend against the pliers **(b)**. Curl loops as instructed in project directions **(c)**.

Inset Bezel Frame

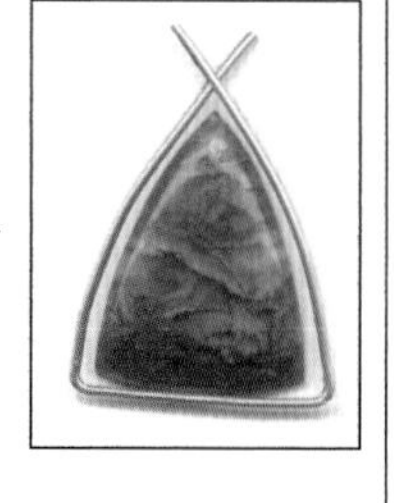

For an inset or beaded bezel, set cabochon inside frame and make sure that, when closed at top, cabochon sits easily inside it with a little room to spare. Trim ends so they are even. Make loops as instructed in project directions.

Closed Hoop

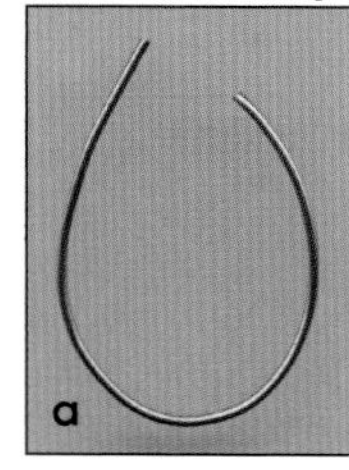

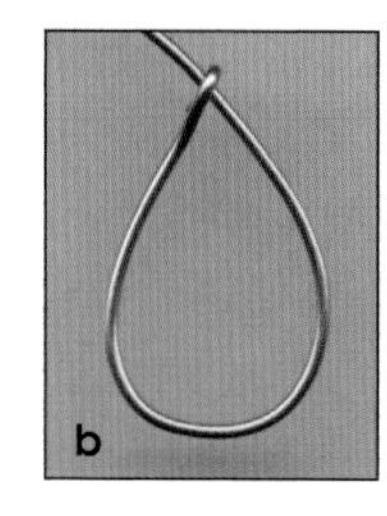

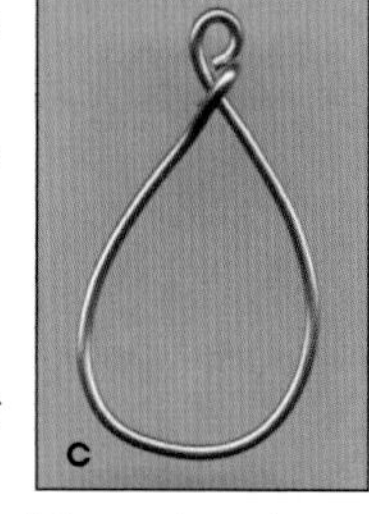

Begin as for Basic Frame, but make one side of frame about ¼ in. (6.5 mm) longer **(a)**. Turn a loop sideways on short end, bring long end through loop **(b)**, and curl a second loop above first loop **(c)**.

Wraparound Bezel Frame

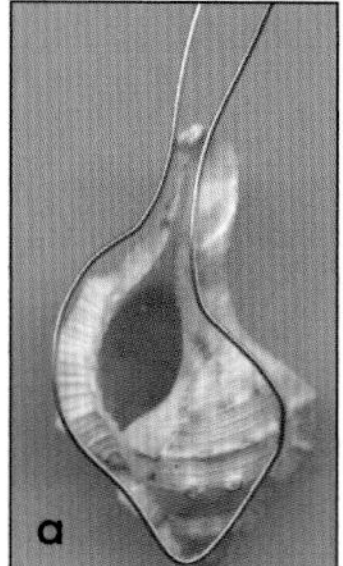

Make a wrap-around bezel frame in the shape of the object being bezeled, but smaller than the object itself, so that it cannot slip out of the frame when finished **(a)**. Make loops as instructed in project directions. **(b)**

Inset Ring Bezel Frame

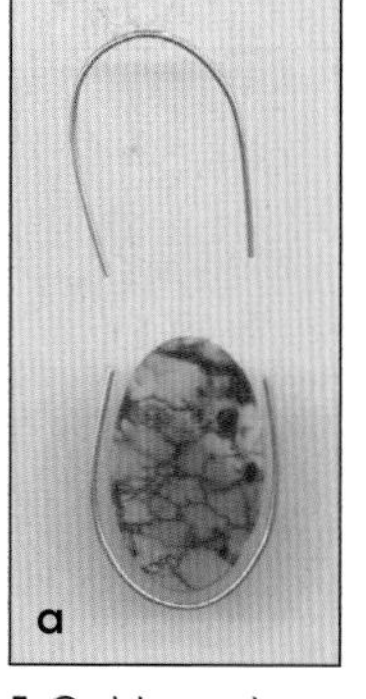

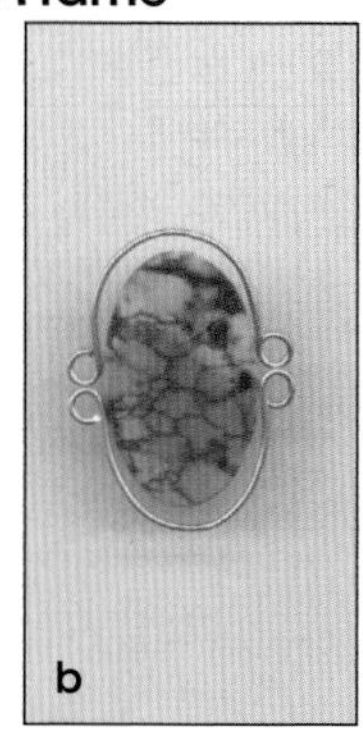

1 Cut two pieces of 20-gauge wire to length specified in project instructions. Form into "U" shapes (or shapes specified by shape of cabochon), making large enough for a row of thin wires to fit between frame and cabochon **(a)**.

2 Turn a loop toward outside at each end of each "U." Place pieces of frame "loops to loops" to gauge fit. Clip short bits from ends of loops and turn loops down again as needed to get correct fit **(b)**.

3 When instructed, use short pieces of 28-gauge wire to join two sides of frames together by coiling 4–5 times around both 20-gauge wires at points where loops meet. Clip tails.

ANCHORING WIRES

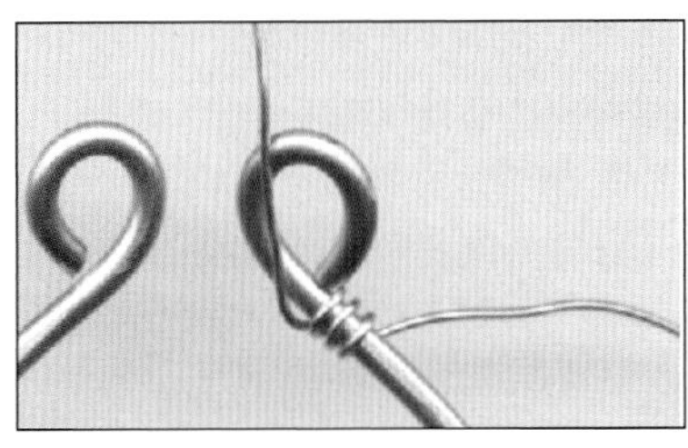

To anchor a new wire in place, leave a 1-in. (25.5 mm) tail and coil wire three times tightly around frame or wire as instructed.

FINISHING OFF

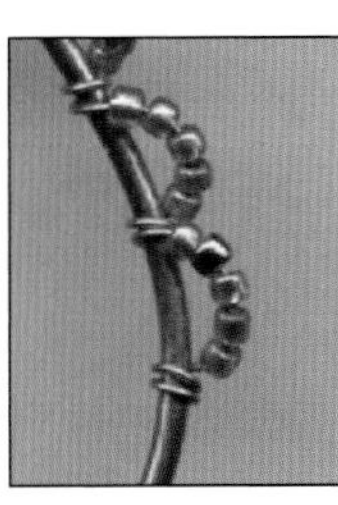

To finish off a wire, coil it tightly twice around the frame or wire as instructed. Clip tails unless otherwise instructed. Using chainnose pliers, press ends flat so no sharp ends protrude.

ADDING NEW WIRE

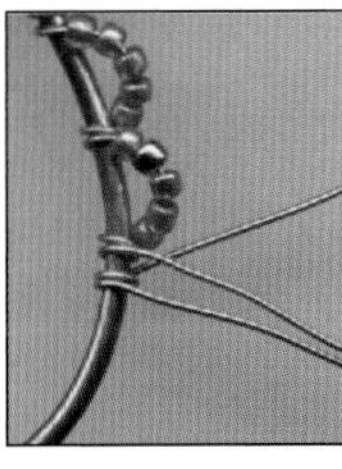

To add in new wire if the old one breaks or runs out, finish off previous wire and anchor new wire by coiling on top of, or right next to, previous coils.

MAKING BASE ROWS

Beaded Outer Base Rows

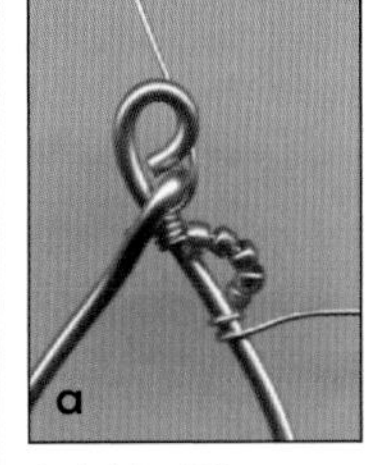

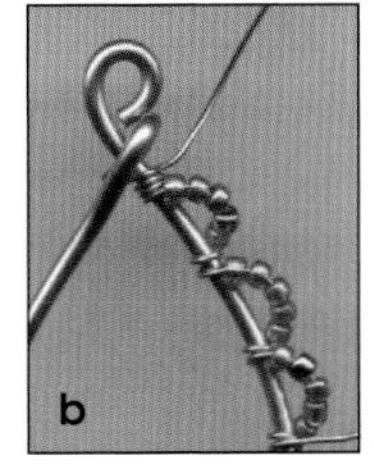

Add to 28-gauge wire the number of beads called for by project instructions. Wrap wire up over and across frame and then down under and around it **(a)**. Holding bead(s) in place above frame, coil tightly around frame one more time. Repeat as instructed **(b)**.

Unbeaded Outer Base Rows

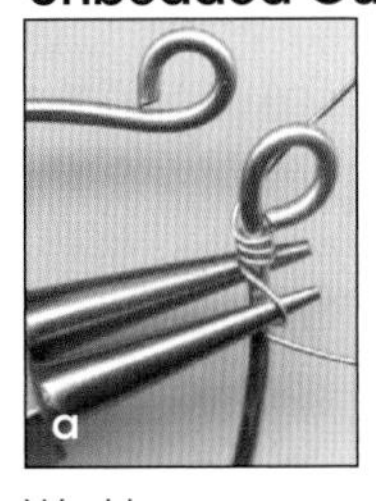

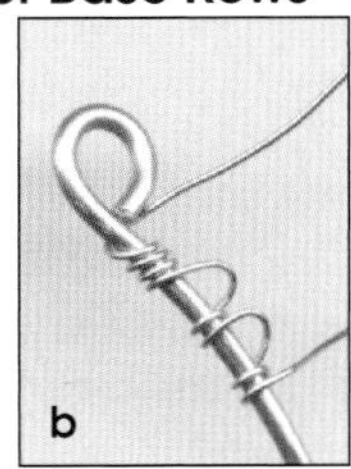

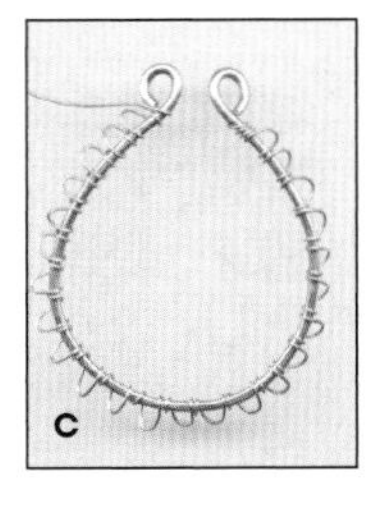

Working near tips of pliers for small arches or farther up for larger ones, hold frame just below anchor point between jaws of pliers. Wrap wire up over top jaw of pliers and across frame and then down under and around it **(a)**. Coil wire tightly once more around frame only. Repeat as instructed **(b)**. Nudge arches around frame until evenly spaced, with equal number on each side of frame **(c)**.

Unbeaded Inner Base Rows

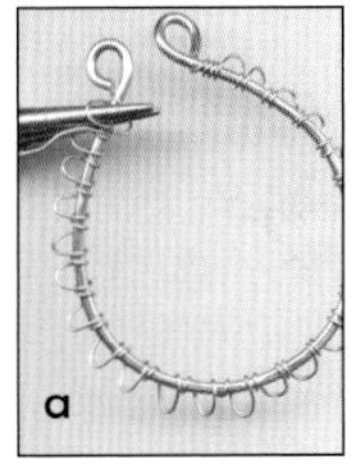

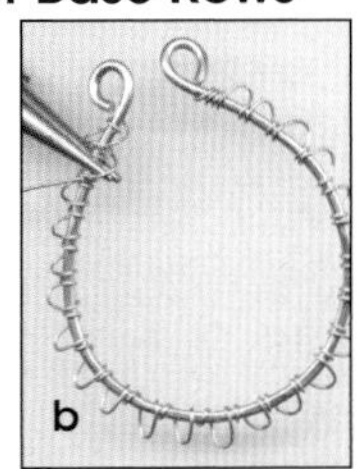

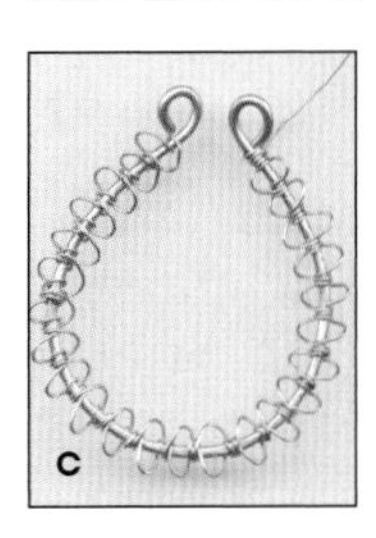

Insert bottom jaw of round-nose pliers into designated arch of outer base row and, gripping frame between both jaws, wrap wire up over top jaw of pliers and then across the frame and down around and under it on top of coils made previously (if any) **(a)**. Coil wire once more tightly around frame on top of other coils **(b)**. Repeat as called for by project instructions. Clip tails unless otherwise instructed **(c)**.

REARRANGING ROWS UPRIGHT (for Bezels)

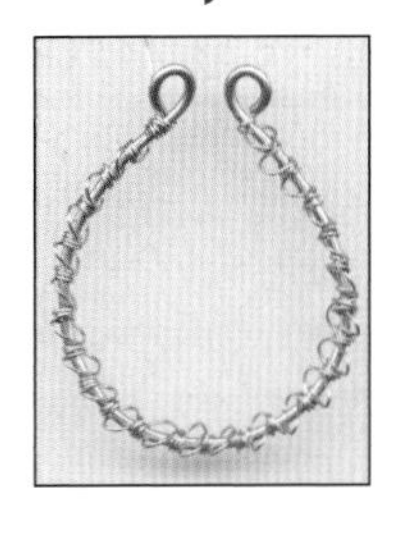

Nudge both rows 45° around frame so that one row is standing up from front side of frame and the other toward back side. Rows will now be referred to as front and back rows.

Technical Basics

MAKING BASE BEZEL ROWS

Unbeaded Outer Base Bezel Rows

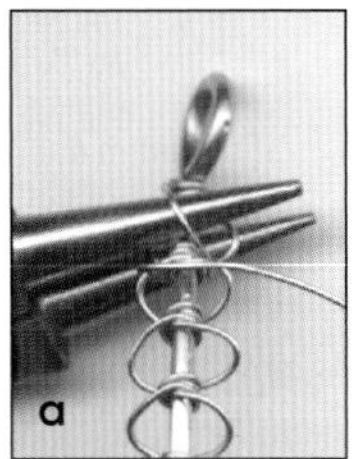

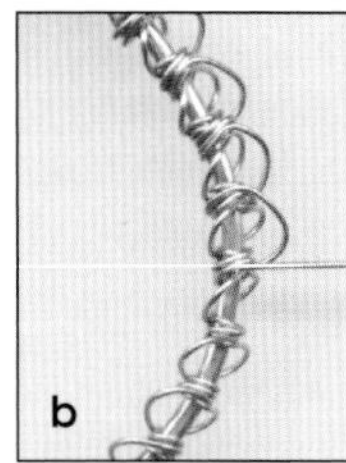

Rearrange base outer and inner rows to their upright position, and anchor wire as instructed. Begin working back around frame in opposite direction. Grip frame with roundnose pliers across first pair of arches. Wrap wire up over top jaw of pliers and then across frame and down around and under it just prior to next pair of arches **(a)**. Coil wire tightly again around frame between arches, working on top of the coils already made. Grip frame across next pair of arches and repeat as instructed **(b)**.

Beaded Outer Base Bezel Rows

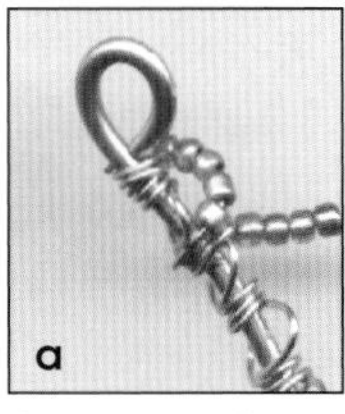

Rearrange base outer and inner rows to their upright position, and anchor wire as instructed. Begin working back around frame in opposite direction. Add beads as specified. Wrap wire up over and across frame and then down under and around it just prior to next top and bottom arches. Holding bead(s) in place above frame wire and working over coils previously made, coil wire tightly around frame again **(a)**. Repeat as instructed **(b)**.

BUILDING ONTO BASE BEZEL ROWS

Anchoring

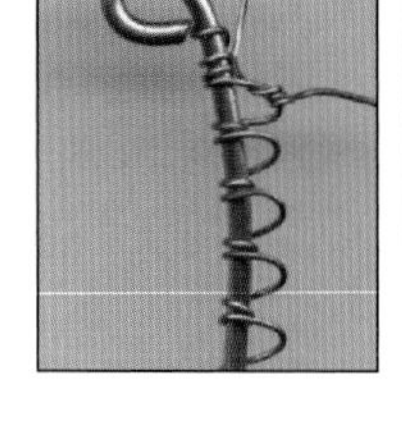

Anchor wire to arch as instructed by coiling it tightly twice around top of arch. If you are working into a beaded arch, coil it between two of the beads.

Unbeaded Arches

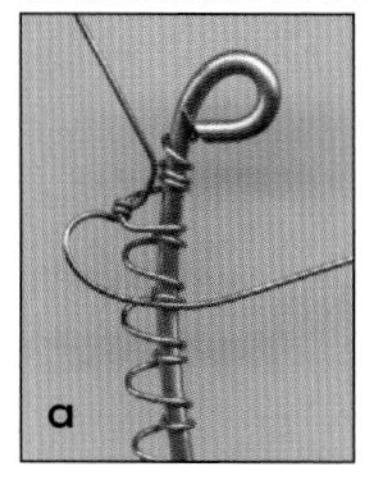

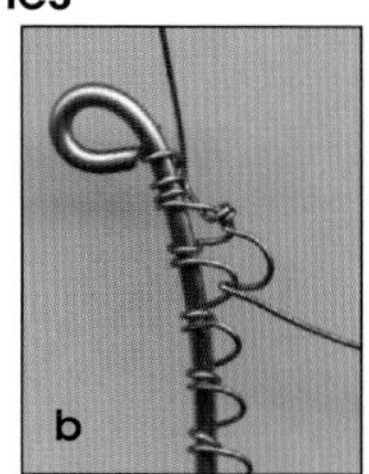

To make an unbeaded arch, use your thumbnail to curve wire slightly, close to anchor point **(a)**. Draw it through next (or designated) arch, being careful not to kink, until it forms a new arch similar in size and shape to those already made. Holding new arch firmly in place, bend wire sharply upward against top of base arch **(b)**. Coil wire tightly around top of base arch twice. If you are making an arch into a beaded arch, coil the wire around arch between beads as instructed.

Beaded Arches

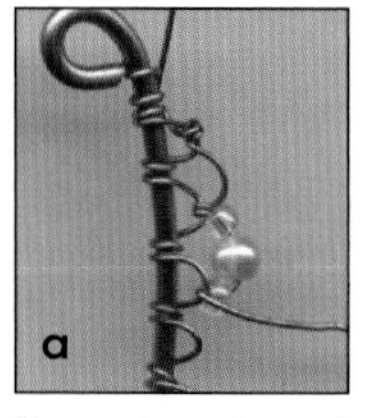

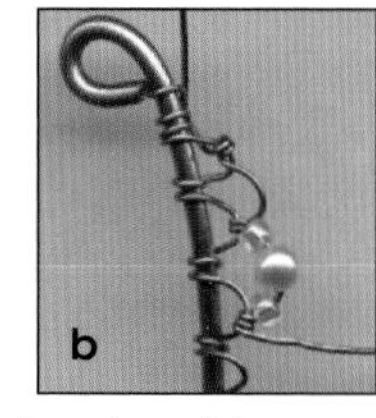

To make a beaded arch, add desired bead(s) to wire. Draw wire through next (or designated) arch, being careful not to kink. Pull wire tight so bead(s) are firmly seated between two base arches **(a)**. Coil wire tightly around top of base arch twice **(b)**.

FINISHING BEZELS

Lacing Up Bezels

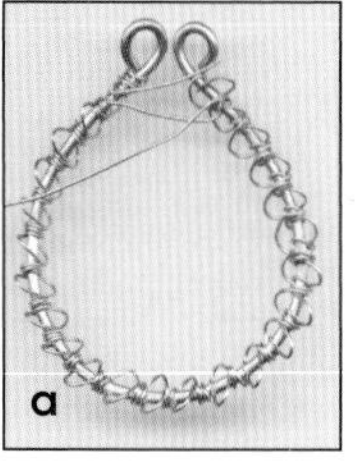

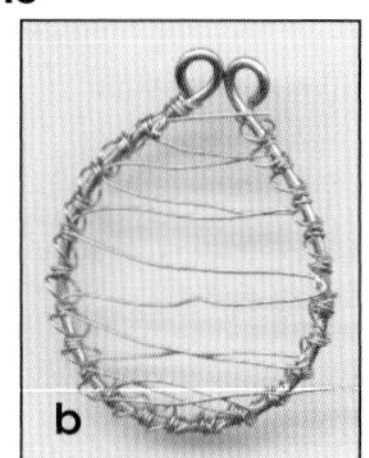

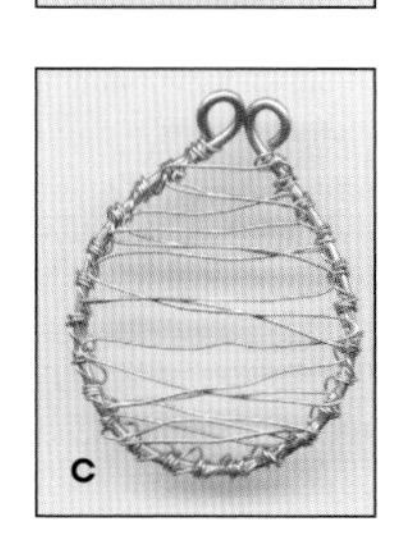

Anchor wire in first back arch of bezel (or as instructed). Skipping corresponding arch on opposite side of bezel, draw wire through next arch. Holding arches upright so they can't lean toward center of bezel, bend wire toward opposite side. Skipping one arch, draw wire through next arch (like lacing a shoe) **(a)**. Continue lacing back and forth across back of bezel, making sure that pressure of wire is not causing back row of arches to start leaning toward center **(b)**. When at bottom, work back toward top, using skipped arches. Finish off **(c)**.

Tightening Bezels around Cabochons

Insert cabochon into bezel, and gently press front rows of arches down across face **(a)**. Using round-nose pliers, insert tips into first two arches and, pulling inward toward center of bezel and down toward face of cabochon, squeeze loops together. Move down one arch and repeat. Continue for each pair of arches all around bezel. Repeat as needed to secure cabochon **(b)**.

TWISTING WIRES

Twisting a Main Stem

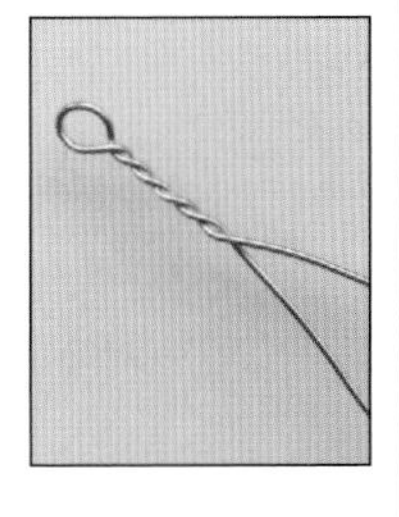

Hold two wires about 1/8 in. (3 mm) or so apart between thumb and forefinger of left hand, 3/8 in. (9.5 mm) or so from point where twisted section is to begin. Holding the frame, loop, or motif between thumb and forefinger of right hand, twist it several times. Begin backing left hand away from twisted portion bit by bit, about 1/8–1/4 in. at a time, still holding two wires just slightly apart between thumb and forefinger of left hand as you continue to twist with right as instructed.

Note: Over-twisting will cause wire to become brittle and breakable. Under-twisting will make lace spindly and weak.

Adding a Bead to a Main Stem

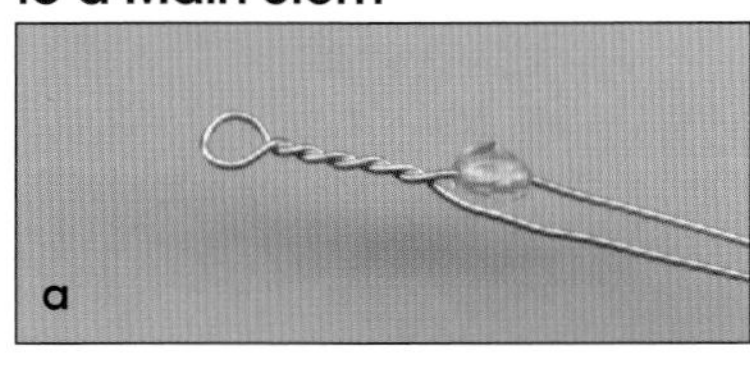

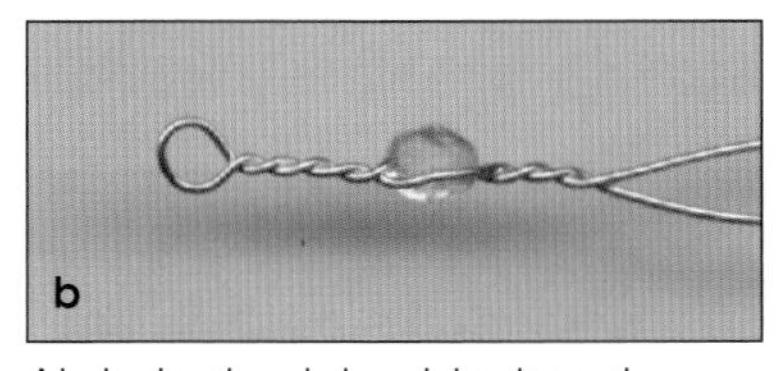

At desired point, add a bead to one wire **(a)**. Hold both wires just after bead or motif between thumb and forefinger of left hand. Holding bead between thumb and forefinger of right hand, twist several times **(b)**.

Twisting Branches

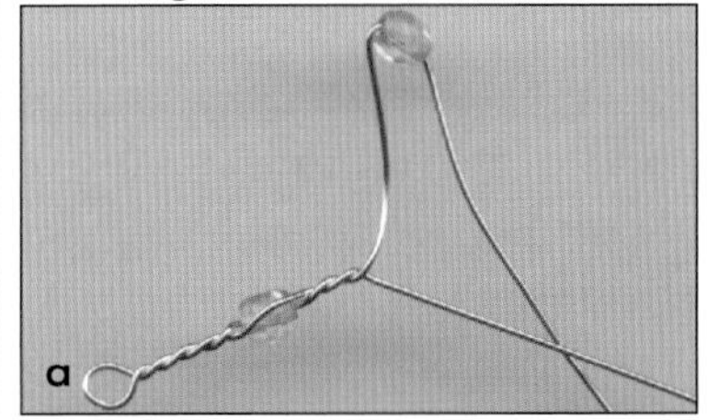

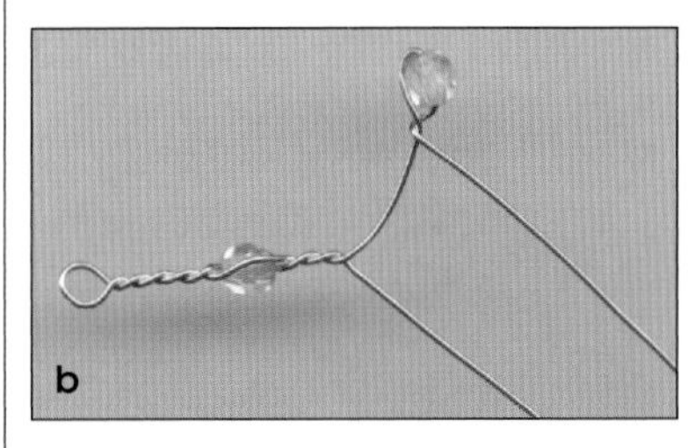

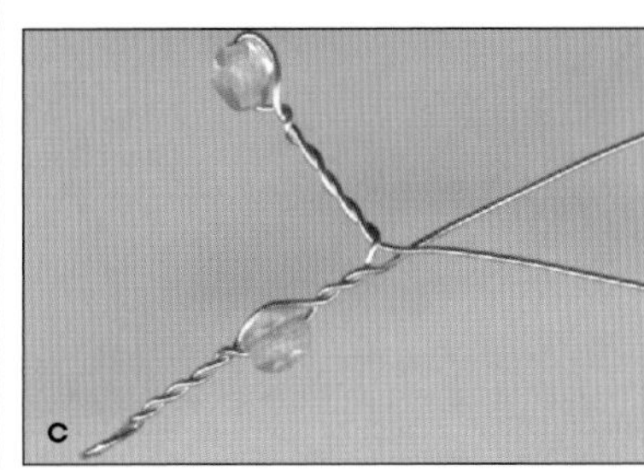

Using only one wire, add bead(s) and position at instructed length from already-twisted section. Fold wire back toward main twisted section **(a)**. Hold both wires between thumb and forefinger of left hand close to bead or motif. Holding bead or motif between thumb and forefinger of right hand, twist several times **(b)**. Continue twisting back to main section **(c)**.

Tweaking

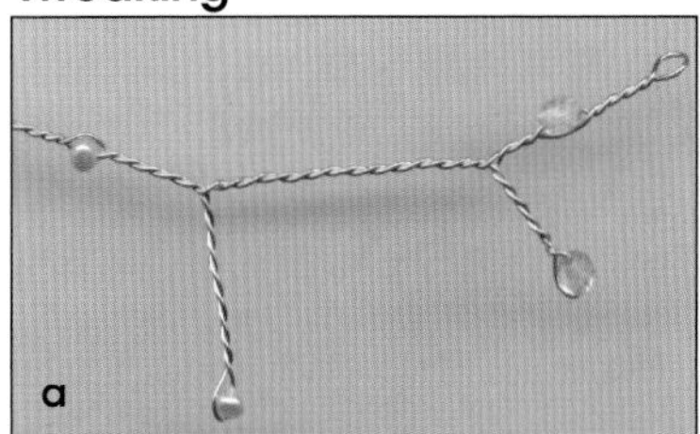

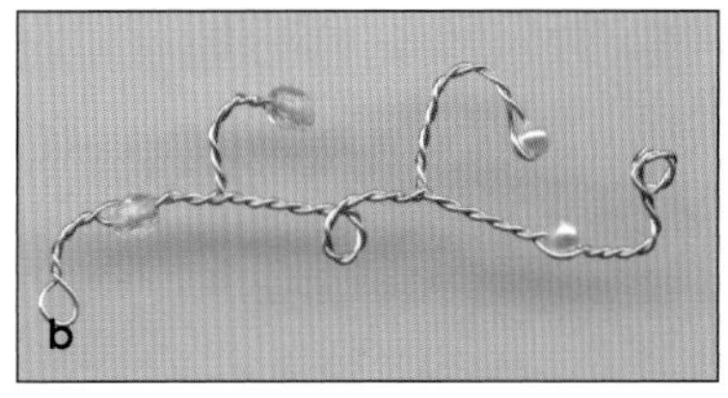

Using roundnose pliers, curve, curl, and/or loop stems and branches so they twine gracefully instead of sticking out stiffly **(a, b)**.

Shaping

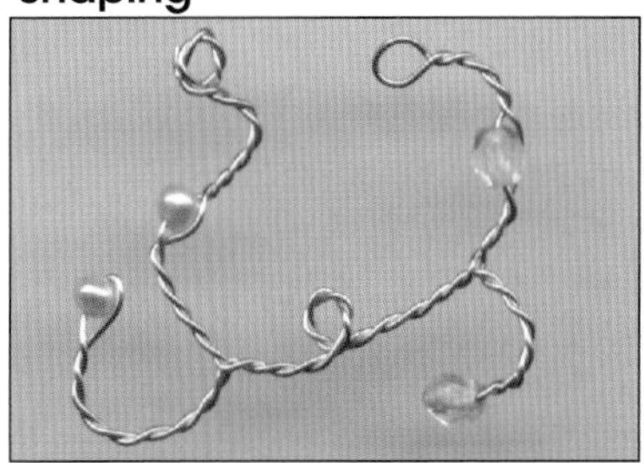

Using your fingers or pliers as needed, nudge lace a little bit at a time to define its overall shape.

Troubleshooting Your Technique

If twisted portion looks as if one wire is wrapped around the other, hold wires a bit farther apart with left hand as you twist with right.

If you are having trouble controlling length of twisted sections, try bearing down with thumbnail of left hand at point where twisted portion should end.

If you are having trouble getting bead or motif well secured at correct distance from starting point, press down on both wires with thumbnail of left hand just below bead. Give 2-3 half-twists before continuing to twist down the "branch."

Technical Basics

TWISTING WIRES cont'd.

Adding New Wire

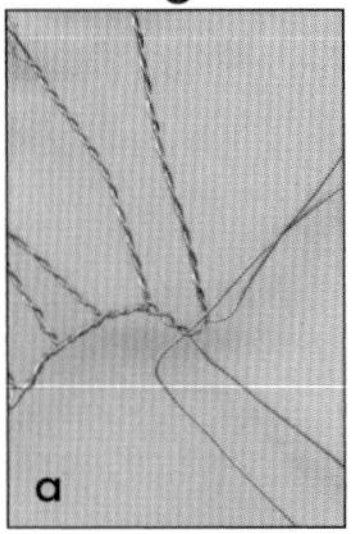

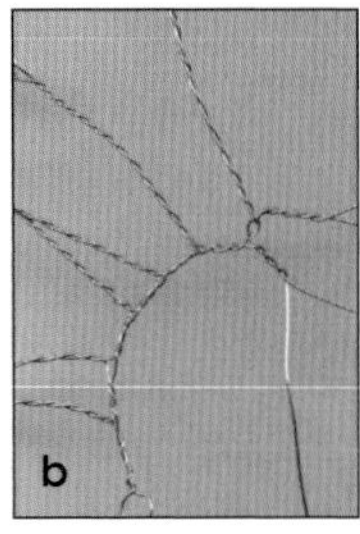

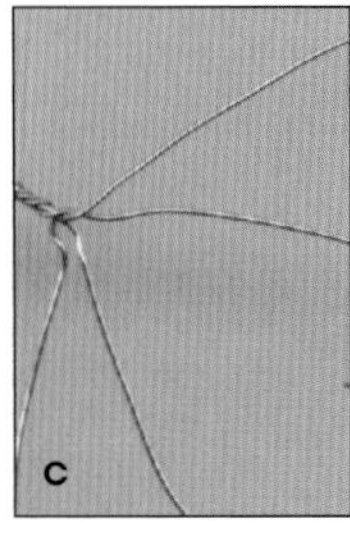

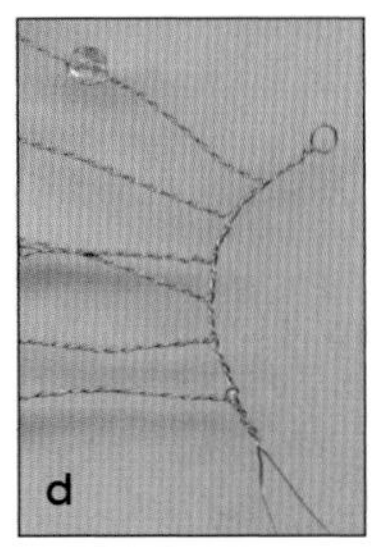

If you run out of wire (or if wire breaks), fold new wire at its halfway point and lay it across nearest stem/branch intersection **(a)**. Twist each new side with one tail of old wire for about ½ in. (13 mm) **(b)**. Twist two twisted portions together **(c)**. Clip old tails and press down with chainnose pliers so no sharp ends stick out **(d)**.

SCULPTING WIRE

Making Triple-Layer Arches

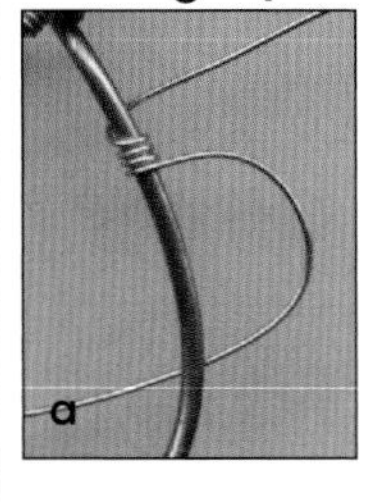

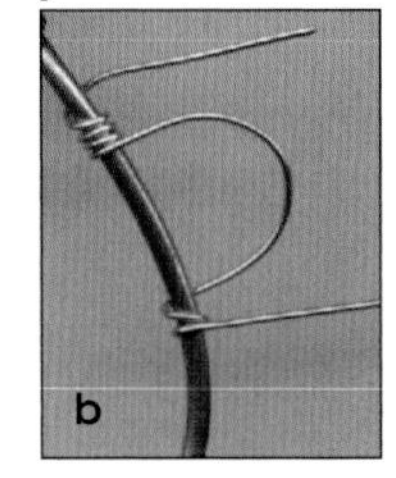

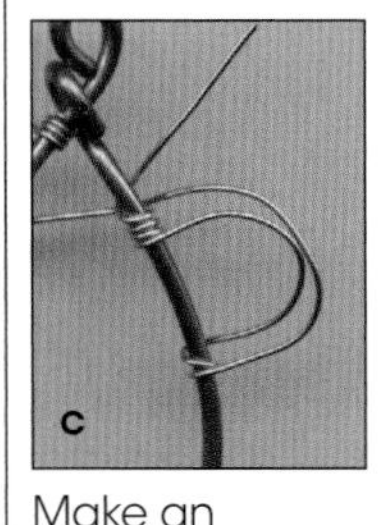

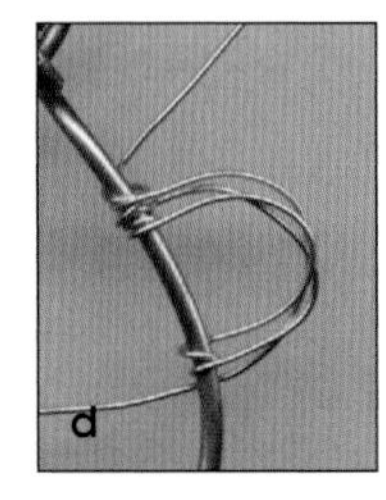

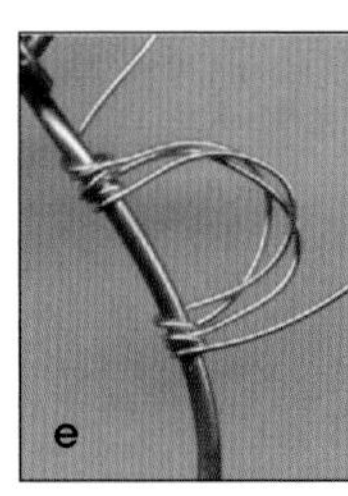

Make an unbeaded arch of size instructed **(a, b)**. Doubling back, make another arch the same size over the first **(c)**. Working back the opposite way, make a third arch over the second **(d)**. Coil wire around frame twice tightly **(e)**.

Making a Triple-Layer Outer Base Row

Make a series of triple-layer arches as above.

Crinkling Triple-Layer Arches

Using roundnose pliers, grip all three wires of arch near base and give them a 45° curl downwards. Move pliers about one-fourth of the way along arch and give wires a 45° curl upwards. Repeat process around arch, alternating downwards and upwards curls.

Making a Five-Petal Flower

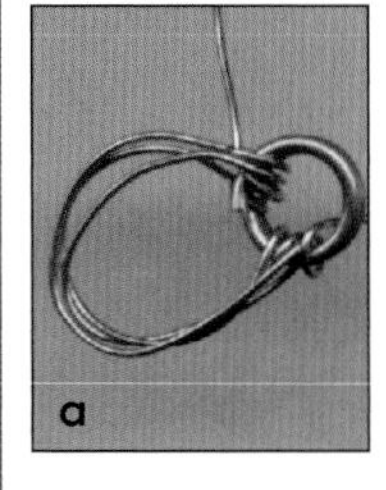

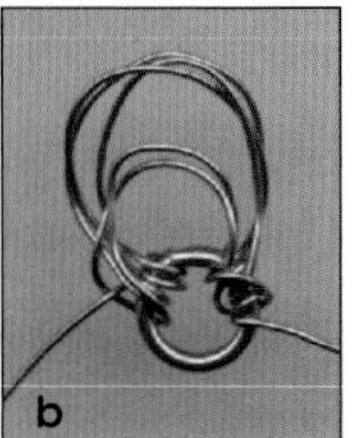

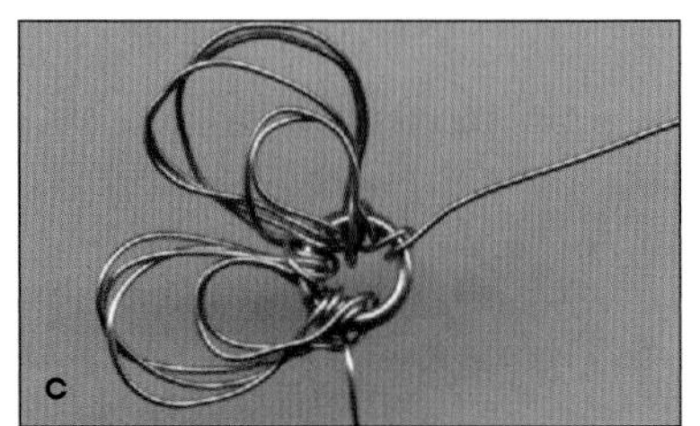

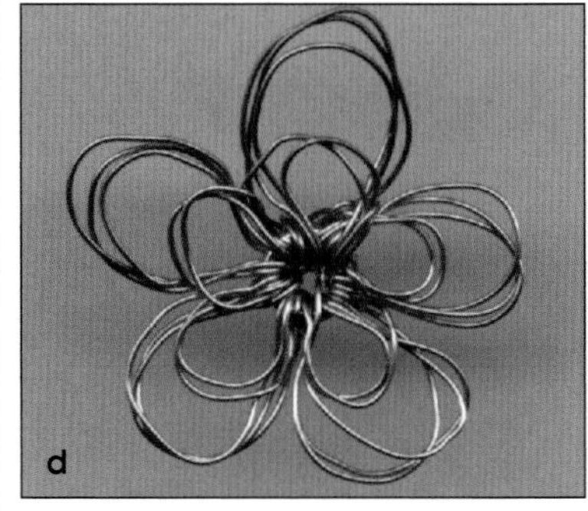

Note: Sizes of wire, rings, loops and arches will be specified by project instructions. Also, you will not be able to insert your pliers far enough into the jump ring or loop to make large enough arches, so make unbeaded arches as you would for a second outer row of filigree or bezel arches (see *Building On To Base Rows: Unbeaded Arches*). Anchor wire on a double jump ring or loop. Make a large triple-layer arch **(a)** and, doubling back, a smaller double-layer arch across large one, anchoring with second coil only after third and fifth arches or as necessary to secure **(b, c)**. Repeat process five times, sliding arches around ring as needed for symmetry **(d)**. If ring gets too crowded with wires, insert tip of roundnose pliers into it and push to open up more space.

Making Sculpted Points

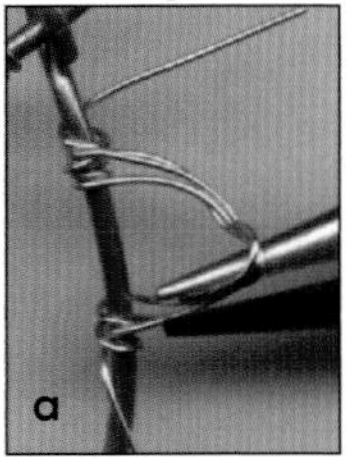

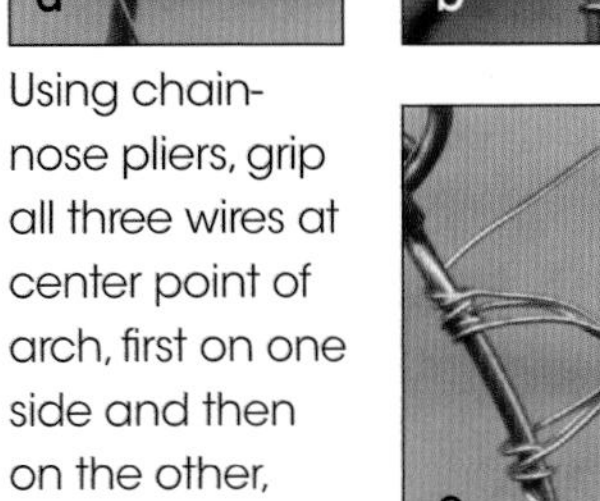

Using chain-nose pliers, grip all three wires at center point of arch, first on one side and then on the other, bending wires outwards to create a tip **(a, b)**. Squeeze tip gently between jaws of pliers if needed to get sharper point **(c)**.

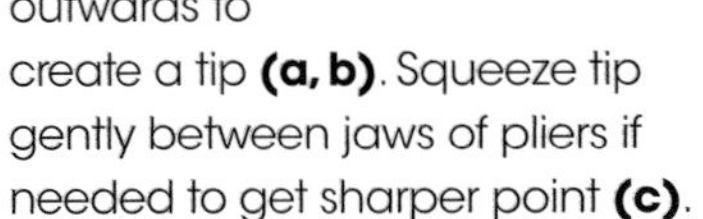

MAKING CURLICUE LACE

Note: Curlicue lace is random, so these instructions are just suggestions.

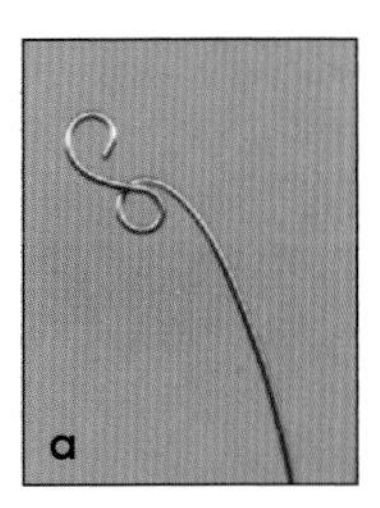

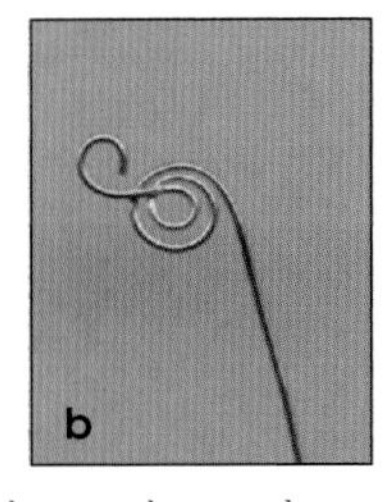

Using 20-gauge wire and round-nose pliers, begin with a small loop at one end of the wire. Move pliers to a point just after the first loop and form a loop in the opposite direction **(a)**. Switch to chainnose pliers and gradually coax the wire into a spiral, bringing it around to the point farthest from the original loop **(b)**. Move the pliers to a point just after the spiral. Turn a loop in

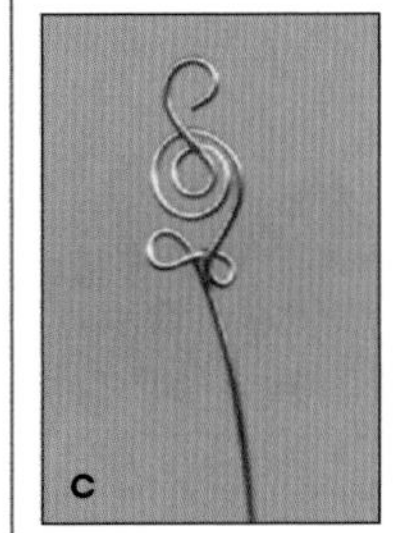

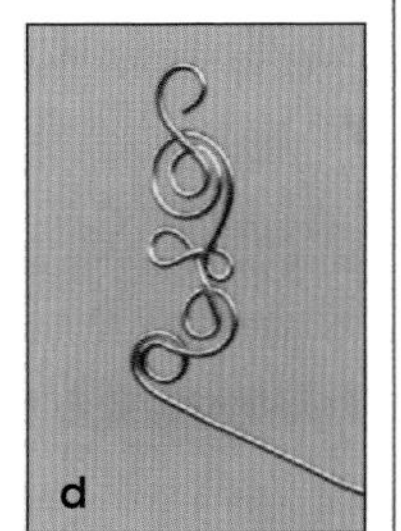

the opposite direction **(c)**. Continue making loops, spirals, twists, and turns, changing directions as necessary to form the lace into the desired shape **(d)**.

ATTACHING LACES TO FRAMES

Tacking Laces in Place

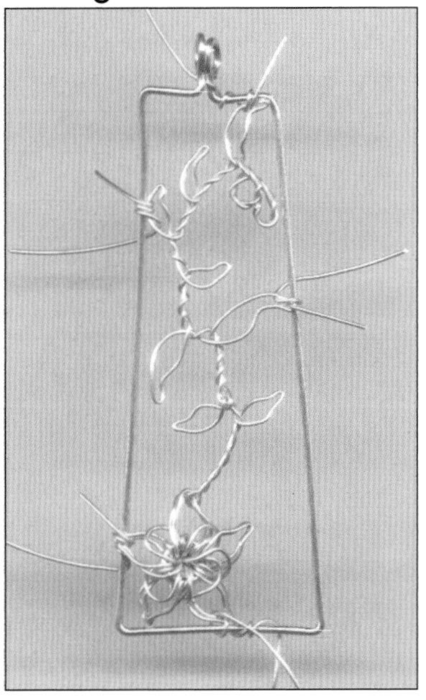

If desired, you may use scraps of wire to wrap around frame and lace at each projected point of contact. To do this, insert wire through lace, bringing other end of wire around frame and back through filigree again once or twice as needed to secure. Do not pull tacking wire too tight, or it will be difficult to remove later.

Coiling Lace Directly onto Frame

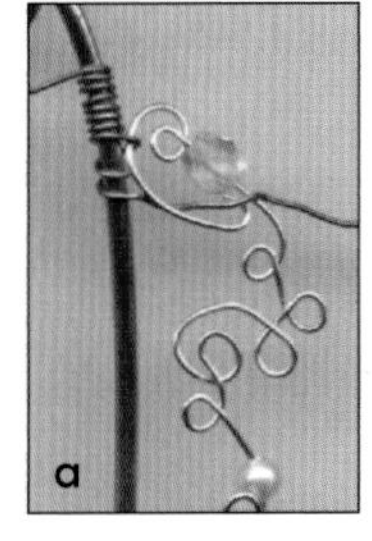

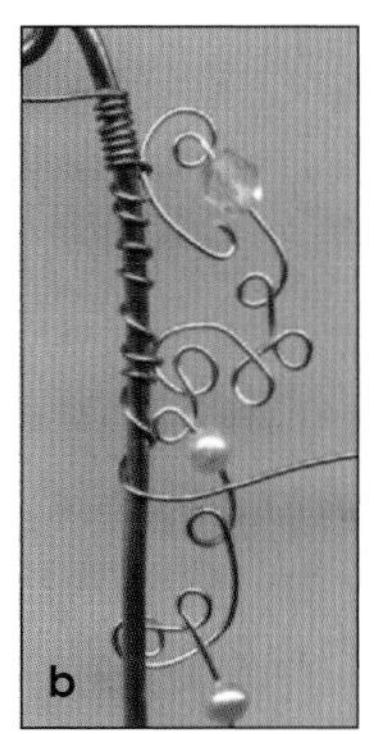

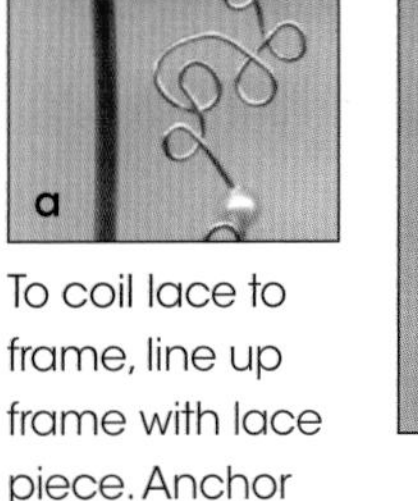

To coil lace to frame, line up frame with lace piece. Anchor wire onto frame at point as instructed. Coil wire around frame as directed by project instructions until first point of contact is reached. Coil wire into designated arch or other designated place on lace piece and then around frame twice **(a)**. Continue coiling around frame until you reach next point of contact and repeat **(b)**.

Attaching Lace Directly to Frame with Beaded Arches

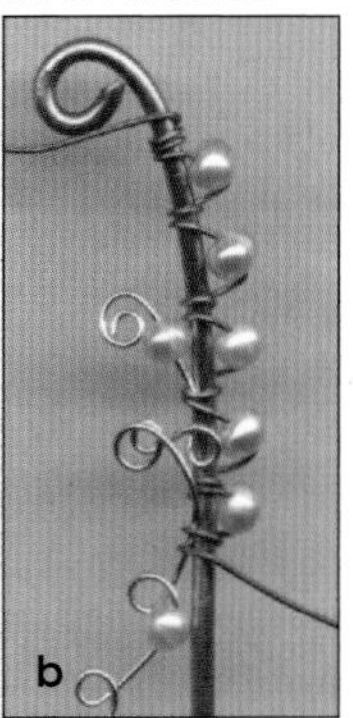

To attach lace to frame with beaded arches, make beaded arches as directed by project instructions until first point of contact is reached. Add bead(s). Coil wire into designated place on lace piece and then around frame twice **(a)**. Continue making beaded arches until you reach next point of contact and repeat **(b)**.

Technical Basics

ATTACHING LACES TO FRAMES cont'd.

Attaching Lace to Base Row of Arches

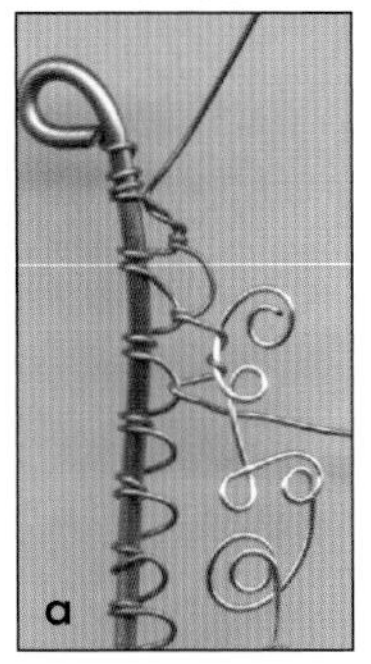

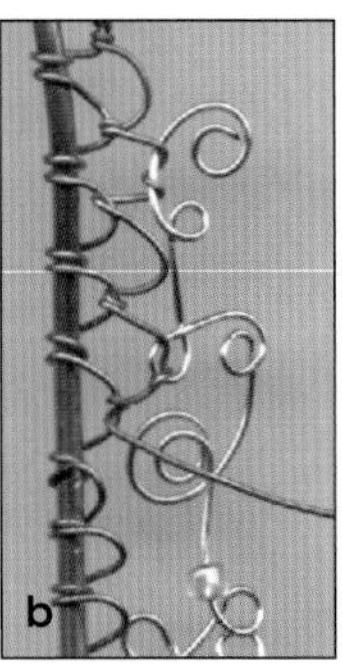

Anchor wire in arch as instructed. Make unbeaded arches into each arch of base row until you reach first contact point. Take wire through lace. Coil tightly once all the way around that point on lace. Bring wire back around and through next base arch and anchor there **(a)**. Continue making unbeaded arches up to next point of contact and repeat **(b)**.

JUMP RINGS

Single Jump Rings

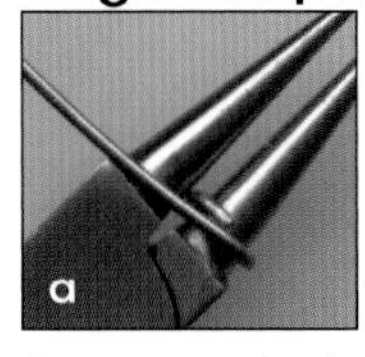

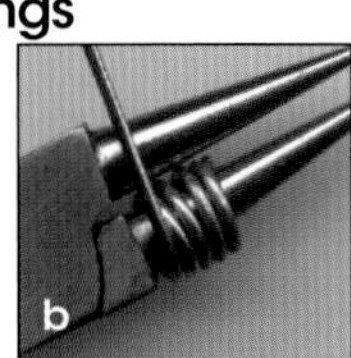

Grasp very end of wire between jaws of roundnose pliers at the fat end and roll them so that wire coils tightly around one jaw. **Note:** Make sure that beginning end of wire is on the side toward tip of pliers **(a)**. Continue rolling, opening pliers, grasping again, and rolling some more until you have the instructed number of rings **(b)**. Using wire cutters, clip off one ring at a time **(c, d)**. Once rings have been cut from coil, there will be a bur from the pinch cut, particularly on the side of ring that was toward recessed side of cutter when being

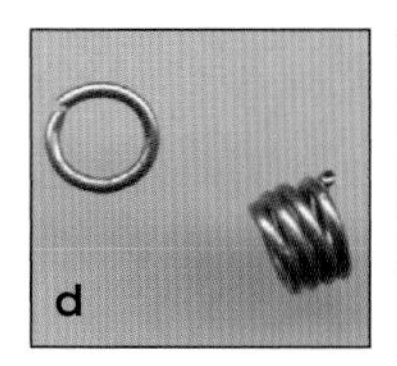

clipped. Trim that side on each ring with the cutters turned the other way (with back side of cutter, where blade is flush). You also may use a metal file to smooth the ends.

Double Jump Rings

Make as for jump rings, coiling only twice around the roundnose pliers. Clip even with beginning end of wire.

POST EARRING BACKS

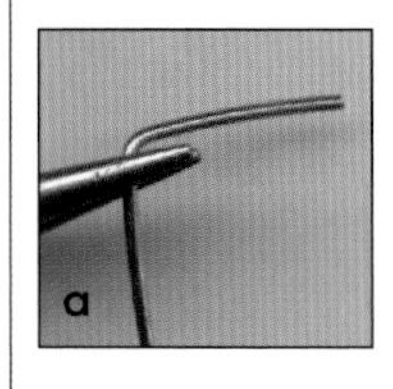

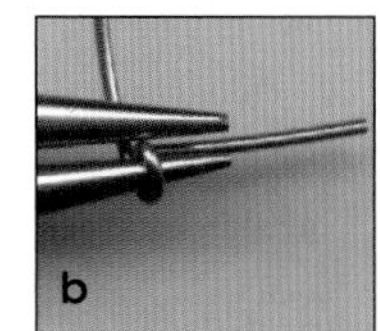

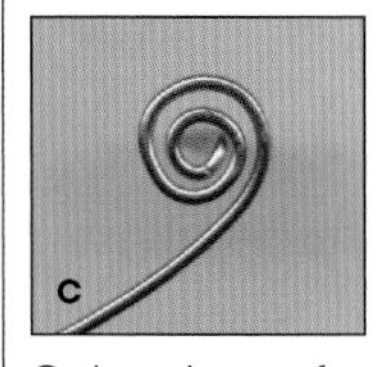

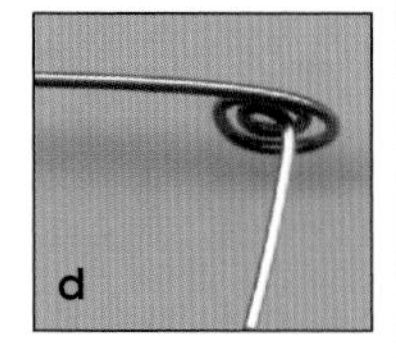

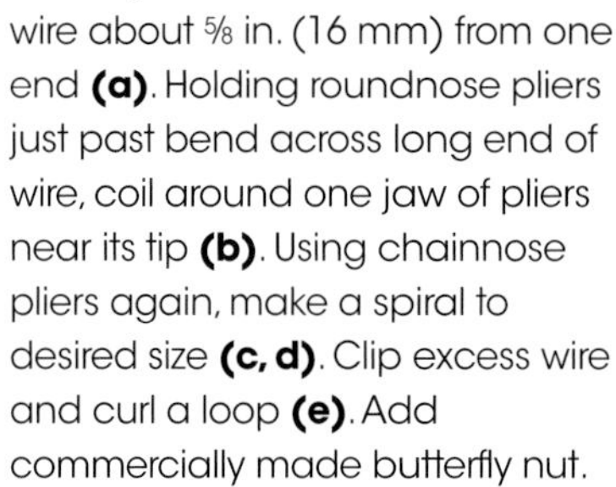

Cut a piece of 20-gauge wire to instructed length. Using chainnose pliers, make a 45° angle in wire about ⅝ in. (16 mm) from one end **(a)**. Holding roundnose pliers just past bend across long end of wire, coil around one jaw of pliers near its tip **(b)**. Using chainnose pliers again, make a spiral to desired size **(c, d)**. Clip excess wire and curl a loop **(e)**. Add commercially made butterfly nut.

CLASPS

Basic Hook-and-Eye Clasp

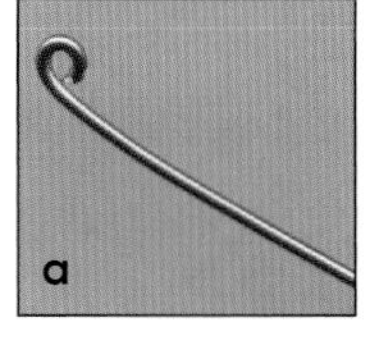

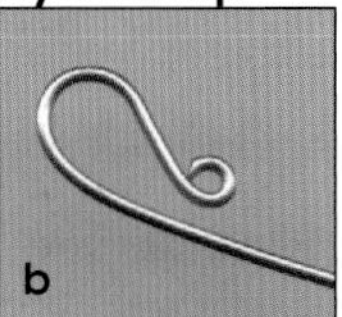

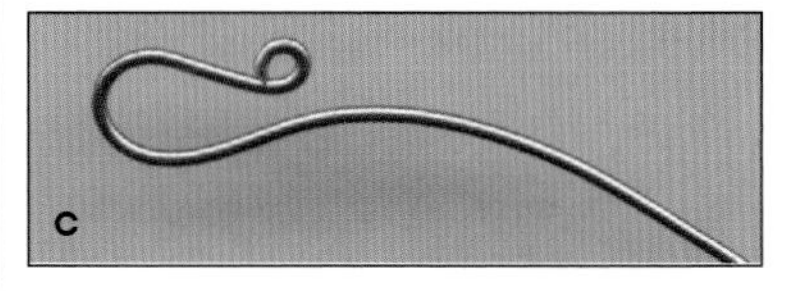

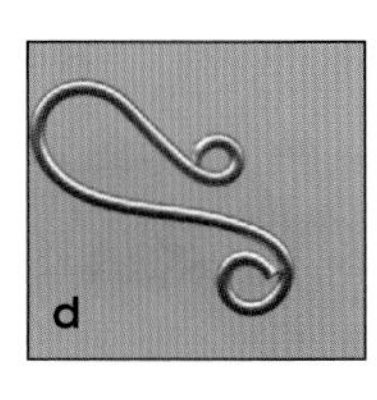

Hook: Using roundnose pliers and a piece of 18-gauge wire of length specified in project instructions, turn a small loop at one end of wire **(a)**. Grasp wire slightly above loop and make a loose curl in opposite direction **(b)**. Using thumb, curve wire slightly about even with beginning loop **(c)**. Clip wire about 1 in. (25.5 mm)below beginning loop. Curl another loop in same direction as long curve **(d)**. Hammer to strengthen.

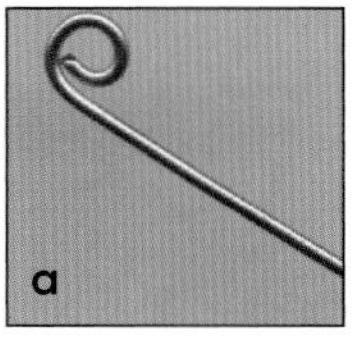

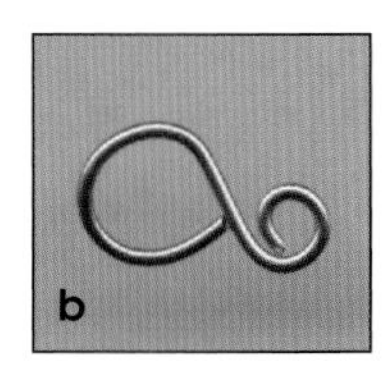

Eye: With remaining wire, curl a loop at one end as shown **(a)**. Grasp wire slightly above loop and make a loose curl in opposite direction. Clip wire **(b)**. Hammer to strengthen.

Spiral Point Clasp

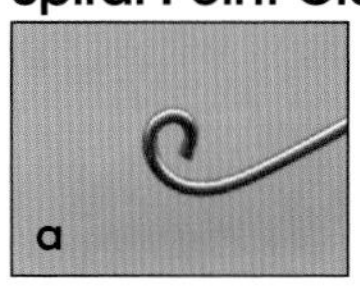

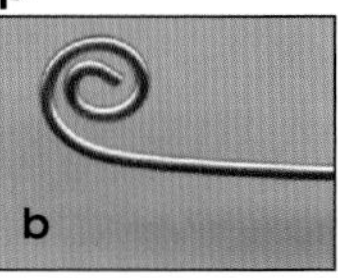

Eye: Using 18-gauge wire and roundnose pliers, curl a loop at one end **(a)**. Using chainnose pliers, grasp across flat sides of loop and gradually coil a spiral **(b)**. Grasp

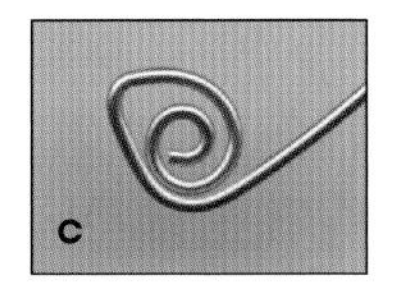
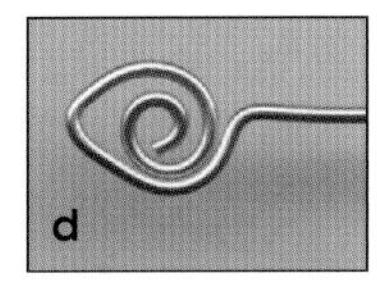
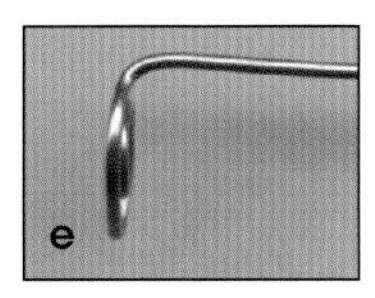
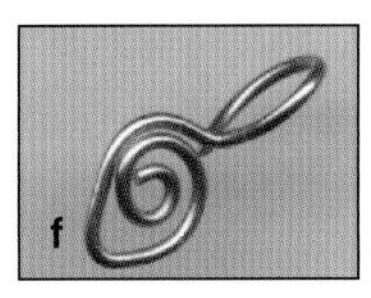

long wire just below spiral and bend it sharply upwards, making a "V" shape **(c)**. Bring wire on around to opposite end of spiral and bend outwards away from spiral **(d)**. Hammer spiral section. Bend wire again just above spiral as shown in **(e)**. Using roundnose pliers, make a loose curl back down to base of spiral. Clip wire **(f)**. Place eye section of clasp on anvil with spiral hanging over edge, and hammer loop to strengthen.

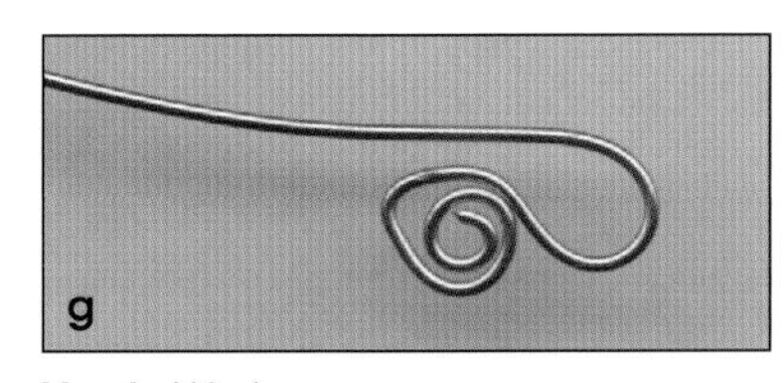

Hook: Work as for eye through **(c)**. Using roundnose pliers or fingers, grasp long wire above spiral and make hook shape as shown in **(g)**. Clip wire about even with bottom of "V." Using roundnose pliers, curl a small loop up toward top of hook **(h)**. Hammer to strengthen.

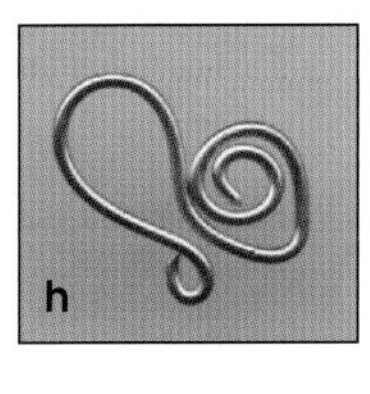

Hook-and-Bar Clasp

Hook: Cut one 2¼-in. (57 mm) piece of 20-gauge wire. Grasp with roundnose pliers at center point and bend wire around one jaw of pliers into a "U" shape, keeping ends the same length **(a)**. Using

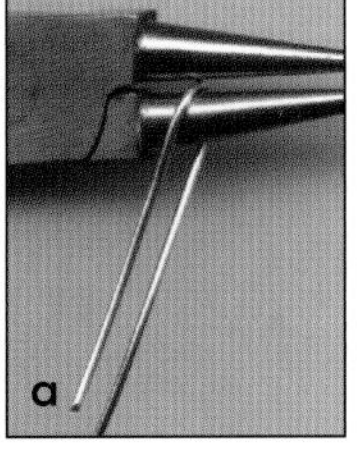

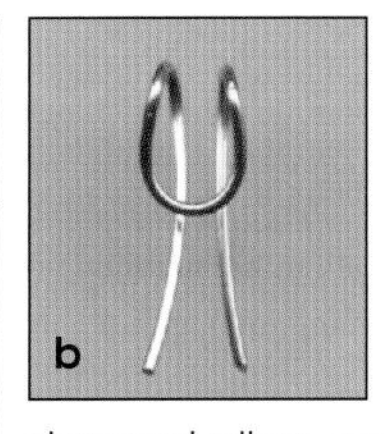
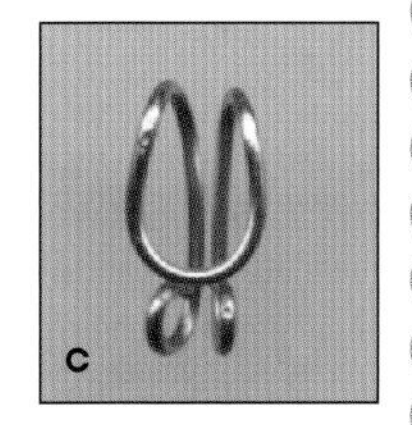

stepped pliers, curl curved end over **(b)**. Using roundnose pliers, turn loops under at both ends **(c)**. Using stepped pliers, curl curved end of hook outwards slightly.

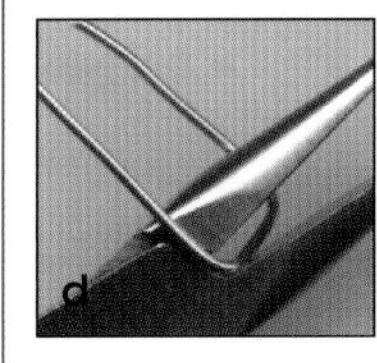
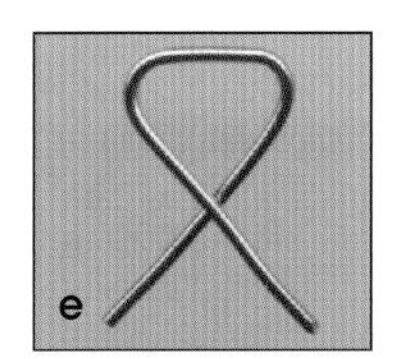
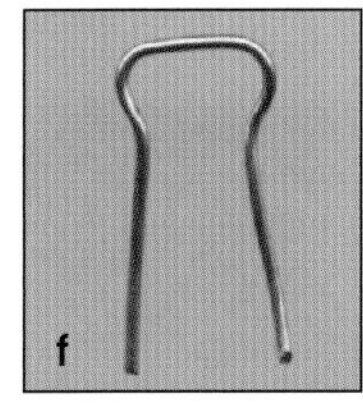
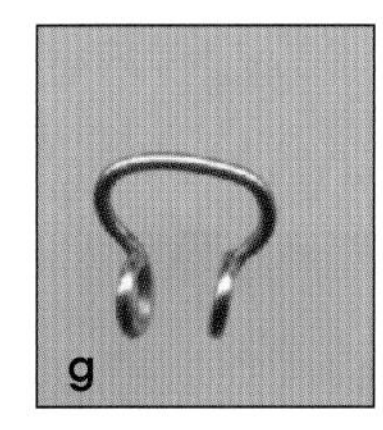

Bar: Cut one 1½-in. (38 mm) piece of 20-gauge wire. Grasp with chainnose pliers at center point and bend wire around jaw of pliers, keeping ends the same length **(d)**. **Note:** Be sure your bar is wide enough to accommodate your hook. Using roundnose pliers, bend each side farther inward **(e)**. Using roundnose pliers, bend back outwards again **(f)**. Trim tails to about ½ in. (13 mm) and turn a loop under at each end **(g)**.

SPIRAL POINT MOTIF

Work as for spiral point clasp through **(c)**. Make a loop as shown. Hammer to strengthen.

Tools

Wire cutters: Choose sharp pliers with a fine point at the tip for precise cutting, especially in crowded areas.

Roundnose pliers: Narrow jaws with a fine tip are necessary for making small loops and curves.

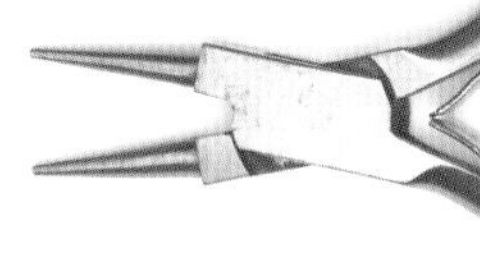

Chainnose pliers: A narrow tip helps get a precise grasp in crowded areas.

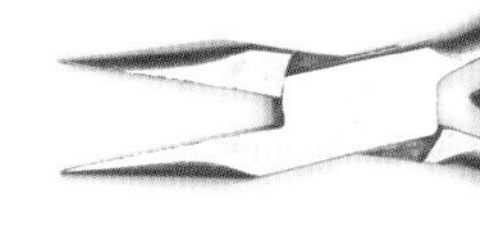

Ring mandrel: Used to gauge ring size, the heavy plastic version is fine.

Hammer: Use any hammer with a flat, unmarred head.

Anvil: A 2½ x 2½-in. (64 x 64 mm) flat metal-plate-style is the right size.

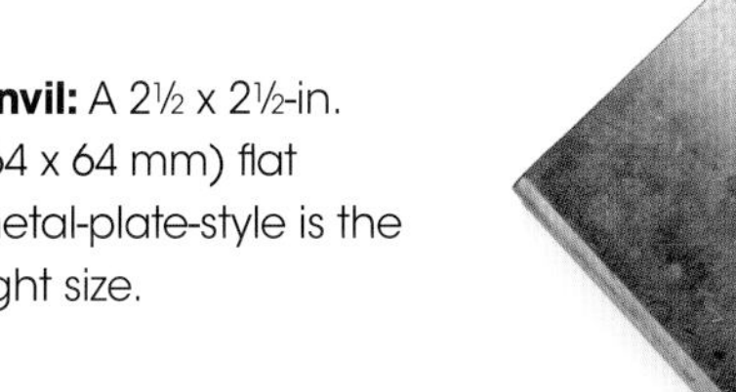

Stepped Pliers: Stepped pliers help make consistently sized loops.

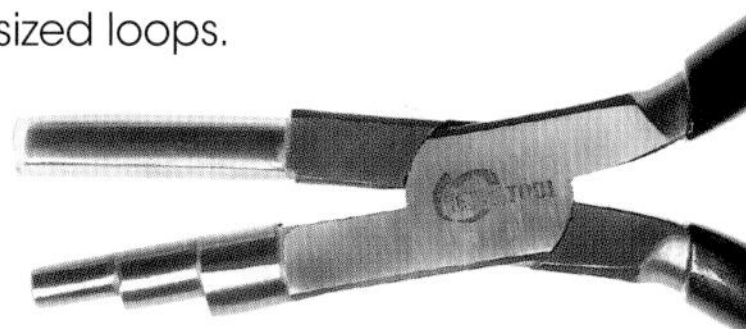

Materials

WIRE

Note: The wire requirements stated in the project instructions are estimates only. The exact lengths needed may change depending on variations in the sizes of arches, the degree of twisting, and so forth.

Hardness/Softness:

Half-hard wire: Maleable enough to be shaped without too much difficulty, half-hard wire is nevertheless stiff enough to hold its shape once formed, making it suitable for making frames.

Dead-soft wire: Dead-soft wire is more flexible and less likely to become brittle when manipulated than half-hard wire, making it suitable for the lacy portions of these pieces.

Note: Some of the wire called for in these patterns is very fine. The lacy portions do, however, remain flexible, and require careful handling and storage. You may opt to make your pieces a bit stronger by using a slightly heavier gauge of dead-soft wire instead (i.e. 26-gauge in place of 28-gauge), but they will be more difficult to make and will lack the delicacy that the thinner wires produce.

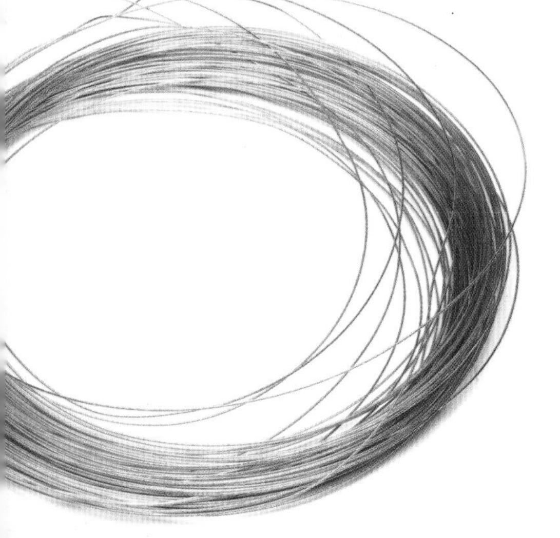

Type of Wire:

Precious metal wire: Sterling silver and 14k gold-filled wire are available in both dead-soft and half-hard.

Note: If you opt for sterling silver or gold-filled for the lacy portions of your pieces, be sure you choose dead-soft.

Craft wire: Often called "artistic" wire, craft wire is almost always dead-soft unless marked otherwise. It is made of base metal, usually copper. Less expensive than dead-soft sterling or gold-filled wire, it comes in a variety of colors that can add exciting dimensions to your lacy wire pieces. However, craft wire's sheen is much more likely to dull over time. Slow this process by storing your wire pieces in a closed container away from the light.

Note: Some craft wires have coatings that can easily be nicked when twisting or cutting wire, allowing bare metal to show through. These are less appropriate for most lacy wire jewelry patterns.

Niobium and Titanium wire: These wires, while beautiful, are too brittle to withstand much manipulation, making them unsuitable for the lacy portions of your pieces. They are not perfect as substitutes for the half-hard frame wires, either. since the anodized coatings often come off when brought in repeated contact with other wires.

Memory wire is a base metal wire that is extremely stiff. It is intended to "remember" its original shape, and will not withstand much manipulation.

Note: Do not use your regular wire cutters on memory wire—it will nick the blades and ruin the cutters.

BEADS

The patterns in this book call for beads in a wide variety of shapes and sizes, and made from a variety of different materials. The exact beads suggested may be difficult to find at times, but a multitude of good substitutes are available on the market. It's best to select beads that are within a millimeter or two of the called-for size, since significant size changes may affect the proportions of the piece. In some cases, larger or heavier beads may also weigh down the laces, causing the pieces to sag or lose their shape.

Beads made of most any material—glass, plastic, crystal, and stone—can be used effectively in most of these project instructions. Be somewhat careful when selecting metal beads—some may be too heavy for the finer laces.

FINDINGS

Findings are the extra elements that are necessary to finish a piece. They include clasps, earring wires and posts, headbands, barrettes, combs, jump rings, double jump rings, pin backs, and head pins. Some of the findings in this book are handmade, but commercially made findings can be substituted if desired.

GLUE

A good epoxy glue is called for in a few of the patterns.

Soul of Somanya

Creating Art, Transforming Lives

The Krobo beads used in *Lacy Wire Jewelry* come from the little town of Somanya in the Eastern Region of Ghana, West Africa. A traditional art form of the Krobo tribe, they are made of recycled glass and are extremely labor-intensive to make.

In 2007, after an issue of *Bead&Button* magazine containing one of my jewelry designs somehow found its way into the hands of a group of Krobo bead artisans, I was invited to go to Ghana to teach jewelry making. What began for me as a desire for an interesting busman's holiday quickly evolved into a determination to help these hard-working people raise their standard of living above the barest subsistence level. Thanks to the unshakable determination of a young Ghanaian man named Arkuh Bernard Tettey, we were able to begin a self-empowerment project that would significantly increase the demand for Krobo beads while providing work for a group of disadvantaged Krobo youth whose employment prospects—and therefore life prospects—would otherwise be very grim. We named the project, "Soul of Somanya."

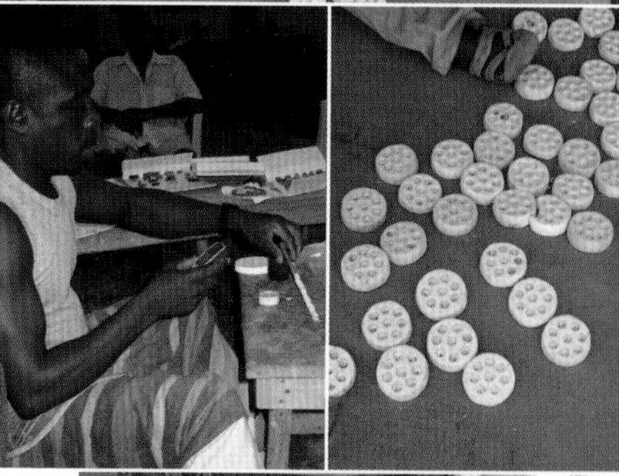

For me personally, Soul of Somanya has been the end to a long search for my true vocation. For the people of Somanya, it is, we hope, the beginning of an enterprise that will grow and benefit more and more of the Krobo people. Currently, we are helping 10 young people in Somanya develop marketable jewelry and other products using these beautiful Krobo beads. After shipping to the U.S., I, with the help of a fast-growing group of volunteers, market the products here and overseas. Every single penny of the proceeds from our sales goes exclusively to fund the project.

The bead makers of Somanya begin by going to a neighboring village and digging clay to make their own wood-fired kilns and bead molds. To make the beads, they pound pieces of glass into a powder in a huge mortar and pestle and then sift it, adding ceramic powders as needed to get the desired base color. They then siphon the powder into the molds, which consist of thick clay plates with holes hollowed out of them. A casava stick is inserted into each bead-to-be. The molds are then inserted into the kilns using a long-handled spatula. The casava sticks burn out during the first firing, leaving a hole open for stringing.

The beads are then loosened in their molds and cooled. Once they have been washed and dried, they are placed on skewers. Using a small pin-like instrument, the bead maker then paints on one color of ceramic glaze to begin his or her design. Once the first glaze has air-dried, the beads go back in their molds and then back into the kiln. The process is then repeated for each color used.

To shop for the beads used in these projects, and to view pictures and read stories about the people involved in Soul of Somanya, visit soulofsomanya.net.

About the Author

Melody MacDuffee has been designing jewelry for 20 years. Her work has been shown in juried competitions in several states. She teaches internationally and manages the class program for her local state-of-the-art bead store. Melody is the author of *Boutique Bead & Wire Jewelry*, the coauthor of *Beaded Edgings*, and has contributed to dozens of other beading books and publications.

More Ways to Enjoy Wirework!

Incredible Ideas for Every Style!

Inspired Wire guides wireworkers of all levels through a personal journey of design and creativity. Clear instructions, a unique building-block approach to basics, step-by-step photographs, and an eight-page gallery of the author's work make this book a stunning addition to any jewelry maker's collection. 36 projects in all.

62564 • 112pgs • $21.95

Making beautiful, delicate silver filigree jewelry is easier than ever! Jewelry artist Jeanne Rhodes-Moen demystifies the process in this clear and thorough guide. Packed with dazzling full-color photos, *Silver Threads* features detailed, illustrated instructions for twelve stunning projects that range from simple pendants to more-complex necklaces.

62210 • 112pgs • $22.95

This all-new collection features projects that move from the basics to a comfortable challenge of increasing complexity. The fresh, fashionable ideas include a mix of metals (copper, bronze, silver) and introduce exciting elements (rivets, metal blanks) and new tools (dapping block, hole-punching pliers).

64186 • 112pgs • $21.95

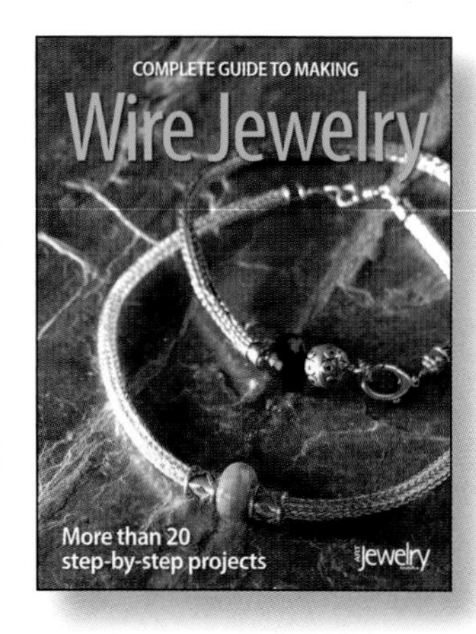

More than 20 exciting projects from *Art Jewelry* magazine introduce fundamental wireworking techniques, including wrapping, coiling, weaving, chain mail, cold connections, and soldering. Shape wire into beautiful necklaces, earrings, bracelets, rings, and more!

62540 • 112pgs • $21.95

P11586

Buy now from your favorite bead or craft shop!

Or at www.KalmbachStore.com or 1-800-533-6644

Monday – Friday, 8:30 a.m. – 4:30 p.m. CST.
Outside the United States and Canada call 262-796-8776, ext. 661.

XB